WITHDRAWN

HARVARD LIBRARY

WITHDRAWN

The Greek and Hebrew Origins of our Idea of History

The Greek and Hebrew Origins of our Idea of History

Paul Merkley

Toronto Studies in Theology
Volume 32

The Edwin Mellen Press
Lewiston/Queenston

Library of Congress Cataloging-in-Publication Data

Merkley, Paul.
  The Greek and Hebrew origins of our idea of history.

  (Toronto studies in theology ; v. 32)
  Bibliography: p.
  Includes index.
  1. History (Theology) 2. History--Philosophy. I. Title. II. Series: Toronto studies in theology ; 32.
  BR115.H5M34 1987   231.7'6'01   87-11136
  ISBN 0-88946-820-6

This is volume 32 in the continuing series
Toronto Studies in Theology
Volume 32 ISBN 0-88946-820-6
TST Series ISBN 0-88946-975-X

Copyright © 1987 The Edwin Mellen Press

All rights reserved. For information contact:

The Edwin Mellen Press   The Edwin Mellen Press
P.O. Box 450   P.O. Box 67
Lewiston, New York   Queenston, Ontario
USA 14092   CANADA L0S 1L0

Printed in the United States of America

to Gwen, my wife:

*Her children rise up and call her blessed;
her husband also, and he praises her:
"Many women have done excellently,
but you surpass them all."*

                        Proverbs, 31 : 28–29 (RSV)

CONTENTS

Chapter One: Prolegmena: Our Civilization's
                Dynamic View of History 1

Chapter Two: Herodotus: His Enquiries into History 15

Chapter Three: Elements of the Ancient Greek
                Theory of History 49

Chapter Four: Elements of the Ancient Jewish
                Theory of History 67

Chapter Five: The God of Israel and the History
                of World Empires 117

Chapter Six: Convergence of the Graeco-Roman
                and the Jewish Theories of History 149

Chapter Seven: The Gospels as Historical Testimony 199

Chapter Eight: Christ, the Lord of Time 245

Endnotes   265

Index   285

Acknowledgements

I am grateful to Carter Elwood, Chairman of the Department of History, and to Naomi Griffiths, Dean of Arts of Carleton University, for their encouragement of this project, which has been so long in preparation.

The Faculty of Arts of Carleton University provided financial assistance towards completion of the manuscript, which was prepared in its final form, with great skill and patience, by Joseph Goski.

Note:

Unless otherwise noted, all Biblical references are in the New English Bible version.

Journeymen of the historical craft ... have been trained to live according to the law. That law is what the profession calls methodology, that is, the way in which one should go about studying history and doing research and writing. This methodology was based in its inception either upon Biblical affirmations about the reality of truth or upon Newtonian-Darwinian concepts of scientific certainty.... Now, the historian, along with most other intellectuals in the modern world, long ago concluded that Biblical faith was irrelevant, that it did not validate his methodology; he has long since ceased to see its meaning for his methodology. No sooner had he repudiated the Biblical foundations, however, than scientists themselves began to undermine reasons for believing in scientific certainty. These two great erosions have by our own day gone a long way toward destroying the intellectual and faithful foundations of historical methodology....

[M]ost historians go about their daily work on the common sense assumption that historical truth must have its own existence because otherwise their work would be meaningless and their careers a fraud. They live not in total darkness but, it might be said, in the dim light of natural revelation. And in many instances they live scrupulously, morally, righteously, by the law of historical method. For them it is no longer a divine law, handed down on some Sinai; they know the law's formalities, not its life. But it is a seemingly viable way of professional life. Carefully observed, it enables one to write acceptable monographs and to teach seminars of his own.... [But] living by the law as historian amounts to precisely the same thing and has precisely the same inevitable results as living by the law in all of life. We are not able to fulfill our true vocations, that is, to be good and faithful historians, because we simply do not have it in us to fulfill the law's demands.

Arthur Link, "The Historian's Vocation"*

* Arthur Link, "The Historian's Vocation", in C.T. McIntire (ed.), *God, History, and Historians: An Anthology of Modern Christian Views of History* (New York: Oxford University Press, 1977), 375-376.

That in the dispensation of the fulness of times he might gather together in one all things in Christ, both which are in heaven, and which are on earth.

– Ephesians 1:10 (KJV)

Chapter 1:

Prolegomena: Our Civilization's Dynamic View of History

Every ideology that presents itself in this age for the serious consideration of active men and women in whatever corner of the globe, presents itself as the right answer to one universal question:

How can the whole of the human past be told as a single story,
- positing something common to all human origins
- having a single, linear direction
- bringing us all to this common global crisis which presages a common global conclusion?

The universal recognition that there can be only one history of mankind is the *differentia specifica* of our present historical epoch. The authority of each and every ideology presently in contest for the allegiance of intellectuals and the masses of men is dependent on the plausibility of the theory it offers in explanation of this outcome—that is, on how it offers to describe how all men everywhere in the globe have come to share in one destiny. That is, it depends on its theory of history.

In our own generation, the proposition that the whole story of mankind can and must be told as World History imposes itself on every thinking person everywhere, like it or not, because we are in fact all caught up in the one global crisis. There is now no practical possibility that history could take one direction for some of us and a radically different direction for others.

To judge among the various ideologies in contest for people's allegiance everywhere in the world today we have to have a secure notion of what constitutes historical knowledge, how historical judgements can be made, what constitutes historical fact, what it is possible for history to say to us with its own authority. In short, we must have a clear *theory* of history.

The globalizing of human destiny

In the following chapters we are interested in finding the origins and the premises of our theory of history. It would be perverse indeed to neglect the most conspicuous clue in our search for these: namely, the fact that it was our European civilization that began and that has throughout dominated the process by which all the peoples of the world have, in the course of the last four centuries, been brought to share one destiny.

The work of exploration and penetration (which usually involved colonization, and always involved some forms of exploitation) of all the extra-European civilizations was a large and complex process, which engaged the most philanthropic as well as the most villainous characters in our civilization. The only feature in this complex story that concerns us here is this: that in the course of this work our civilization brought all men everywhere to an understanding of the possibility and the necessity of telling the whole story of mankind as a single, linear story. We gave to all the extra-European populations of the world the gift of history. We taught them the elements of our theory of history. *And we gave them their own history.*

These gifts were made possible as a result of the practical work of the globalizing of human destiny, founded on the explorations and imperialistic penetrations of the extra-European civilizations which began in the sixteenth century. The story thus begins with the triumph of our material power and practical skills. But it ends in this last half-century in an intellectual and spiritual triumph: the conquest won by our theory of recital of the human past over all those which were indigenous to extra-European civilization. It ends in the establishment of "World History" as the foundation of all political ideologies.

A direct way of testing this proposition is to examine the biographies of all the major nationalist leaders of the extra-European world of the past half-century. These include such persons as Mao, Ho Chi Minh, Nehru, Kenyatta, Bourguiba, Mugabe. Common to all these lives is the experience of discovery of western life and ideas (not necessarily while living *in* the West), followed by the discovery of some model for telling the past of their own people (now defined as a "nation", in terms of the model of European history), followed by the elaboration of a political ideology based on this model of European nationalism.

As an example, we take the case of Mohandas Gandhi. As he himself has told the story, it was during his months in England as a student of law at the Inner Temple that he discovered the history of India, and with it his personal faith, as well as the first elements of his political program.

> "One of the most significant facts about the life and vocation of Gandhi," Thomas Merton pointed out in his essay, 'Gandhi and the One Eyed Giant', was his discovery of the East through the West". It was a discovery that in a way he shared with the whole of India, for by the initiative of European scholars in the nineteenth century, ancient Indian history was re-created, the serious study of Sanskrit literature was begun, and the Indian vernaculars were treated seriously and became literary languages. Perhaps, indeed, the greatest gift the British gave to India was her past, which before they came had been lost in the pseudo-history of the Brahmins. In Gandhi's case the gift was dramatically direct. He went to England looking for the know-

ledge that made Englishmen powerful. He learned instead his first lessons in the knowledge that had once made Asians wise.[1]

The historical dynamism of our civilization derives from its "realism" about this life-in-time, which students of comparative religion often argue is the most fundamental point of contrast between the religious world-view of Judaism, Christianity and Islam (on the one hand) and all other religious world-views.

The religious faith-systems alternative to our own all have (a) at a minimum, doubts, or (b) at a maximum, the strongest objections to investing cumulative and irreversible significance to deeds done in time. Class *a* (which would include the classical religions of the Hellenistic world and, with different emphases, the classical religions of China) have their doubts about the enduring significance of deeds done in time because they tend to identify enduring meaning with reason or some principle of order within either nature or spirit, in the light of which singular meaning can only be ephemeral. Class *b* (which would include Buddhism and Hinduism) absolutely reject the possibility of an enduring meaning attaching to deeds done in time because they identify meaning only with Eternity, which they insist can only be a property of Being-as-a-whole. Since singular meaning is deficient meaning (in class *a*) or no meaning at all (in class *b*), neither *a* nor *b* is interested in making a case for meaning-in-history, which ostensibly deals with an accumulation of such singular meanings.

Likewise, religious faith-systems which are alternative to our own have all tended at a minimum to discourage reflection on the possibility that consequences of decisions that we make in this lifetime extend beyond the plane of our singular life-in-time (on the ground that nothing can be known about such possibilities); or positively to denigrate such speculation (on the ground that eternity is a property of being-as-a-whole, and cannot be relevant to the case of the singular deeds of all men.) This bias has, in one form or another, marked the idea-systems or the faith-systems of the civilizations which are alternative to our own; and this fact justifies Albert Schweitzer's observation that our civilization has had "a uniquely world-and-life-affirming" (as contrasted to "a world-and-life-denying") mentality.

This historical realism sets our religion in a class by itself. We should expect that it should have left its stamp on Christian civilization; and that when one came to the comparative study of civilizations this unique bias of our religion would be reflected in some peculiar, characteristic way. And indeed it has. Our civilization has been the most dynamic of the civilizations. It is our civilization which is responsible for having brought all the previously isolated civilizations of the world into contact with one another and created the reality of one global history. Something unique in the realm of ideology is needed to account for the uniquely dynamic behaviour of our civilization in world history. The globalizing of human destiny traces to our development of a vision of the possibility of such a single, global human destiny. This in turn traces to the dogmas of Christian faith regarding the origins and the ultimate destiny of all men, and of God's program for individual salvation.

The ascendancy of the European model for the recital of the past

It was in fact our civilization which brought the previously separate histories of all the other civilizations of the globe into contact with one another, with the result that these previously separate histories are now organized and told in terms of the convergence of those separate histories into *one* global stream.

This development has several distinct stages, but it is practical to tell this story of the convergence of separate human histories into one world history as beginning in the sixteenth century, when certain technological developments made it possible for Europeans to set out on the great voyages of discovery which eventually brought all the civilizations of the globe to the knowledge of one another, beginning the process of involving their civilizations in the preoccupations of ours, and (to a distinctively lesser degree) of ours in theirs. Our economies are now linked together by global networks of exchange of goods, money and services. Our communities are linked by global networks of exchange of ideas, information and entertainment. This exchange has made us aware of each other, as rivals for space, for resources, for opportunities of expression. They make possible expressions of sympathy and of hatred that reach around the world. The diverse faith-systems and idea-systems which until our own time governed without challenge in separate spheres of allegiance, now confront one another everywhere in the globe, competing with one another for the allegiance alike of the populations indigenous to the civilizations out of which they grew and of populations which are only now learning of them for the first time.

For more than three centuries the extra-European peoples experienced an increasing implication of the Europeans in their lives and an increasing displacement of their civilizations' values and preoccupations by those of the Europeans. Most went through a long period of colonization by one or more of the European states. Then, in the second quarter of this century there began a process of turning-out the European masters and replacing European imperialist regimes with new regimes of indigenous leaders. To accomplish this, intellectuals and political leaders reared in the indigenous faith-systems and idea-systems of the extra-European world had to learn the political philosophies and techniques of the Europeans. *They had to master the history that the Europeans told in explanation of the origins, development, and legitimacy of their imperial regimes, in order to make the counter-claims for the new nations upon which they intended to rear their new regimes.* They had to learn to think like Europeans, which is to say to think historically.

Everywhere in the extra-European world intellectuals had to develop a case for the necessity of their new regimes. And everywhere the case had to be made out of the same materials mined from the *one global* scheme for historical recital. The story of all regimes founded

Prolegomena 7

since 1776 is told in terms of the struggle for liberation from European-colonial domination, the beginnings of this story being in the Age of Discovery, dating (as we have seen) from the sixteenth century. In the case of extra-European regimes, the very content of the nationality allegedly expressed in that state traces to this story of European conquest and the boundaries of such nationalities are set down in the terms of the maps produced by the European conquerors in the days of their empire.

The histories of regimes older than 1776, whether European or extra-European, centre on the role played by the particular nation-state presently governed by that regime in the sequence of world-wide military, economic and diplomatic struggles that began in the eighteenth century, and which were continuations into the larger canvas of European power conflicts of even longer standing. Certain stations in this story are obligatory for all: Yalta (1945) for even the youngest regimes; Versailles (1919) for those of middle age (in terms of diplomatic seniority); Berlin (1878), Versailles (1871) for some; Vienna (1815) for others; and for the oldest Paris (1783), Utrecht (1713)—and so on along this track.

In all state-run schools everywhere in the world, national history is told as a significant section (often the most important section; invariably the most edifying section—but still a section) of the one global story. The model for this story is called World History. Other traditional types of recital of the story of the past continue to exist in the world, in the European as well as the extra-European sections. But the model of World History has pre-eminent authority in the world of power: it is appealed to (a) when rulers defend the legitimacy of their regime to their citizens; (b) when citizens speak of their rights and when they speak of the performances of their rulers; (c) when the rulers speak to each other; (d) when rulers speak over the heads of other rulers to *their* citizens or subjects. Within any particular political jurisdiction a particular sub-community may understand itself in terms of some other form of recital of the past, and may refer to this when it confronts another sub-community or the community as a whole. Thus, Canadian Baptists, or Canadian Ukrainians, or Canadian Eskimos have their own myths, legends, or just unstructured memories which may be more important to some than world history. So too with the Kikuyu tribe of Kenya, or the Samaritans of Israel, the Kurds of Iraq or the Meo of Vietnam. But when they make their case for the sympathy of the whole nation or of the world community, they have all got to appeal to world history. They must all have a well-considered case for where and how that esoteric (and usually ancient) recital of the past fits into the one global model in terms of which all political power is measured out in this twentieth century A.D.

The Soviet Government and the Government of the United States; the Communist Party of the U.S.S.R. and the dissidents who distribute *samizdat*; the Republicans and the Democrats; the Walloons and the Flemings; the Maronites, the Shi'ites, the Sunnis and the Druse— when two sides line up to debate their rights before the world, they must draw upon the same model for giving structure to the whole human past. They must appeal to the one World History. One chronological scheme ("A.D./B.C.", or "B.C.E./C.E.". as the Jews prefer) is in force everywhere. There are alternative schemes, as for example the traditional Jewish which reckons from the date of Creation giving the years 5743 beginning in October 1982 C.E., or the strictly lunar Islamic calendar, which reckons from the Hegira (June 622, according to the European calendar), giving the year 1403 beginning in October of 1982 C.E. But these traditional calendars are never used when addressing the world communities of scholarship, business or diplomacy. The universal chronology is a very recent accomplishment, but is now so thoroughly assumed that it takes great imagination to understand how impossible it was to have any discussion of world history before it.

Theory of global history in the post-Christian world

There is a powerful irony in the fact that the beginnings of the practical business of bringing all the world's civilizations into contact with one another and setting them onto a common historical course tending to one common historical destiny, coincides with the beginning of the end of Catholic European civilization. For our present purpose it should suffice to offer as benchmarks the dates of Henry of Portugal ("the Navigator") (1394–1460), to mark the beginning of the story of Europe's exploration of the East; the dates of Columbus (1446?–1506), to mark the appearance of a New World; of Martin Luther (1483–1546), to remind us of the schism within European Christianity; of Machiavelli (1469–1527), to remind us that we are into the distinctly secularizing phase of the Renaissance; and of Bacon (1561–1626) and Descartes (1596–1650), to indicate the beginning of the end of medieval-Christian theology's domination of learning. The practical business of globalizing human destiny began under the auspices of a united religious ideology, and the vigour which our civilization was then displaying to the alternative civilizations which it assaulted and began to undermine was the vigour that comes from ideological unity. But soon that ideological unity was demolished, and it is clear that the vigour our civilization displayed through the centuries of its main work of globalizing human destiny (the early seventeenth through twentieth centuries) was the vigour of a civilization deeply divided—its frustrations displaced into aggressions against the certainties of the faiths of other civilizations. The process ends in the post-Christian era, with our civilization having a steady narrowing range of initiatives left for it to take, but taking these with proportionately increasing vigour, a vigour which owes nothing any longer to religious zeal, but rather to insecurity and self-loathing.

There is no longer anywhere on the globe any political jurisdiction in which Christian confession is formally responsible for shaping public policy or is even generally perceived to be dominant in determining the content or form, the substance or even the themes of culture, controversy or entertainment. There is likewise no corner of the globe where the Christian gospel is not being proclaimed, in direct confrontation with some one or more indigenous religious confessions or secular ideology. There is no community anywhere in the world (provided that it is larger than a mere village, and provided that it has at least a handful of citizens educated beyond mere literacy) where a merely indigenous religion or ideology can make its way without having ready answers to all the other religions and ideologies that have been, like itself, brought to the global community's attentions as the end-result of the process of global discovery initiated by Christian Europeans in the sixteenth century.

In addition to their ideas and their technology, Europeans brought their political preoccupations with them to the four corners of the globe. The latest chapter in that story begins in the aftermath of a half-century of civil war within the European civilization (beginning with the Great War of 1914–1918.) The Europeans are now aligned in two camps, led by two great powers, each nearly hegemonous within its separate camp, each possessing the power to destroy the other utterly, but only at the risk of destroying all life on earth altogether. The rivalry between these two powers has been projected (not without much distortion) upon the rest of mankind, so that no people in any corner of the globe is unaware of it; so that no one anywhere can think that he escapes the implications of that struggle. The basic ideological quarrel which is at the heart of the schism within the European mind is now globalized. The scientific-technological genius of the Europeans has so far arranged that when one of the principals makes even the merest feint at the other, the military damage is borne somewhere else than in the West, always by Third World bystanders, not yet by the principals.

It has always to be stressed that it is our civilization that has been responsible from the beginning for bringing about the present reality of One World. It was the energies of our civilization that brought the fate of all men everywhere in the globe into the matrix of the great controversy that now divides our present post-Christian civilization into two military-political blocs. This controversy is supposed by the leadership and the masses on both sides to be founded in unbridgeable differences about the meaning of man's destiny on this earth. These differences trace to a revolt against the authority which the Christian religion once had among us, the seeds of that revolt having been planted in that same Age of Discovery which began the process of globalizing the sway of our civilization. While the intellectuals (let alone the masses) of the extra-European world have trouble unpacking the history of this revolt (both on its side as a story of ideas and on its side as a story of political deeds), they have been brought by the history of the period since 1945 to understand that they cannot do without the esteem of the leaders of either the Communist or the Free World camp, and that it has never proved possible to have both together for very long. Their intellectuals understand that Marxism-Leninism's appeal to European intellectuals turns on its claim to provide an absolute and scientific explanation for the very historical dynamism that brought the extra-European civiliza-tions into the orbit of European civilization. Marxism-Leninism is (from the perspective of extra-European intellectuals) very much the child of its Christian parent in the matter of its dynamic view of history (its "world-and-life-affirmation".) But these intellectuals know also that Christians reject the interpretation of history that the Marxist-Leninists offer, and that the Marxist-Leninists, for their part, reject the supernaturalistic explanations without which the parent Christian theory of history would be utterly unrecognizable.

• • •

Christian civilization gave to the world a model for telling the whole story of mankind's life on this earth as a single, linear story, to which in theory belong all the separate stories that all the distinct nations and tribes of the world tell of themselves. The proposition that the whole story of mankind could and must be told in this way once commended itself to the civilization which invented it because it followed from the story we told of the origins of mankind, and the related story of God's work of salvation which belonged to the recital of the history of Israel, and to the Life, Death, Resurrection and Ascension of Jesus Christ, the origins and extension of the Church, and the expectation of an ultimate global conclusion to all, as drawn from Jewish and Christian eschatology.

The apparent eclipse of that vision raises many questions. Is it possible to have the dynamic vision of history and history's meaning without the faith-propositions of Christianity? Was there ever a necessary link between the two, or was the connection merely fortuitous? Is there a historically-necessary link between the historical-seriousness of Christian dogma and the historical vitality of Christian civilization? Can the historically-vital view of our civilization survive the devastation of its creed? Is the historically-vital philosophy of our civilization portable? Is the theological component expendable? optional? or already discredited (as held by Marxism-Leninism) as an impediment to further "progress" in the line of history?

This book argues three principal theses:

The first is that history is the bearer of the largest meanings that men can know.

The second thesis is that this confidence in the noetic possibilities of history is inseparable from confidence in the central assertions of dogmatic Christian theology.

(It follows from this that decline of the prestige of these assertions must lead to a decline in confidence in the authority of history.)

The third thesis is that the necessary link between vital theory of history and the premises of dogmatic Christian theology is itself a singular product of a singular historical process.

Vital theory of history is not a possibility of abstract thought. There is only one vital theory of history which is capable of defending its own distinct authority against the rival authorities of philosophy and science—and this is the theory accomplished by our civilization over many centuries, and which received definitive form in the first several generations of the Christian Church. The premises of this theory of history—our civilization's theory of history—cannot be separated from this dogmatic foundation without loss of its entire rationale. In other words: there is no possibility of *defending* vital theory of history before an audience that does not know the articles of our faith and the story of our civilization.

To make the whole case for vital theory of history would be to tell the whole story of our civilization. Even the largest of multi-volumed works cannot do this. Thus (we argue) the whole case for our theory of history is never fully graspable. It is no less than our history. *But*, we can make a beginning towards defense of our theory of history by reminding ourselves of where and how the discipline of World History began. In the next two chapters, we go to the record of the beginnings of reflection on world history in our civilization. We go first to the ancient Greeks—not because there is evidence for believing that reflection on world history began earlier there than it did among the ancient Jews (in fact, the evidence is to the contrary), but because there among the Greeks the beginning of the process is easily fixed (as it is not in the case of the Jews.) We begin with Herodotus, "the Father of History".

Chapter 2:

Herodotus: His Inquiries into History

> In this book, the result of my inquiries into history, I hope to do two things: to preserve the memory of the past by putting on record the astonishing achievements both of our own and of the Asiatic peoples; secondly, and more particularly, to show how the two races came into conflict. (Herodotus, *The Histories*, Book I, *cap.* 1.)[1]

The word "history" derives from the Greek *histor* (ιστωr).[2] This word refers to a person who had the confidence of a community and was called in to settle legal disputes, in the days before political life became so complex and social contacts so diffuse that it became necessary to invent courts and lawyers and judges. In a dispute, for example, about a property line or grazing rights, the *histor* had to examine which of the rival stories was the true one, or nearest the truth. The inquiry that led to his verdict was called istorih. When, in the fifth century B.C., Herodotus undertook to explain how public affairs had come to their present state, he called his work *history* and himself an *historian,* alluding to this office and this officer as prototypes.

The primary qualification of the *histor* was *not* the gift for telling a story. On the contrary, it was the gift for listening to stories and dealing critically with them. He needed industry to track down all the stories that were worth taking into consideration; sensitivity, to deal patiently with them; strict moral sense in weighing the rights and wrongs of the issues; and critical intelligence, to discover consistencies and inconsistencies.

Down through the many centuries since Herodotus there have been countless scholarly discussions of this question of the special character of historical inquiry. It is deeply significant that speculation about the task of the historian began here, with Herodotus' evocation of the *histor*. It is a good rule of thumb that the soundest scholarship in our field is that which hits upon this affinity between historical inquiry and forensic inquiry. The valid reverse of this rule is that the measure of the incompetence of speculative theory of history is exactly proportional to the distance from the truth of this insight.

The most explicit statement of this theme in the contemporary literature is the famous section on the historian-as-detective, "Who killed John Doe?" in R. G. Collingwood's *The Idea of History*.[3] Collingwood considers in this section the gifts which the historian requires, how these are related to the gifts of forensic inquiry, and how these both differ from the gifts of other sorts of scientific inquiry. Although Collingwood does not directly allude to the etymological clue in the word *histor*, his observations are distinctly in the spirit of Herodotus. The historian (like the detective) is called in because the peace has been disturbed, and justice must be done. Calling in the historian amounts to acknowledging that the facts about the past are not uniform. To get at the truth means hearing out a variety of stories, weighing the motives of the parties who tell them, "getting behind" the stories (as Collingwood put it) making the documents reveal what their authors intended to conceal. The historian, like the detective, covets the maximum number of accounts and the multiplication of contradiction. He may go into his enquiry with firm views about what is possible under the sun, but he is always ready to hear out yet another account, on the possibility that it will convince him to accept new truth about human or natural or divine possibility, in the light of which he will change his definition of historical fact.

Herodotus was born somewhere between 490 and 480 B.C.—that is, at some point during the years when the Greeks turned back the invasion of the "Asiatic peoples" who were the subjects of the Persian

Empire. In the last years before his death (which was probably in 425), he saw the beginnings of the conflict between the leading Greek states (the Peloponnesian War, 431-404), which, as it turned out, ruined the possibility that the Greeks would be able to remain their own masters. The occasion for his "inquiries into history" was the depressing disunity that had succeeded to the exhilarating unity that had made possible the defeat of the Persian tyrant. Herodotus believed that an understanding of the events that had brought the Greeks into conflict with the Asiatic peoples would cause his fellow Greeks to appreciate what was at stake in the preservation of their unity, restoring the sense of proportion necessary for a resolution of their differences.

The first step in this task was to fix "responsibility for the quarrel." (Book I, *cap*. 1) But fixing responsibility, he found, required him to go all the way back, as far as reliable records would allow, to tell the whole story of how all of the principals came to be involved in the Wars. And this in turn (he found) required him to re-examine and offer fresh judgements of his own upon all of the quarrels that marked the stations in the originally separate histories of all the communities of men who were ultimately brought into that war. Given that that war engaged all the known communities in what civilized men believed was the whole civilized world, it followed that Herodotus was committed to bringing within one matrix of interpretation,*the whole story of mankind*. Two separate tasks were therefore involved: (i) to sift the whole record of the past of each community; and (ii) to align the discrete histories thus achieved into one global history. What we might call the theorem of world history was first proposed in scholarly terms by Herodotus.

Gathering the materials of World History

To explain how the conflict came about, Herodotus had to step back to the immediately previous chapters of history and describe the power realities in the world at the time of the completion of the Persian

Empire. This then leads to telling the story of the Lydian Empire, Persia's immediate predecessor as the great power of western Asia. And from this point, Herodotus leads us back into the several histories of all the nations that found themselves caught up in these empires, together with the stories of all the previous empires with which he was familiar.

This was no easy task:

> His sources for all this material were very mixed—personal observation, oral hearsay and tradition, literary sources and documents. Of his personal observation it need only be repeated that this was the man who crossed the entire eastern Mediterranean to check a single fact.... The conditions facing a traveller of the fifth century B.C. presented such almost inconceivable difficulties that Herodotus' journeyings and personal observations can scarcely be comprehended or credited. It is true that oral traditions were more extensive than we can easily appreciate since they continued to be handed down on a large scale even after writing had been introduced. Yet they were also incomplete, untrustworthy and contradictory. Herodotus cites verbal reports from forty Greek states and almost as many foreign countries.... [Where they were available, he consulted written sources. Thus,] eastern inscriptional records, archives and official chronicles and land surveys, are explicitly or implicitly referred to on a number of occasions. It is because of all this material that the oriental sections of Herodotus' work are the richest in biography.... Herodotus' choice of the Persian Wars as his theme was exceptionally audacious. Hard facts about the subject were desperately few.... Never has any practitioner of history had a more difficult task than its father.[4]

There is a long tradition of recurring assaults upon Herodotus' practice and his theory of history, beginning in the generation immediately following his death.[5] Most people associate the campaign against Herodotus with Voltaire, who called him "the Father of Lies;" but this is a typical instance of the ingrained tendency of moderns to think that critical intelligence was a discovery of the century of the Enlightenment. There was, in fact, nothing new in any of the charges which Voltaire brought against Herodotus (E.g., see below p. 219). But Herodotus' reputation for integrity and sound method has been restored and improved following each of these assaults, so that today there is no reason in a book like this to dwell on the case for allowing him his traditional title: "the Father of History".

On the question of Herodotus' general reliability in the presentation of facts (as the knowledge of the geography and of archeology, and the state of the sciences generally then allowed), the best judgement now is that, if anything "he actually erred on the side of over-scepticism" in most of the sort of matters where he has been accused of naivety.[6] On the question of his fairness in dealing with ideologies and political loyalties not his own, he is now seen as standing well above the standards that our own contemporaries have got accustomed to: "[Herodotus] claimed it was one of his principal tasks to describe the achievements of eastern non-Greeks, and the promise is amply fulfilled by a magnificent series of portraits of great Persians. All this was too advanced for many Greeks, with their local patriotisms, and more than five hundred years later Plutarch (who had other and more parochial reasons for his dislike) still saw him as *philobarbaros*, a pro-barbarian or lover of wogs.... Such tolerance was part of a widely ranging, cheerful broadmindedness. The object of all travelling was to learn, and it was this spirit of enquiry, revealed in a hundred passages, which gave 'history' its modern meaning."[7] And on his critical intelligence in the handling of conflicting testimony, he usually gets high marks today: "'My business' [Herodotus wrote, VII: 152] 'is to record what people say. But I am by no means bound to believe it—and that may be taken to apply to this book as a whole.' These are the words of good sense that went with a critical eye and ear. There was no line of professional historians for Herodotus to draw upon. Yet his exceptionally intelligent and observant attitude to his material was what created the line of professionals which has continued from his day to ours."[8]

The mainstream of theorists of history (again, best illustrated by reference to Grant's *The Ancient Historians*)[9] does incline to blame him for his attachments to the superstitions of his time: his readiness to invoke divine explanations in historical causation, his credulity regarding the real force of omens; and so on.[10] But here we come to the heart of the secular-modernist's unhappiness about the origins in religion of our theory and practice of history. And of this we will have much more to say in the following pages.

Herodotus' project of a world history was not unprecedented. The work of certain predecessors had already brought to light the difficulties in such a project. There was, first, the massive task of gathering the discrete histories of all the discrete communities whose lot had involved them in the conflict between the Persian and the Greek alliance; then of tracing the sequence of cause and effect behind all of this; and finally of reconciling discrepencies both of story-telling methodology and of ideology so that they could be fitted into one chronological framework, and the whole told as one linear narrative.

Significantly, Herodotus' precursors, like Herodotus himself, were "Asiatic" Greeks. That is, they lived in the Greek-colonized communities of what we call Asia Minor. These were the first Greek communities to come under the threat of incorporation into the Persian Empire, having been in the closest commercial, social and intellectual congress with all the other nations of the East for several generations. The intellectuals of these Asiatic-Greek cities were in fact the pioneers of all the principal philosophical and scientific disciplines which the Greeks established. (W.F. Albright speaks of this ferment of critical inquiry among the Ionian Greeks as one facet of a generalized search for philosophical modes of understanding which occupied the higher culture of Phoenicia, and which finds expression in the biblical *Book of Job*.)[11]

There is good reason for the primacy of the Asiatic Greeks in the intellectual inquiry of this period. The Ionian Greeks of Asia lived on the frontier between the Greek world and a plurality of other worlds. Like medieval-European intellectuals of the generations confronting the Moslem world at the time of the Crusades; like European intellectuals of the "Renaissance" generations, confronting a newly discovered world beyond Europe, and discovering at the same moment a new interpretation of their own past world made possible by re-examination of the Graeco-Roman past—the Ionian Greeks were driven by the discovery of the plurality of worlds of meaning, to search for principles which would allow discrimination between what is false and what is true. As the history of philosophy is conventionally (and I suspect correctly) told, it was the Greeks of Asia Minor who first conceived the necessity and the possibility of philosophy. This intellectual project coincided in time with the first stages in the incorporation of these communities into the Persian empire.

Before history, there was "epic", The *Iliad* and The *Odyssey*. According to J.B. Bury,[12] it was during the Sixth century B.C. that Greek intellectuals began to express impatience with these epics as vehicles for a satisfying recital of the past. There was too much that they left unexplained, or which they explained in terms of marvels. How could human beings apply to their present lives stories in which the active figures are gods and demigods, in which the human race appears in a mostly passive role? When did these events really happen? Was the world so much different then that gods and demigods did move among men? Some bold souls were beginning to conceive the possibility of finding a path leading back to those days by research in the rolls of temple-priests and great families. Efforts were being made to harmonize scattered and contrary traditions, to establish schemes which would bring into conjunction the separate succession-lists of princes and rulers, and thus to establish synchronisms, that is, chronological milestones from which to measure forward and backward on the terrain of the past. In short, "crude and rudimentary processes of what we may call historical inquiry" were established; and the recital of past-events was "becoming quasi-historical in form".[13]

Inquiries of this sort required the medium of written prose. The Greeks had only recently adopted the alphabet from the Phoenicians,[14] and this made it possible to fix in writing the oral literature (all retained in the memory, in poetry) and then move on to discussion in writing of its meaning. From this it was an easy, but vitally important step to prose narration. "Prose meant a break with the old view that the past was something variable with each poet, and in any case only recoverable by inspiration from the muse."[15] The effective use of prose called for a calmer tone of address. The poet's inspiration, conveyed by the effects of metre and rhyme, has the effect of shouting down the critical instinct. The persuasiveness of poetry is inseparable from its ecstatic effects; when prose is the medium, authenticity is conveyed by effects that almost entirely exclude the ecstatic.

Several processes were therefore coming to critical pressure at the same moment (i) the Ionian Greeks' exploration of the East; (ii) their discovery of the uses of prose; (iii) the beginnings of philosophy; (iv) the beginnings of critical history; (v) the beginnings of the Graeco-Persian conflict. Herodotus' *Histories* were inspired by the conviction that his generation stood at the critical moment of decision which was the outcome of, and therefore must serve as focus for telling, the whole sequence of human and divine decisions which amounts to world history.

Herodotus singles out as an inspired precursor one Hecataeus.[16] An Ionian Greek, Hecataeus (c. 550-476) travelled throughout the whole of the Persian empire to detail the geography and to gather the histories of the component peoples of that Empire, with a view to fitting them into one framework of recital. The crux of this whole ambitious project, Hecataeus recognized, was to find a governing chronology.

Herodotus

Establishing the beginning of world history

Incredible though this must seem to ourselves, who have inherited the results of the labours of centuries of scholarship in these matters, the recognition of the need for one governing chronological convention came very late in the history of the development of the idea of history—and thus very late indeed in the history of the invention of human philosophy. In fact, as we shall be considering later, the Greeks never came to accept with quite the seriousness of our own later civilization this essential requirement for coherence of historical understanding.

Hecataeus was the author of a number of genealogies of aristocratic families (including his own). His labours in this field evidently caused him some considerable soul-searching. It was customary for good Greek families to recite a chain of names of the heads of the family going back only a few generations before the family's history was declared to have begun in a liaison between some female member of the family and a god. Hecataeus had at his disposal only a few tools. The Greeks had never felt anything like the passion for record-keeping that we have for so many centuries assumed to be incidental to the condition of civilization. Scattered throughout the Greek speaking world there were temples where one could find lists of priests or priestesses indicating, sometimes, an exact number of years of presidency, but for the most part no more than mere lists of succession. Hecataeus worked out a rule of thumb reckoning forty years as a generation and this became an agreed convention with the historians of Herodotus's generation and their successors[17]. There are, thus no well established dates in Greek history before the seventh century, and this is because the benchmarks of later Graeco-Roman historiography were all drawn from Near Eastern history as that became available to the generations beginning with Hecataeus. Greek historians never did establish a conventional date from which all dates could be reckoned despite several obvious candidates (e.g., the Trojan War, the Persian

War.) Some Greek historians came to the practice of using the Olympiad, a cycle of four years starting in what we reckon as 776 B.C.; and later still, Roman historians occasionally followed the example of Livy (d. 17 B.C.) in reckoning from the agreed date of the legendary foundation of Rome (by our reckoning, 753 B.C.). But no hard and fast convention for such dating was ever achieved by the historians of the Graeco-Roman world.[18]

Using the rather flimsy apparatus of Spartan king-lists, Hecataeus worked his own genealogy back through sixteen generations to "the settlement of Miletus by colonists from the Greek mainland (c. 1000 B.C.)—the founder of the line being a God."[19] Herodotus tells the story of Hecataeus' experience when he recited this genealogy to the priests in the temple of Thebes:

> [The Egyptians] declare that three hundred and forty-one generations separate the first king of Egypt from the last I have mentioned—the priest of Hephaestus—and that there was a king and a high priest corresponding to each generation. Now to reckon three generations as a hundred years, three hundred generations makes ten thousand years, and the remaining forty-one generations make 1340 years more; thus one gets a total of 11,340 years, during the whole of which time, they say, no god ever assumed mortal form.... When the historian Hecataeus was in Thebes, the priests of Zeus, after listening to the attempt he made to trace his family back to a god in the sixteenth generation, did to him precisely what they did to me—though, unlike Hecataeus, I kept clear of personal genealogies. They took me into the great hall of the temple, and showed me the wooden statues there, which they counted; and the number was just what I have said, for each high priest has a statue of himself erected there before he dies. As they showed them to me, and counted them up, beginning with the statue of the high priest who had last died, and going on from his right through the

whole number, they assured me that each had been the son of the one who preceded him. When Hecataeus traced his genealogy and connected himself with a god sixteen generations back, the priests refused to believe him, and denied that any man had ever had a divine ancestor. They countered his claim by tracing the descent of their own high priests, pointing out that each of the statues represented a *'piromis'* (a word which means something like 'gentleman') who was the son of another *'piromis'*, and made no attempt to connect them with either a god or a demigod. Such, then, were the beings represented by the statues; they were far from being gods—they were men. (II:145)

The whole of Herodotus' great undertaking could come to grief on this rock. In fact: Greek self-esteem and the whole enterprise called Greek philosophy is put to its severest challenge right here.

It was an axiom of Greek religion that before there was a world of men there was a world of gods, who lived out a certain set of adventures (traces of which have been whispered into the ears of poets) and who then withdrew to live in more fastidious settings—but not before certain of them had mated with certain among the first generation of mortals in this world which had previously belonged exclusively to the gods. The noble families derive from these liaisons. Because the gods were not subject as we are to the limitations of space, they must have held sway—the same gods, that is, must have held sway in all corners of the globe at the same time. An adventure told (by Hesiod, for example) of the god Pan happened in Hellas, but also in Egypt, in Phoenicia, in Syria, in Italy, and so on. Proof of this, said the Greeks, is to be seen in a well known feature of what we would call "comparative religion": the tendency for similar tales to be told of ostensibly different deities or demigods or heroes in different cultures in far-flung places. The key to co-ordinating the separate histories of the many families of man is therefore to trace back the genealogies of great families (priests serve especially well for this purpose, since they always retain some confused perceptions of the mythical foundations of their dynasties), until one reaches those local stories that clearly echo the stories the Greeks would recognize as belonging to the age when the gods were withdrawing from the world of men, leaving traces of their liaisons with mortal women, and dropping hints of their other adventures into the ears of the poets.

When the priests of the Egyptian cult showed Hecataeus, and later Herodotus, that long line of statues of their high-priests, they could not have guessed how agonizing was the threat thus posed for these historians. Hecataeus *knew*, as a first premise of his religion, that the gods had withdrawn from human affairs sixteen generations ago; and that prior to that withdrawal they had lived in this world and governed it. That was the Golden Age. Everything depends upon this truth. Civilization is impossible without it. It never occurred to the Greeks that civilization was something that human nature worked its way up to. They thought it was self-evident that common human character, tied as it is to appetite, which is in turn fixed in the need for survival, did not have any intrinsic capacity to *rise* to anything—certainly not to moral philosophy (without which there is no basis of consent to government.) If there was culture in the world, it was because there was order; and if there was order, it was because there was government; and if there was government it was because there was moral philosophy; and if there was moral philosophy it was because there was an aristocracy to whom had been given gifts of intelligence and fragments at least of higher-than-merely-human understanding which was their legacy from a sexual liaison between a divine being and a human woman during the age just before the gods withdrew from active governance of the world from within the world. For political philosophy, moral philosophy, aesthetics (*inter alia*), there are many implications to this premise. We cannot pursue these here. Our only present concern is to note that this dogmatic-theological premise is the cornerstone of Herodotus' theory of history.

Herodotus

Belief in the universal jurisdiction of the gods of the Greek pantheon, linked to the belief in the Golden Age, gives Herodotus the key to organizing world history. The question that men must answer before they can begin to construct a history of mankind is: how do we know that there is anything in common to the past experience of men everywhere in the world? This is *practically* speaking, tantamount to asking: how do we begin our story? *What* is the point—or *where* is the point—or *when* is the point where we can *link up* all of the separate stories that all of the separate communities of men tell about themselves?

It will not suffice merely to *insist* that human nature is always and everywhere the same. (Cultural anthropologists tell us that wherever a society has lived in isolation for a long period the word for "people" is identical with the name of the tribe. Contemporary leaders of "native-American" movements of protest against the effects of the Europeanization of such cultures usually insist that "liberation" from that *history* must begin with restoration of these original names: "Dene" (in the case of North American "Indians"), and "Inuit" (in the case of the "Esquimos" of Canada, Alaska and Greenland)—both terms having the meaning of "the people".)

The key to bringing all of history into one account is therefore not a theory about universal human nature. There is too much that is strange to us in the present practices of other "people", and much more that is absolutely unrecognizable to us in what men of different nations tell us about their past—especially since every community of men seems to insist that in the earliest chapter of its history there was something unique—usually uniquely-active dealings between their fathers and the Divine. Herodotus had heard many plausible tales about creatures that are not human like us, but not animals either. (Book IV: 24f.) He did not doubt that there are gradations of animality between dumb creatures and the human species; and therefore he sensibly rejected the challenge of defining the content of human nature.

Herodotus' aim is to link together and combine into one story the history of the world of men; and for this purpose what he needs is not an anthropology but a global event within time—something to be found in all the records of civilized men that points to our having shared in a common and global (common *because* global) human adventure, to which we can give at least an approximate date in time. Herodotus brings the knowledge of this common and global human adventure into his study of history from what we would call dogmatic theology: it is the legend of the Golden Age. This theological *a priori* is the basis for his synchronism. It is also the answer to the question: how can we know that our experience of humanity has been a universally-shared experience?

Word mythology and world history

We should note in passing the contrast between Herodotus' solution to the question: how can we begin our story of world history?, and that which is offered in the Jewish tradition and echoed in the Christian. In these latter, the answer is: we all derive from a single set of parents. The definition of what is human (anthropology) derives from what we are told of the circumstances of the creation of the first couple, and the conditions under which they were told to live their lives. If we start with this premise, there is no room for conjecture about gradations of animality between the human and other living creatures (as there *were* for Herodotus.)

Perhaps the most appropriate text for comparison of the Greek and the Judaeo-Christian theories regarding the link between anthropology and history is Paul's speech at Athens (*Acts*, Chapter 17.) We note especially verses 26 and 27: "He created every race of men of one stock, to inhabit the whole earth's surface. He fixed the epochs of their history and the limits of their territory." According to the Judaeo-Christian theory, we are permitted to go back beyond Herodotus' frontier (his own generation minus fifteen generations approximately), or any other frontier, and find the recognizably human material for our history in the story of the common parents of all mankind.

We leave aside for now the many difficulties bound up with this theory. (We return to the issue below, Chapter Four.) Our only immediate need is to make Herodotus' theory as clear as possible by showing it in contrast to its rival. In a very real sense, all subsequent controversy within our civilization about theory of world history turns on the choice between models like Herodotus' and models like St. Paul's. *Both originals stood on dogmatic-theological premises.* But it is possible to express the choice between them in non-theological terms. The question is: how is it possible to tell the whole story of mankind as a coherent, single, and unilinear story? And the rival answers are: (a) because there is a point where institutions of human community begin to emerge in many places under the impact of similar forces which reveal some global logic; or (b) because everything that is human has the same beginning in one and the same moment in time.

We know (said Herodotus) that there was a Golden Age when the gods lived in this world. But who knows how long that age went on? (Does it even make sense to speak of "length of time" in connection with that Age when the immortal gods lived in a setting which, if it satisfied *them*, must have been much different from our world of seasons and weather and growth and decay?) But we do know that there came a "time" when the gods began to withdraw from their life within this world. Everything that is unquestionably human, everything that history can deal with, is recognizable from that time forward, since government and all kinds of human community, art and civilization were the gifts the gods left behind to men as they withdrew. Herodotus' rule for organizing world history is: search out each and every one of the separate stories that each and every discrete human community tells about itself; find for each story the place where human government began (it will be at the point where, reading backward in the line of succession of human rulers we come to the divine founder); confirm this point by checking for parallels between stories told of this founder and the stories we know of the divine founders of our own Greek dynasties; then link the separate stories together at that point —because that point is known to coincide *roughly* everywhere in the civilized world.

Returning to the lists of succession of Egyptian priests: if Herodotus were to admit that the line of human government goes back among the Egyptians several generations further than the frontier of sixteen generations prior to his own, several unthinkable consequences must follow:

(i) Egyptian civilization is older than the Greek. That is, the date of the withdrawal of the gods of the Egyptians is so much further back that we do not reach it even when we have counted all the way back to the first high-priest recorded by the Egyptians, three hundred and forty-one generations prior to Herodotus' time.

(ii) We have denied the universality of the rule of the Gods known to the Greeks. For, if Zeus was the chief of the gods sixteen generations prior to Herodotus' own time, in the golden "time" of which the poets speak, he was also (under different names) the chief of the gods in Syria, in Palestine, in Italy—and in Egypt.

We are speaking here of the relation between the world of myth and the world of history, and of how the Greeks conceived the connection. The issue is of course much more complex than I have made it out to be. An excellent discussion is in B.A. Van Groningen, *In the Grip of the Past: Essays on an Aspect of Greek Thought*:

> [T]he Greeks often imagine a chronological no man's land between the mythical and the historical past.... [For example, with respect to the link between the Spartan kings and Heracles,] Herodotus enumerates eighteen ancestors who separate king Leonidas, the hero of the Thermopylae, from Heracles. Leonidas was killed, as everybody knew, in the year which we call 480 B.C. The Greeks assumed, as a rule, that approximately three generations make a century. The conclusion was obvious: If Heracles'

life is considered in a purely historical way, he lived some seven centuries before Leonidas. Our chronology would say, in the eleventh or twelfth century B.C. The mythical past to which Heracles belongs here is made to coincide with an exact period in the historic sense of the word through a simple arithmetical operation. Of course it does not matter in the least that all the calculations referring to him do not arrive at the same result. We must, however, not forget that Heracles lived in the mythical sphere; the nature of his achievements proves it. None less than Zeus was involved in his birth, and, at the end of his career, the son of Semele obtained his place among the Olympians. In his figure the human and the divine are intertwined and he belongs to the two forms of the past. In his life the two close in upon each other. To speak more correctly, the Greeks considered the same hero, according to the tale which was told, as living now in the one, now in the other past, just as Thebes is sometimes a real city, that of Epaminondas for instance, and sometimes a mythical one, that of Cadmus and Oedipus.

Heracles is no exception. The same considerations apply to numerous other heroes, probably to all of them. Long ago it has already been remarked that practically all of them are placed close to each other in a very limited number of generations, roughly, between 1400 and 1100 B.C. On the other hand, the past of the gods themselves, to which their personal history as well as the genesis of the universe belong, does not admit of any such chronological fixation.

To sum up, the whole past presents itself to the Greek, if we neglect all differences of level, as consisting of three fields of light. Nearest to him lies the historical past of which his own present is the direct continuation. The pure mythical past of the gods lies at the greatest distance. It borrows its splendour essentially from the same source of light as the time of the gods, but in practice it stands in the historical light as well, although, as a rule, the transition is blurred.[20]

(iii) If we deny the possibility of the universal rule of the gods known to the Greeks, we deny the possibility of a universe of order. For, if different gods ruled in Egypt, how could we know that these gods had the same mind and the same purposes as the gods we know? If there are other gods, independent of those we know, they might have other purposes for men than those that we acknowledge.

(iv) If there are other gods with other purposes for men, there is no hope of finding a common and globally-valid moral basis for the activities of different human communities, and no way of linking their stories together and telling them as one story, tending in one direction towards a meaning that we can all recognize.

How does Herodotus deal with this challenge? The answer is in the first line of our excerpt: the Egyptian priests are (though they don't know it) "the priests of Zeus". Whatever they might claim with respect to the long line of priest-rulers,

> Nevertheless, before their time Egypt was, indeed, ruled by gods, who lived on earth amongst men, sometimes one of them, sometimes another being supreme above the rest. The last of them was Orus the son of Osiris—Orus is the Apollo, Osiris the Dionysus, of the Greeks. It was Orus who vanquished Typhon and was the last god to sit upon the throne of Egypt.
>
> In Greece, the youngest of the gods are thought to be Heracles, Dionysus, and Pan; but in Egypt Pan is very ancient, and one of the 'eight gods' who existed before the rest; Heracles is one of the 'twelve' who appeared later, and Dionysus one of the third order who were descended from the twelve. I have already mentioned the length of time which by the Egyptian reckoning elapsed between the coming of Heracles and the reign of Amasis; Pan is said to be still more ancient, and even Dionysus, the youngest of

the three, appeared, they say, 15,000 years before Amasis. They claim to be quite certain of these dates, for they have always kept a careful written record of the passage of time. But from the birth of Dionysus, the son of Semele, daughter of Cadmus, to the present day is a period of about 1600 years only; from Heracles the son of Alcmena, about 900 years; from Pan the son of Penelope—he is supposed by the Greeks to be the son of Penelope and Hermes—not more than about 800 years, a shorter time than has elapsed since the Trojan war.

It is open to anyone to believe whichever of these two traditions he prefers; I have already stated my own opinion. If indeed these gods had been publicly known and had grown old in Greece, like Heracles, the son of Amphitryon, and Dionysus, it might have been said that the two last-mentioned were men who bore the names of previously existing gods; but the Greek tradition is that Dionysus, as soon as he was born, was sewn up in Zeus' thigh and taken to Nysa, which is in Ethiopia above Egypt; and as to what happened after the birth of Pan, tradition is silent. It is clear to me, therefore, that the names of these gods became known in Greece later than the rest, and that the Greeks trace their genealogy from the time when they first acquired the knowledge of them. (II:145)

Coming to terms with the Egyptian and other rival Asiatic schemes for giving order to the past, constituted for the Greek historians the first critical challenge in their work of establishing world history. The fascination of this story lies in the way in which this apparently merely technical exercise (the working-out of a synchronism for the various king-lists and priest lists that came to hand) is in fact charged with the gravest philosophical and religious challenges. The gist of the problem is that before there can be any discrete-national history there must be a world-history. There is no telling the story of Lydia, for example, until we find where it links up to the story of the other kingdoms which were its neighbours—because the significance of the history of Lydia is a function of its effects on other nations and their effects on it. But we cannot relate one to another without synchronism. So, the very notion of history begins its life in our civilization as world-history

Purpose in History

It was Herodotus who introduced the project of world-history to our civilization. The foundation-stone of his theory of human history is his theorem that the story had to be told as a set of originally scattered discrete national stories coming into focus in a moment of time: the moment of confrontation between the Greek and Persian alliances. This moment of confrontation is the *kairos*—the moment requiring decisive response from this generation of Herodotus' contemporaries.

But, equally, it is not possible to talk of a *kairos* without talking of Purpose. And such Purpose (as a matter of logic) has to be larger than any of the purposes of any of the human and divine agents in the story; and larger even than the total of all their purposes. This Purpose is the *telos* of history—the purposive End toward which all events are striving.

The study of world history was first proposed and first attempted by a man who believed (in his own words) "that the hand of God is active in human affairs;" and furthermore that "it is plain" that this is the case (IX:101.) Quite apart from other evidence that we have from Greek literature, we could assume from the fact that Herodotus earned a living reading his Histories aloud to the people of Athens,[21] that this view was shared by the mass of his contemporaries. Assuming this agreement about basic meanings, Herodotus sets out "to put on record the astonishing achievements both of our own and of the Asiatic peoples", and "more particularly, to show how the races came into conflict" (I: 1.) At each step of his story, Herodotus assumes that the men whose deeds he is describing are responsible for how things are turning out. There is no question of resort to abstract, generalized or neutral forces. To understand what we must do in face of today's crisis (Herodotus is saying) we must know where right lies. And to know where right lies we must be prepared to listen to the whole story of the human past up to this point. It is as though all the races of mankind had come to Herodotus to tell him all of their stories so that he could judge what their rights are—and what is right in this hour: two faces of the question of right, somehow related. Whatever can be judged he judges, from merely technical or practical decisions (a general has two routes open to him, and he goes north rather than south; there is ostensibly "nothing to choose between them" [as we would say], but somehow in the whole economy of purpose that ties all life together something real is attached to that choice, and the outcome reveals whether he was "right") to those decisions which even the dullest can recognize as involving issues of right and wrong. We have already noted the significance of Herodotus' placing the historian in the line of succession from the *histor*—the man whose task was to set things right. The issue of what is *right* is always near to the surface in Herodotus' story-telling. Those who have been responsible in the past for "astonishing achievements" have the *right* to be remembered. There is a deeper sense in which the telling of history helps *to set things right* between the human race and the gods. And there is a deepest sense of all in which the history itself is *accomplishing right*.

Herodotus took with him into his "inquiry" for meaning in the whole of history the attitude that follows from what Immanuel Kant called "the supreme principle of morality". Herodotus believed that there was an economy of right which governed everything in the human world. Every human action had moral significance and moral consequences. The sum-total of all human actions goes into world history. But in addition one has to include the actions of the Divine. There can be no basis for all the subsidiary meanings in terms of which we understand our lives unless there is a largest-of-all-meanings, a meaning-of-meanings which works to establish right and to put down wrong.

For their confidence in the possibility of meaning in history, Herodotus and his generation saw sufficient evidence in "the starry heavens above and the moral law within". And on the question of the moral responsibility of all the human actors within history, they likewise would have followed Kant: "The knowledge of what everyone is obliged to do [is] within reach of everyone."[22]

Herodotus makes it clear that every inch of the terrain of history is governed by moral meaning. Our point of entry (the point where our "interest" is engaged) into the story of world history is our singular understanding of the moral meaning of our own deeds. This sets us on the path that leads to recognition of the moral dimensions of the deeds of the actors in history. There is no understanding what is happening in history unless we make judgements of right and wrong. (Of what use would the *histor* have been to the community if he begged off judging the rights and wrongs of the stories put forward by the complainants?) As the themes get more complex, the moral implications become greater—but the difficulties of judging correctly get greater too. At a certain point along this line we get to see certain features of the largest meanings that govern history. And we see enough to know that they are moral too. But there is no possibility that our mortal intelligence can follow all the way up to the heights where divine purpose is dominant. Because the gods are interested in history on its higher reaches—and because their *interests* are not ultimately continuous with ours—we must not pretend that we can interpret all the features of the meaning of history. But we do know that its meaning is consonant throughout with "the supreme principle of morality", "the moral law within".

The gods are not mocked

It is not worth offering citations in proof of Herodotus' *invariable* practice of judging in moral terms historical actions. Whenever a human deed is described, a moral judgement is implied or explicity ascribed. But it is worth pausing at some typical examples of those places where we get glimpses of the largest meanings—the meaning-of-meanings.

The first principle of Herodotus' historiography is a Greek equivalent of the Biblical principle, that "God is not mocked". We know what is right and what is wrong: this is general issue to all human beings, and needs no explanation. In certain kinds of crisis, where routine ethical practice does not give us the precedents we need, we have to consult the gods through those formal avenues of approach provided by traditional religion: these are omens, auguries, and oracles (a typical example is I:91; also, *inter alia*, VI:29; VII:6, VIII:77.) We must also remain alert to messages that come through dreams (a typical example is VII:14-20; also, *inter alia*, I:34, 107, 209, II:141, III:124, 149, VI:107.) It has to be stressed that for Herodotus both common sense and piety are behind the obligations to make use of all these superstitious avenues: it is downright immoral to doubt the real presence of the divine will in all "signs", and such immoral neglect is always punished. It is, however, normally sufficient to listen to "the moral law within".

Herodotus' basic operating assumption is that brutal behaviour is punished within the sphere of this life (that is, within history.) The challenge for the student of history is to find the sequence of cause and effect connecting the evil deed and the divine punishment. Sometimes punishment follows immediately; and the appropriateness of punishment to sin is in these cases often so obvious that proverbs are built upon the story.

Sometimes, however, the guilty appear to have escaped. Nonetheless, long afterwards, punishment follows. In these cases, thoughtless people will fail to see the connection; and this is what gives rise to the impious notion that the gods do not really care about human behaviour. It is essentially the weakness of memory that explains the temptation to think that evil can be done with impunity. It takes no skill to see that history is full of defeat and frustration. What does take skill is to learn to recognize the sad news in history as the outcome (*teloi*) of sinful human deeds. *The historian's work is therefore essentially to discipline the memory so that it learns how to trace back from effect to cause in the chain of moral consequences.*

Here (from VII:133-138) is a rather complicated story whose meaning ordinary readers would never see without the assistance of disciplined historical memory.

When Xerxes began his invasion of Greece (486), he sent messengers to the Greek states inviting them to submit (by making a token offering of earth and water, to be carried back to Xerxes.) But he made an exception of Athens and Sparta, the reason being that when on a previous occasion his predecessor Darius had sent messengers (in 492) with the same message to all the Greek states, "at Athens they were thrown into the pit like common criminals, at Sparta they were pushed into a well—and told that if they wanted earth and water for the king, those were the places to get them from." Herodotus does not know "just what disagreeable consequences were suffered by the Athenians"; but he assumes there were such. "Perhaps," he muses, "it was the destruction of their city [in 480] and the country-side around it—though I do not myself believe that this happened as a direct result of their crime." What seems to be lacking in the Athenian case is some obvious feature in the outcome that shows its appropriateness to the crime—something *relevatory*.

"The case is clear, however, with respect to the Spartans". In Sparta there is a temple dedicated to Talthybius, who was Agamemnon's herald, and whose descendants (the Talthybiadae) still served in that office. For a long while after this incident, the Spartans could get no favourable omens from this temple. The significance of this ought to have been clear right away. But apparently it was only Xerxes' decision *not* to send messengers prior to his invasion that set men to making the connection. The ghost of Talthybius had been affronted by his descendants' violations of well-understood rules of diplomatic behaviour which overrode political differences and the passions of wartime. Talthybius would have to get satisfaction. As the seriousness of all of this ultimately dawned on the Spartan people, they tried to set things right, by calling for two volunteers to go to Xerxes, to offer their lives in atonement. Xerxes, however, was so impressed by the courage of these messengers, Sperchias and Bulis by name, that he declined to set things right: he would not, he said, "behave like the Spartans". "He had no intention of doing the very thing for which he had blamed them, or, by taking reprisals, freeing the Spartans from the burden of their crime". The ghost of Talthybius remained unsatisfied.

Thus, "long afterwards—during the war between Athens and the Peloponnese" the true outcome took place—

> and in this, I think, the hand of God was clearly to be seen. That Talthybius' anger should have fallen upon *ambassadors*, and should not have ceased until it was fully satisfied, was only right; but that it should have struck the sons of the very men who visited the Persian king because of it—that the objects of it should have been Bulis' son Nicolaus and Sperchias' son Aneristus—this to me at least is clear evidence of divine intervention. What happened was that these two men were sent by the Spartans on a mission to Asia and were betrayed by Sitalces son of Teres, the king of Thrace, and by Nymphodorus son of Pythes, a native of Abdera; they were made prisoners at Bisanthe on the Hellespont and taken to Attica, where they were put to death by the Athenians in company with Aristeas son of Adeimanthus, of Corinth. This, however, took place long after Xerxes' invasion of Greece, and I must get back to my story.

It is important to stress that in this matter of moral accountability men are only up to a certain point reckoning with each other; ultimately, they are reckoning with the divine. Note that in this story the people of Athens and the people of Sparta committed the same offence against the messengers of Persia. In the case of Athens, the punishment may or may not (Herodotus is unsure) have been received in 480 at the hands of Persia. But somewhere in the economy of history a price was paid for this sin, and we can be sure that it was an appropriate one. In the case of Sparta, it is not Persia (who, if the gods are left out of the account, is the offended party) that hands out punishment. In fact, Persia cancels the debt owed to herself and sends the Spartan agents back to settle with the gods. The gods then choose Athens, Sparta's original partner in sin, as the instrument of punishment. The moral appropriateness in this last touch is one of the clues which persuade Herodotus that the deaths of Nicolaus and Aneristus are the outcome of the historical event which set this causal sequence in motion.

Another example, from Book IX, might help to make this same point.

During the seige of Athens, Persian troops assaulted the temple of Demeter at Eleusis. Much later, it came about that the two battles which decided the outcome of the Persian War took place on the same day, one at Plataea and the other at Mycale. In both cases, the action took place near precincts sacred to Demeter. Regarding Plataea, the amazing fact was that "though the battle was fought close to the holy precinct of Demeter, not a single Persian soldier was found dead upon the sacred soil, or even appears to have set foot upon it, while round the temple, on unconsecrated ground, the greatest number were killed. My own view is—if one may have views at all about these mysteries—that the goddess herself would not let them in, because they had burnt her sanctuary at Eleusis". (IX:65)

At Mycale, Greek soldiers came ashore from their ships to meet Persian soldiers already landed.

> During the advance [of the Greeks], a herald's staff was found on the edge of the beach, close to the water, and at the same time the rumour flew through all the ranks that the Greeks had beaten Mardonius in Boeotia [at Plataea]. Many things make it plain to

me that the hand of God is active in human affairs—for else how could it be, when the Persian defeat at Mycale was about to take place on the same day as his defeat at Plataea, that a rumour of the kind should reach the Greek army, giving every man greater courage for the coming battle and a fiercer determination to risk his life for his country? It was another odd coincidence that both battles should have been fought near a precinct of Demeter of Eleusis. . . . Moreover, the rumour that Pausanias' men had already been victorious at Plataea was perfectly correct; for Plataea was fought early in the day, but the action at Mycale did not take place until evening; and the fact of this concurrence of dates—the same day of the same month—was proved when they reckoned back a short time afterwards. (IX:100)

It stands to reason that immortal gods do not have to settle with mortals immediately. The consequences of the sins of one generation, indeed, may not show up in the lifetime of the sinners. This raises "technical" problems for the historian, who must use diligence and imagination in tracing back from outcomes to morally appropriate but remote initial actions. It raises as well profound philosophical problems. To illustrate how Herodotus handles this problem we take the case of Croesus king of Lydia (Book I). It was Lydia (on Herodotus' reading) that set in motion the process that led to the Persian wars: the apex where meet all the separate destinies of all the previously discrete communities of civilized men. Lydia's harassment of the Ionian Greek states had gone on for generations (I:7-25), but it was Croesus (who reigned c. 560-546) who actually put an end to their independence, incorporating them into his Empire, which then appeared the secure master of western Asia. It is said that Croesus consulted the Athenian lawmaker Solon for a verdict on the question: "Who is the happiest of Men?", expecting that Solon (who was visiting Lydia at the time) would be forced by the evidence of Croesus' success and Lydia's prosperity to name Croesus himself. But Solon infuriated Croesus by declining to answer "until I know that you have died happily". For, "God is envious of human prosperity.... Great wealth can make a man no happier than moderate means unless he has the luck to continue in prosperity until the end.... Until he is dead, keep the word 'happy' in reserve. Till then, he is not happy, only lucky" (I:32).

No man was ever more scrupulous than Croesus in worshipping his own gods, and respecting the cults of others. He was rewarded with consistently favorable omens at times of sacrifice and even received what he took to be a promise of ultimate success on the grandest scale from the oracle of Delphi. And yet, at the end Croesus lost the whole of his empire to the Persian king Cyrus, and found himself a prisoner, standing on a great funeral pyre along with fourteen other captives, about to be burnt alive by Cyrus. Remembering in that moment the advice of Solon, he called out that wise man's name in despair. Cyrus heard the name of Solon, and wanting to know the story that went with it, called for the fires to be put out. At first, it seemed that he was too late:

> While Croesus was speaking, the fire had been lit and was already burning round the edges. The interpreters told Cyrus what Croesus had said, and the story touched him. He himself was a mortal man, and was burning alive another who had once been as prosperous as he. The thought of that, and the fear of retribution, and the realization of the instability of human things, made him change his mind and give orders that the flames should at once be put out, and Croesus and the boys brought down from the pyre. But the fire had got a hold, and the attempt to extinguish it failed. The Lydians say that when Croesus understood that Cyrus had changed his mind, and saw everyone vainly trying to master the fire, he called loudly upon Appolo with tears to come and save him from his misery, if any of his gifts had been pleasant to him. It was a clear and windless day; but suddenly in answer to Croesus' prayer clouds gathered

and a storm broke with such violent rain that the flames were put out.

This was proof enough for Cyrus that Croesus was a good man whom the gods loved; so he brought him down from the pyre and said, "Tell me, Croesus; who was it who persuaded you to march against my country and be my enemy rather than my friend?"

There follows a philosophical discussion between Cyrus and Croesus, about the gods, destiny, and luck. Then, Cyrus acceeds to Croesus' request that his chains be delivered "to the god of the Greeks [that is, to the temple at Delphi] whom I most honoured, and ask him if he is accustomed to cheat his benefactors...."

It is said that when the Lydian messengers reached Delphi and asked the questions they had been told to ask, the Priestess replied that not God himself could escape destiny. As for Croesus, he had expiated in the fifth generation the crime of his ancestor, who was a soldier in the body-guard of the Heraclids, and, tempted by a woman's treachery had murdered his master and stolen his office, to which he had no claim. The God of Prophecy was eager that the fall of Sardis might occur in the time of Croesus' sons rather than in his own, but he had been unable to divert the course of destiny. Nevertheless what little the Fates allowed, he had obtained for Croesus' advantage: he had postponed the capture of Sardis for three years, so Croesus must realize that he had enjoyed three years of freedom more than was appointed for him. Secondly, the god had saved him when he was on the pyre. As to the oracle, Croesus had no right to find fault with it: the god had declared that if he attacked the Persians he would bring down a mighty empire. After an answer like that, the wise thing would have been to send again to enquire which empire was meant, Cyrus' or his own. But as he misinterpreted what was said and made no second inquiry, he must admit the fault to have been his own.... When the Lydians returned to Sardis with the Priestess' answer and reported it to Croesus, he admitted that the god was innocent and he had only himself to blame (I:90-92).

This story of the life of Croesus stands at the very outset of Herodotus' account, not as a vehicle for hometruths about life's ups and downs, but as the first of many parables which convey Herodotus' message on the theme of the moral implications of the incommensurability of singular-meaning and historical-meaning. The story of the life of Croesus can be told in terms that reveal in a rough-hewn sort of way the moral economy at work. It is obvious-ly not the case that the amount and the quality of the retribution which the gods exact upon a man in this life exactly match the amount and the quality of the sin that the same man does in this life. There are enough clues in the circumstances of a man's fate that we get what the gods are driving at. Croesus, clearly, is punished for pride, and for dullness of wit. But he also bears the consequences of the crimes of his ancestors. There is no point crying to the gods for fairness in these matters. *Justice* is what interests the gods—and justice works out only in the longer haul, in the large-scale economy of history which is open to the immortal gods, but not to mortal men. "Fairness", in the everyday sense, has apparently nothing to do with the case. Cosmic questions of right are involved—offences against the gods. The gods set things right, ultimately, in ways that satisfy them and (we must simply accept this) that satisfy the ultimate moral order.

The cycle of fortune

In the long view (that is, from the perspective of the immortal gods) everything is being set right: within the process of history will take place all the outcomes necessary to set right the effects of the crimes of men and nations. This is all done according to the largest of the laws that govern history: namely, the law of the cycle of fortune. (This law is in fact a sub-law of the largest laws that govern the universe, and to which nature is subject and in a real sense the gods themselves. Just how these laws are linked together we shall be considering a little later (pp. 59f.) Every one of the collective entities with which history deals (dynasties, tribes, cities, nations, empires) comes within the aegis of the law of the cycle of fortune with which the gods are accomplishing their purposes in history. The effect of this law is as follows:

(1) any community of men which does not forever remain obscure and powerless (which any may do, if it lacks ambition), but enters into vital contest with other communities of men, may grow in strength to any degree up to the limit of empire over all the other communities of men;

(2) the particular degree reached is determined by the use to which the gods intend to put the community in question; but,

(3) the height of empire is also and at the same time related to the quality of the ambitions of the human rulers of the communities; and,

(4) since the gods are determined to keep human accomplishments from over-reaching suitable limits and thus diminishing their (the gods') own prestige; then,

(5) the limit of empire allowed to a community occurs at the point at which the gods perceive this threat to their own glory.

(6) When this point is reached, the process by which the community reached greatness is halted absolutely, and the process of reversal of fortunes must begin, and must not stop until the community has been returned to the level of powerless it had when its ambitions began.

The economy at work here is undeniably "moral", even though we mortals do not care for it. It is typical of the most spirited men in Herodotus' story that they struggle against it. Thus Xerxes flew into a rage when he was reminded of this logic of history by Mardonius: "You know my lord, that amongst living creatures it is the great ones that God smites with his thunder, out of envy of their pride. The little ones do not vex him. It is always the great buildings and the tall trees which are struck by lightning. It is God's way to bring the lofty low. Often a great army is destroyed by a little one, when God in his envy puts fear into the men's hearts, or sends a thunderstorm, and they are cut to pieces in a way they do not deserve. For God tolerates pride in none but Himself." (VII:10.) But, Xerxes persisted in his ambition: "... we shall so extend the empire of Persia that its boundaries will be God's own sky." (VII:8).

The problem of theodicy

But this law of the fortunes of empires is apparently not continuous with the laws which govern the dealings of the gods with individuals—except in the cases of the extraordinary individuals who are the greatest leaders of men —the "great buildings" and "tall trees" whom only the lightning strikes. Up to a point, what befalls an individual can be understood as the moral outcome of his deeds. But because every individual is also a member of a community, and because the gods are dealing with communities according to the largest laws of history and within a much broader time-frame than that of singular life, a good deal of what befalls a person in this life will depend upon where the community to which he belongs stood in the cycle of its own destiny when he was born into this life. This aspect of man's fate is controlled by "luck"—a technical term in Herodotus with this exact meaning. There is thus no absolute correlation between the sum-total of all that befalls a man in this life (his whole "fortune") and his singular-behaviour. Only in the case of giants of history like Xerxes ("world-historical figures", to anticipate Hegel) are the moral outcomes of singular destiny exactly appropriate to the moral outcomes within historical destiny.

If it were a matter of absolute importance that things should be set right between man and man in this life of time, we would have to concede that history does not amount to a story of triumph of right.

But if we allow ourselves to tell the story within a time-frame broad enough to take in the economy disclosed in the rise and fall of empires, there is no problem in telling history as theodicy. The fact is that fairness to individuals is not a governing concern when the gods are directing history.

It will already be obvious what, from a Christian point of view, is lacking in this characteristically Greek view of the moral meaning of history: namely, the perspective of *eternal singular* destiny. There will be time enough to develop that theme. But we must stress here, what modern commentators have largely denied or suppressed: namely, the absolute confidence of Herodotus and his contemporary audience that history's meaning is ultimately moral—that there is a meaning-of-all-meanings which it accomplishes. There have been certain Christian theorists of history (a good example is Bossuet) who have insisted that pious history is history told as theodicy, without shadow or remainder. But these theorists have never held their Christian audiences for very long. Most Christian theorists of history have settled for saying that we can see enough of the economy of divine retribution and reward within history to extrapolate some of the patterns of the operation of meaning-in-history, and that these are sufficiently satisfying that we can live confidently with the darkness of the rest. In its mainstream Christian theory of history admits that rewards and punishments seem not to be distributed equitably on history's own plane (this life-in-time.) And thus Christian theory of history looks beyond history for a satisfying answer to the question how history itself can be told as a story that illustrates the meaning-of-all-meaning. In this crucial sense, Christian theory of history is more realistic than that of Herodotus.

These are the foundations of Herodotus' theory and practice of history:

We cannot think historically, without thinking globally (subsuming all national and other local histories within the recital of one world-history.)

We cannot describe things historically without thinking teleologically.

We cannot think teleologically without thinking theologically.

The clue to history's meaning (if we are prepared to think theologically) is our knowledge of what the gods require of us. What specifically we must do is deducible from this *kairos*—the present state of crisis in which our human community finds itself. The *kairos* also, necessarily, contains the clue to how we must organize our history.

These propositions amount to the original contribution of Herodotus to historiography. They are likewise his permanent legacy to historiography, as valid today as in his own time. Theory of history that attempts to bypass these hard-earned insights subverts *history's authority*—which might equally be called its power to contradict the knowledge that derives from any other authority: philosophical, scientific or ideological.

Chapter 3:

Elements of Ancient Greek Theory of History

Herodotus' understanding of the significance of the Persian Wars

Herodotus was inspired to write his *Histories* by the conviction that his generation stood in the midst of a time of decision (a *kairos*) which was the immediate outcome of the Persian War. The Persian war was itself the outcome of all the previous decisions made by men and by gods within the realm of history. As the *telos* of all of history to this point, the war was of *absolute* and *inclusive* significance.

Herodotus felt it necessary to show that his account took in the histories of virtually all the populated sections of the globe. He insists that beyond countries familiar to himself or directly known to the peoples who are included in his *Histories* there are only uninhabitable deserts, endless oceans, and barren areas of ice and snow. He has heard many rumours of populations beyond these frontiers, but is convinced that these are fantasies or old-wives' tales. Though he admits the possibility of the existence of quasi-human creatures in some of these places, these, by definition, do not belong in his account (III: 100-118 and IV: 17-50.) He makes desperately bad guesses about the size and shape of the geography beyond southern Europe, North Africa and the Middle East. "Asia", he insists, "is inhabited only as far as India", "Europe is as long as the other two [Africa and Asia] put together" (IV: 42). And he compounds his culpability in this by (in his own words) "laughing at the absurdity of all the map-makers" (IV: 36) who would jeopardize his book's claim to universality by positing vaster lands and greater oceans beyond, and islands in the oceans. It is absolutely essential that the Graeco-Roman conflicts be seen as inclusive. If it falls short of inclusivity, it might have less than the absolute meaning upon which Herodotus insists.

Likewise, the absolute significance of the Graeco-Persian conflict is related to the ultimate character of the issue involved. It was a contest between tyranny and freedom. This theme controls the organization of the material and runs through the entire book. It takes distinct polemical form at critical junctures. For example, he reports a debate about the relative merits of the principal alternative forms of government (democracy, oligarchy and monarchy) that takes place among the principal claimants to the throne of Persia, following the death of Cambyses (521). The debaters agree that ideally democracy is the noblest system—though its weaknesses are admitted; but they decide for monarchy, because it alone fits the situation of empire over subject peoples. To illustrate the essentially arbitrary character of such regimes, Herodotus tells us that they then agree that the next emperor should be the one whose horse neighs first after the sun comes up. Darius cheats; and wins (III: 80-88.)

Another exchange on the ideological issues takes the form of a debate between Xerxes and Demaratus, a defector in his camp from Sparta. It is a very modern-sounding debate. Xerxes spots the weakness in government based upon the consent of the governed. If men are truly free, they will exercise that freedom by running away from battle. So "free" men are bound to lose their freedom in war. The fear of death is man's real master. Tyrants know this, and use men's fear of death at their hands to drive their subjects into battle. Demaratus answers: men living under democracy "are free—yes—but not entirely free; for they have a master, and that master is Law, which they fear much more than your subjects fear you. Whatever this master commands, they do; and his command never varies; it is never to retreat in battle, however great the odds, but always to stand firm, and to conquer or die" (VII: 101-105.)

Put another way, what is at stake is the Greek way of life. The Athenian envoys who rally the other Greek states to support them in the war are clearly speaking for Herodotus—and for the thesis of his *Histories*: what is at stake in this contest is "the Greek nation—the common blood, the common language, the temples and religious ritual; the whole way of life we understand and share together" (VIII: 144.) "We shall never be traitors to Greece" (IX: 7.)

The loss of Herodotus' vision of history

The sad fact is that Herodotus' work failed of its purpose. Herodotus' vigorous patriotism was already regarded as "old fashioned" when he wrote.[1] Herodotus' "straightforward contrast between Greek freedom and Persian depotism ... [and his] antithesis between the Hellenic and Persian spirit had become established during the Persian wars and is enshrined in Aeschylus' *Persae*. But by 425 the generation which heard Aristophanes making mild fun of Herodotus' remarks on the origins of the east-west struggle [in his *Acharnians*] no longer thought of Persia in quite the same hostile way. Indeed the country had ceased to be in the forefront of their thought, because they had been plunged for the past six years in the Peloponnesian War between Greek and Greek. That is why Herodotus felt it so imperatively necessary to evoke those events of half a century earlier in which the Greeks had been united together in freedom's cause."[2]

Herodotus failed to impress his vision of history upon the Greeks. It died with him. He was right to fear that the intra-mural conflict among the Greeks would result in the loss of Greek solidarity in defense of Greek values. People lost the sense that history could have much meaning. The vision of telling the whole of history as a single, linear story, organized teleologically, so that all the previous decisions of men are invested with absolute moral meaning and the consequences of all accumulate, culminating in a present moment of decision for the readers—these *conditions* of Herodotus' historiography were simply too hard on people.

Even if his contemporaries had agreed to believe that it had been right and necesary to organize the whole story of the past towards the *kairos* which was the Graeco-Persian war, of what relevance was that model to later readers, in the wake of the Peloponnesian War? Before long, the centre of power shifted, and so did the centre of real interest for those who were given to speculating on the largest meanings. History (in Herodotus' sense) surely could not answer the largest questions in the minds of the Greeks. And this was simply and obviously because it could no longer be organized in Herodotus' way: working back from a present moment of decision for the Greeks, as the embodiment and champions of liberty. The centre of decision in the real world of power was shifted, with the assistance of the Greeks themselves (now subjects of the Empire of Macedon), to the East. Eventually, the centre would shift again westward—but bypassing Greece—to Rome.

It is impossible to separate cause and effect here. Did the loss of the Greeks' sense of seriousness about history follow from their loss of political significance? Or was the latter the effect of the former? No doubt the relationship was reciprocal.

Greek historiography after Herodotus

Necessarily, the enthusiasm of Herodotus (and Hecataeus, and presumably other immediate precursors whose names we do not know) for gathering, sifting, and organizing the basic materials of history, went into eclipse along with Herodotus' confidence in the noetic value of history. A vital tradition of historiography requires both a lively habit of speculation about theory of history (how it should be organized, what meanings it bears) and a lively and persistent attention to the task of gathering and giving order to new historical materials. Even the most enthusiastic admirers of the Greek tradition of historiography (J.B. Bury, for instance) have conceded that the Greeks were unable to sustain interest for very long in the practical side

Ancient Greek Theory of History 53

of historical scholarship. Even the best historians, before and after Herodotus, were shockingly vague about chronology, and showed a surprising lack of imagination when it came to using available documentation.[3] J.B. Bury speaks, for example, of Hellanicus of Lesbos (roughly a contemporary of Herodotus) whose work as a compilor of historical annals was, Bury says, the best the Greeks ever achieved:

> His whole chronology of the thirty-five years after the Persian war was arbitrary; and it illustrates how in the absence of records precise chronology is hopeless.... There were numerous stones at Athens, officially inscribed and precisely dated, from which, if they were all preserved a modern student would probably construct without difficulty and with absolute certainty an exact chronicle of Athenian history in the fifth century. But it never occured to Hellenicus to look for them, and in this he was only like most other Greek historians. The Greeks used such records when they came across them, but as a rule they did not seek them out systematically. Was the labour of deciphering them too laborious? It is remarkable that Thucydides describes a sixth-century inscription, which he quotes, as written "in faint characters"; yet a portion of that same inscription which has survived seems to a modern epigrapher quite clear, after more than two thousand years.[4]

In plain words: they didn't try very hard.

There was among the ancient Greeks no tradition of hereditary scribes, responsible for keeping detailed archives, working them up at intervals into annals, and passing the documents and the job down from generation to generation. The lack of archives and annals seriously inhibited the work of the historians; but equally, the historians' failure to perceive the need for these inhibited the extablishment of such an office.

M.I. Finley writes:

No one before the fifth century tried to organize, either for his own time or for earlier generations, the essential stuff of history. There were lists—of the kings of Sparta and the archons of Athens and the victors in the various games. They could provide a chronology, if we knew what happened in the archonship of X or the reign of Y; but we do not know, except in a few isolated instances about a few isolated events. Law codes and individual rulings were recorded somehow, but there were no proper archives, and they soon disappeared from sight for the most part. This combination of negatives—the absence of annals (like those of the kings of Assyria), the indifference of poets and philosophers, and the loss of public documents—is irrevocable. Unless a generation is captured on paper and the framework of its history fixed, either contemporaneously or soon thereafter, the future historian is for ever blocked. He can reinterpret, shift the emphases, add and deduct data, but he cannot create the framework *ex nihilo*. That is why we can write the history of the Persian wars thanks to Herodotus, and the history of the Peloponnesian War, thanks to Thucydides, but not the history of the intervening fifty years, not for all the writers of tragedy and conedy and all the inscriptions and material objects unearthed by modern archaeologists.

Contemporary archaelolgy is a highly refined, highly professional and technical procedure. Carbon-14 dating and similar techniques will one day produce firm evidence undreamed of in the world of Thucydides. Yet it would be a great mistake to explain our superior knowledge of Mycenae solely by reference to scientific advances. Technically, Schliemann and Sir Arthur Evans had little at their disposal which was not available to fifth-century Athenians. The ancient Greeks already possessed the skills and the manpower with which to discover the shaft-graves of Mycenae and the palace of Cnossus, and they had the intelligence to link the buried stones—had they dug them up—with the myths of Agamemnon and Minos, respectively. What they lacked was the interest: that is where the enormous gap lies between their civilization and ours, between their view of the past and ours. A reverse example comes from their use of literary evidence. Thucydides and his contemporaries knew the full corpus of lyric and elegiac poetry, but they made less use, and less skillful use, of this material for historical analysis than we make of the few scraps which have survived in our time. Again neither technique nor intelligence is a useful criterion; only interest will explain the difference.[5]

This complaint against the Greeks (for vagueness about the exact detail of the past and especially about chronology) is not something that modern scholars have invented, out of their frustration with the sources. They had this same reputation in the ancient Eastern world. The Jewish historian Flavius Josephus (c. 37 – c. 100 A.D.) dwelt at length on this matter (in his *Contra Apion*) and offered some plausible thoughts on its causes. The "decisive" cause of the feebleness of their historiographical tradition, wrote Josephus, is that "the Hellenes have never exerted themselves to keep public registers of current events;" and this, in turn, is owing to the lack of anything similar to the priestly castes who have for hundreds of years done this work in Eastern civilizations:

> In Egypt, then, and Babylonia the registration of events was entrusted to the charge of specialists—the priests in Egypt and the Chaldaeans in Babylonia... [And as for the Jews] they were as particular as their neighbours (I shall not go into the question whether they were actually more particular than they were) in keeping records...; they assigned the duty to the high priests and the prophets; and ... down to our own day this practice has been maintained (and, I make bold to add, will be maintained hereafter) with scrupulous exactitude....

Not only did they place this department, from the outset, under the control of the picked men who attended to the service of God, but they took measures to preserve the race of priests unmixed and pure.... The most striking testimony to our accuracy is the fact that the priests in our community can show an unbroken descent, for two thousand years, from father to son as entered by name in the records.[6]

Without citing Josephus, M.I. Finley seconds his verdict regarding the failure of the Greeks as serious historians:

The only people in antiquity who were somehow "modern" in this respect [of total seriouness about historical recordkeeping] were the Hebrews, and the interest which lay behind, and which provoked, their detailed account of the past as a continuum was, of course, a religious one, the story of the unfolding of God's will from the Creation to the final triumph in the future. The Greeks had no such interest, religious or otherwise; whatever the function in the present of Agamemnon, it did not require locating him along a time continuum; it did not matter whether he lived two hundred years ago or four hundred or a thousand.[7]

Behind all this was a deep skepticism about the value of history as a way-of-knowing. "On the intellectual level", writes Finley, "everything was against the idea of history". This is not to say that there is no more history written after Herodotus. But after Herodotus it proved impossible to sustain his confidence that history could be told as a story with meaning of its own and its own authority. Much was still to be written about the past, but it had a relatively low prestige as intellectual work in its own time. Eventually, indeed, the concensus among Greek intellectuals came to be that there was something fundamentally wrong with the notion that significant meanings could be found in history. This was because it was too full of lively event, and could not be brought into a form that would yield anything but trivial meanings—at best, anecdotal illustrations for truth that we already know from intellectual disciplines that are built upon orderly, formal approaches to life.

A useful summary of this situation and its significance for the future of historiography in Western civilization is offered by R.W. Southern.[9] Like several of the other commentators, Southern selects Aristotle's verdict on history as typical of the Greek mind, and of course greatly influential:

> In Aristotle's view history lacks the two main ingredients of serious art—[*viz:*] form and universality. It lacks form because the events of history have no dramatic unity. And since it is the historian's task to record events faithfully, *as* they happened, *when* they happened, and in the order in which they happened, [therefore] artistic form (the famous beginning, middle and end of Aristotle's definition) can have no part in the finished result. Consequently the productions of the historians must be as chaotic as life itself:
>> The historian [says Aristotle] has to expound not one action but one period of time and all that happens within this period to one or more persons, however disconnected the several events may be. [Poetics, 1459 a]
>
> Artistic form is therefore excluded from written history. More important: since the material of history *lacks universality*, the works of the historians cannot have the universal truth which is the hallmark of great art:
>> The historian [says Aristotle] describes the thing that has been; the *poet* the kind of thing that might be. Hence poetry is more important and philosophic than history, for its statements have universal validity, while those of the historian are valid only for one time and place. [1451b][10]

Survival of something like Herodotus' sense of seriousness about history was impossible within the Greek intellectual world, given the premises of Greek philosophy. Its rescue, Southern argues, therefore had to await the discovery of the theory of history developing within the alternative thought-world of the ancient Jews. The theory of history which developed within the Chrisitan world (essentially out of the materials of the ancient Jewish theory, but with an admixture of compatible elements from the Graeco-Roman tradition) depended for its viability on its authority to contradict the ontological approach to life of Greek philosophy. The undermining of the authority of this original Christian theory of history (practically speaking, Augustine's theory of history) begins at the point where Greek ontological philosophy returned to something like the full strength of its original prestige in the Christian world, beginning in twelfth century. Southern argues that "the Aristotelian freeze" (as he calls it) took hold in Europe, and did not let go until the nineteenth. He believes that the recovery of history's prestige had to await the rediscovery of history's true character as "an art of a peculiarly elaborate, exacting and 'artificial' [in the good sense] kind".[11]

The eclipse of history's authority

The conviction grew among Greek intellectuals that Herodotus' teleological vision of history was irrelevant. Ineluctably, they were drawn more and more to make sense of a world in which political power was in the hands of others. Conscious of the superiority of their own civilization over that of the Macedonians, Persians, Phoenicians, Palestinians and Romans, they seemed logically bound to downgrade history (which is ultimately a story of power) as a way-of-knowing.

Increasingly, the best energies of Greek intellectuals went into inquiries into the nature of universe, into those "ontological" disciplines which are antithetical in method and spirit to historical enquiry. The prize for which all the best intellectuals were striving was some confirmation of the perfection which must lie behind the chaotic appearance of life. The study of history sheds no light on the search for the ultimate character of Being—unless it is a negative light. Wherever you reach into history you come up with a limited and specific set of characters and circumstances; and the historians are there, standing in custody of this limited and specific set of *facts*, to tell you that you must take these facts exactly as given. Alternatives to these facts have no standing in reality—no *ontic* reality, as the philosophers say. You are told that the only allowable speculation has to be about the Alexander who *won* the seige of Tyre: there is none allowed on an Alexander who "*lost*." And "speculation" in this context is an extremely confined exercise, since it cannot move to left or right into the realm of alternatives to what is given in the historical record.

But surely, the Greek philosophers believed, our minds were given us to seek after perfection: this *credo* was the starting-point of ontological philosophy. Perfection must, by definition, contain all that is; and if we are not to miss out on all that is, we must speculate on all that is possible. To get the measure of all that is possible, we must deliberately think all that is thinkable. Thus (say the philosophers) to know the whole possibility of meaning within the cosmos we must think the *possibility* of an Alexander who *lost* at Tyre. Not only is this ostensibly braver and nobler than what the historians insist upon, but it seems required by this ubiquitious premise of Greek ontological speculation: that the cosmos must be spherical, because the *All* must contain everything that it is possible to think, and its opposite, and every gradation between. This is clear in nature, in which simple things (seeds, for instance) derive from minute processes that the eye cannot see, grow through stages of increasing strength and complexity, into great things (trees), which realize the whole potentiality contained in the simple beginning—and which, in due course, die, and in decay take us backward down the whole chain to the dust in which is hidden the invisible impulse which will generate a new but identical rehearsal of the same cycle. Since human affairs happen within the same cosmos as nature, this cycle of recurrence must govern there as thoroughly as elsewhere. The true philosopher is therefore not deceived by the linear, irreversible and cumulative apearance of what happens in history: somewhere in the cosmos there is a dispensation in which there is an alternative Alexander, a *loser* of the seige at Tyre, who is as real within that dispensation as Alexander the *victor* of Tyre is real within the dispensation in which destiny has put us.

That we have only Alexander the victor to speculate about is due to our standing at a particular moment in a particular cycle of destiny. There is no absolute *noetic* meaning to this Alexander in the eye of the philosopher. There are untold numbers of cycles of destiny, containing all permutations and combinations of possibility involving Alexander and Tyre and all the other elements in that story. The sum total of all of these is the whole *cosmos*. And furthermore, the deepest Greek thinkers tell us that there is an ultimate dynamic governing the cosmos itself which sees to it that once all combinations and permutations of possibility are played through and the cosmos is full, then each combination is *withdrawn* from reality in reverse order, one afer another, until, after countless aeons the cosmos is emptied of all possibilities but the last. One seed remains in the cosmos. Then the process begins again. And so on, and so on, eternally.[12]

One version of this nearly ubiquitous Greek doctrine of eternal recurrence is offered by "the Stranger" to the young Socrates in one of Plato's dialogues:

> This Universe is sometimes conducted on its path and guided in its orbit by God, while at other times, when the cycles of its appointed time have arrived at their term, it is released from control by God and proceeds to revolve in the opposite direction by itself (which it can do, because it is a living creature endowed with intelligence by the Being who originally constructed it.) The tendency toward this reverse motion is inevitably innate in the Universe.... From these various premises it follows that the

Earth neither rotates itself perpetually nor is entirely and perpetually rotated by God in two contrary revolutions, and again that there are not two Gods rotating it with contradictory purposes, but that (as has just been stated and is the only remaining alternative) it is sometimes conducted by a divine cause outside itself, in which phase it receives an access of vitality and a renewal of immortality from its Creator, while at other times it is released from control and moves by itself. It is released at a juncture which enables it to pass through many hundred thousand reverse revolutions—a feat made possible by the infinitesimal size of the base upon which its vast mass moves with perfect equilibrium....[13]

This cycle (it must be understood) is the ultimate law of the cosmos. The gods are not superior to it. In fact, there are generations of gods that succeed each other and whose powers are appropriate to their particular stage in the cycle of eternal recurrence. Destiny has brought us mortals into the picture when Zeus is the pre-eminent God. He is the son of Chronos ("Time"). History belongs to this phase of things—which, as it happens, is the phase of the gradual self-emptying of the cosmos:

[T]he spontaneous generation of all things for the use of Man ... is entirely foreign to the notion now prevailing, and is one of the phenomena of the previous period [the period during which the universe has been filled to its limits with all possibilities.] In the previous period, the whole circular motion itself, in the first place, was controlled and superintended by God, and the same superintendence was provided locally by the assignment of all the parts of the universe to other controlling deities.... God himself at that time shepherded and watched over Mankind, just as Man, who stands out like a God from among his fellow creatures, acts as the shepherd of other races lower in the scale.[14]

There are (in "the Stranger's" account) periods of increase and decrease of the gods' interest in our activites. But the ultimate drift is downward, towards emptiness.

It is easy to see how fundamentally uncongenial was this sort of speculation to historiography! Nor should we doubt that this mode of speculation was ubiquitous among the Greeks. "The whole of the surviving corpus of literature inherited from antiquity testifies virtually without contradiction that cyclical theory possessed the Greco-Roman world."[15] "In [this] intellectual climate ... there was no place for the lasting significance of unique, incomparable events. Greek speculation was concerned with the cosmos, not with history, which as the sphere of contingency and change was not a proper theme for philosophy."[16]

In the same vein, C.A. Partrides writes:

The idea of recurrence ... is one of the most splendid commonplaces of ancient Greek thought. Throughout the millennium after Homer, the Greeks generally viewed temporality as a cyclical movement. From Greece the idea was passed to Rome, where it was summarily asserted by Seneca when he wrote that "all things are connected in a sort of circle; they flee and they are pursued. Night is close at the heels of day, day at the heels of night; summer ends in autumn, winter rushes after autumn, and winter softens into spring; all nature in this way passes, only to return." This view is encountered almost everywhere we turn, whether it is to Polybius's affirmation of "the cycle of political revolution" (πολιτειων ανακυκλωσιδ), or to Virgil's celebration of the circling centuries (magnus ab integro saeclorum nascitur ordo"), or to Marcus Aurelius' conviction of the "periodical renovation" of all things (περιοδικη παλιγγενεσια)—nor is it necessary to insist on its explicitness in both Plato and Aristotle.

Yet this widespread persuasion that events occur in a series of cycles did not consitute, either for the Greeks or for the Romans, an interpretation of history, much less a "philosophy" of history. Such a possibility was not even entertained by them, not because they were unconcerned with history but because the very nature of the cycles deprived history of any ultimate meaning. Even Polybius, who regarded Rome's conquest of the world as history's apex, still viewed the Roman era as the crest of one of the numberless waves endlessly crashing against the shores of the eternal world.[17]

Nonetheless, history did have a place in the curriculum of the elite. And there are writers of the Graeco-Roman world who can make a very high-sounding case for its value. A *locus classicus* is this passage from Diodorus of Agyrium (c. 90 - 20 B.C.):

> The authors of universal histories deserve the gratitude and recognition of their fellows for the spirit in which they give their labors for the benefit of the race. They have discovered the secret of imparting the fruits, without the perils, of experience, and therefore have knowledge of inestimable value to offer to the readers of their works. Toil and danger are the price of the practical wisdom which is bought by the experience of daily life, and we find that the legendary hero whose experiences were the most extensive had to suffer cruel misfortunes in order to
>
> > See the homes of many men and
> > read the thoughts of their hearts,
>
> while History is able to instruct without inflicting pain by affording an insight into the failures and successes of others. We are further indebted to these authors for their efforts to marshal the whole human race, who are all members one of another, in spite of the barriers of space and time, in one magnificent array.

In attempting this, they have constituted themselves nothing less than the servants of Providence. God, in His Providence, has related in a single system the evolutions of the stars of heaven and the characters of men, and maintains them in perpetual motion to all eternity, imparting to each the lot which Destiny assigns; while the authors of universal histories, in their works, record the general transactions of the world as though it were a single community, and pass the works of Providence through the grand audit of their clearinghouse.

It is a blessing to be given opportunity to improve ourselves by taking warning from the mistakes of others, and in all the chances and changes of this mortal life to be free to copy the successes of the past instead of being compelled to make a painful trial of the present. In ordinary life, the judgment of the older generation is always preferred by the younger on account of the experience which has come to them with time; yet the knowledge which comes by History surpasses individual experience in value in proportion to its conspicuous superiority in scope and content. For every conceivable situation in life the supreme utility of this study will generally be admitted. The young are invested by it with the understanding of the old; the old find their actual experience multiplied by it a hundredfold; ordinary men are transformed by it into leaders; men born to command are stimulated by the immortality of fame which it confers to embark upon noble enterprises; soldiers, again, are encouraged by the posthumous glory which it promises to risk their lives for their country; the wicked are deterred by the eternal obloquy with which it threatens them from their evil impulses; and in general, the good graces of History are so highly praised that some have been stimulated by the hope of them to become founders of states, other to introduce laws contributing to the security of the race, and others to make scientific or practical discoveries by which all mankind has benefited. As a result of all these activities the sum of human happiness is increased, but the palm of praise must be rendered to History, who is the real cause of them all. History may claim to be the guardian of those who have a reputation to keep, the witness against those who have a reputation to lose, and the benefactress of all humanity. Even the entirely fictitious legend of Hell is a mighty instrument for turning the hearts of men to righteousness and fear of God. How much greater, therefore, must we conceive to be the potential ennobling influence upon character of History, the prophetess of truth and wellspring of philosophy?[18]

Notice the steady escalation of the claims for history's value. We begin with the penny-ante argument: history allows us to participate vicariously and with impunity ("without ... pain") in great deeds. Then: we can "improve ourselves by taking warning from the mistakes of others." At the next step, we see history raising the moral sights of its readers, by holding up noble deeds for emulation. This builds by degrees into the argument that society depends upon history for its preservation; for reading history nourishes each generation anew in patriotism. The patriotic spirit depends for its survival on people's confidence that somehow history keeps the best among us eternally alive:

For those who have achieved nothing noteworthy in their lives, the death of the body involves the total extinction of existence; but for those who abilities have won them glory, an eternal remembrance of their achievements is assured by the praises that resound from the divine lips of History ... [All the heroes of the past] who have obtained heroic or divine honors owe the glory which they have earned to the immortality with which their attainments have been invested by History.[19]

From the bottom to the top of this scale of the values that Diodorus assigns to history we are dealing with history's *uses*. There is no thought that history might have a meaning apart from its *uses*. And if it is clear that the supreme *use* of history is for inculcating the virtues which society needs to keep alive, then it is obvious that society defines these values first. There is no thought that history might tell us facts about our condition that could contradict the values that we bring into history, expecting it to confirm them. Every gradation on the theme of how to *use* history seems to be anticipated here in this brief excerpt: from the one that figures in the Department of Education instructions to grade school teachers in liberal-democratic systems to the one which informs the totalitarian ideologies. Where history's ultimate meaning is its usefulness there is no room to make a case for the independent virtue of diligent research and critical scholarship. Nor is there anything capable of sustaining the independent spirit of historical inquiry. Everything tends to stifle it.

Chapter 4:

Elements of the Ancient Jewish Theory of History

Antiquity of Jewish sacred literature

Before turning to comparison and contrast of the Greek and the Ancient Jewish traditions of historiography, it is necessary to get our chronological bearings.

It is not known how long before his death Herodotus completed his *Histories* as we have them; and in any case the exact year of his death is not known (429?/425?). We recall that Herodotus' story begins with review of the relations between the Greek cities of Asia Minor and the Empire of Lydia (founded in mid-seventh century B.C.), concentrating on the reign of its last king, Croesus (c. 560-546). The story of Croesus' defeat by Cyrus II ("the Great") of Persia in 546 provides the transition to Herodotus' section on the history of the Persian Empire. We are given some flashbacks to the history of Mesapotamia and Egypt prior to this Sixth century B.C., but little that has proved of much value to the historians.

The history we have today of these oldest civilizations in the world has been reconstructed almost entirely from materials discovered by nineteenth and twentieth-century archaeology. It is only for the period beginning with the reign of Cyrus (548-529), roughly a century and a quarter before its publication, that Herodotus' *Histories* provides sufficient detail to serve as an historical source in its own right.

As it happens, this same Cyrus is a very important figure in the history of the ancient Jews, and for a number of reasons it makes sense to think of his reign as the point where Greek historiography and ancient Jewish historiography intersect.

History of Israel	History of Greece and Rome
Age of the Patriarchs ? 2000 .... 1825 Abraham	Mycenean civilization at peak c. 1800--c.1400
? 1750 .... 1640 Joseph	
the exodus ? 1280 (or 1260) to 1240 (or 1220)	
crossing of the Jordan 1240 (or 1220)	destruction of Troy c. 1230
period of the Judges c. 1200–c. 1050	Dorian invasions c. 1250–c.1050
United Monarchy Saul c. 1050–1011/10 David 1011/10–971/70 Solomon 971/70–931/30	
division of Israel 930	
	beginning of city states in Greece c. 800 Homer ? c. 800
	Rome founded c. 750
fall of Northern Kingdom (Israel) to Assyria 722	
	age of the tyrants in Greece c. 650–500
reign of Josiah in Judah 640/39–609	
	Solon's constitution 594–560
fall of Jerusalem to Babylon 587/6	
fall of Babylon to Persia (Cyrus) 539	
beginning of return to Jerusalem 538	
Temple rebuilt 537–516	
	establishment of Roman Republic c. 500
	Graeco-Persian War 493–479
	Herodotus 484–425
	Socrates 469–399
	Peloponnesian War 431–404

Cyrus' reign marks the beginning of a hopeful period for the Jews, coming a generation after the most hopeless moment in their history to that date—that moment being the year of the seige and destruction of Jerusalem and its Temple (586) by the Babylonian Empire, under Nebuchadnezzar. (For purposes of orientation, we note the date 594, which was the year when Solon undertook to provide a constitution for Athens. Herodotus' story of the encounter between Solon and Croesus (above p. 41) is, however, regarded as legendary). Cyrus reversed the Babylonian emperors' policy with respect to the Jews (and presumably other subject people whose leaders had similarly been brought into exile into Babylonia). Believing that it was in his own interest and would in fact strengthen his empire to have the gratitude of the gods of his subjects, he encouraged the Jewish leaders to return to Jerusalem; and in fact he subsidized the re-building of their Temple. (This latter was accomplished by 517/516, thus giving the significant figure of seventy years as the traditional reckoning of the Babylonian exile).

During the years of Babylonian exile, the priests and leaders of the Jews carried ahead with renewed earnestness a work begun, and then apparently neglected, during the reign of King Josiah (c. 640-609): the establishment of a corpus of the sacred literature of the nation—the first step in the making of the Jewish Bible.

It is very difficult for a sincere layman to get a grip on the facts of this matter, so recondite and so tendentious is the expert literature, and so divergent are the experts' conclusions. Increasingly, scholars have come to recognize that it is not wise to be dogmatic about the process of the formation of the canon. B.S. Childs writes: "...it should be incontrovertible that there was a genuine historical development involved in the formation of the canon and that any concept of canon which fails to reckon with the historical dimension is faulty.... [However,] the available historical evidence allows for only a bare skeleton of this development".[1]

For our purposes, these few statements (though by no means immune from all critical objection) can be said to be generally agreed. Most scholars believe that at least by 400 B.C. the whole of the Pentateuch (*i.e., Genesis* through *Deuteronomy*) as well as some portions at least of the major Prophets (*Isaiah* and *Jeremiah* and possibly *Ezekiel*), *Job*, at least some of the *Psalms* and of *Proverbs*, and the historical books *Joshua, Judges, Samuel, Kings*, all belonged to the received Hebrew scripture. This canonical literature provided the authoritative code of laws and an account of the nation's history. It was believed that extraordinary (Providential) circumstances had played some part in the preservation of each *Book*, and (going further back) in the preservation of the traditions that preceded the composition of the individual Books. And they further believed that these Books having been separated from other books not selected for inclusion and bound together with others selected, formed a single corpus whose authority was vastly greater than the sum of all their separate authorities, amounting in fact to the authority of the "Word of God".

Herodotus makes no explicit reference to the Jews. Their brief period of significance as a power in the East (roughly the Eleventh to Eighth centuries B.C. (see pp. 170f. below) was real enough while it lasted: recent archeology has made that clear. But it was long past when Herodotus appeared on the scene, and as we have noted, neither he nor any of his sources possessed any documentation belonging to this period (i.e. the Eleventh through Seventh centuries, B.C.). The Jewish people themselves (or at least all but a pathetic remnant) had been removed from their former kingdom into exile in Babylon, and the Temple, together with all its archives, was destroyed. Had Herodotus been writing in the late Fourth century rather than in the late Sixth he would have known of the Hebrew scriptures which were by then circulating among non-Jewish populations and proving of great interest to philosophers, religious inquirers and historians. (See further, pp. 152f. below).

Ancient Jewish Theory of History

Though limited in its perspectives (as we shall see), the Bible of this "first canon" provides virtually the only extensive literary source for the history of the millennium previous to the time for which Herodotus himself serves as an historical source. But the Bible was not available to Herodotus when he laid down the foundations of Greek theory and practice of history. This coincidence guaranteed that Greek historiography was established and developed through its first crucial stages entirely without influence from Ancient Jewish historiography—a much older tradition, and one which (both as theory and as practice) stood on quite different premises. This explains why, when the time came for the first Christian generations to consider what use they would make of historiography, there were two quite distinct traditions existing on the same ground (that is, as a double legacy available to intellectuals everywhere within the Roman Empire, one deriving from Herodotus, the other from the Hebrew Bible).

• • •

It is my experience that the most serious popular misapprehension regarding the history of the Ancient Jews stems from vagueness about the time-frame of ancient history. It is essential that we get the history of Israel in perspective:

> As the Bible presents it, the history of Israel began with the migration of the Hebrew patriarchs from Mesopotamia to their new homeland in Palestine.... [Present scholarship dates this somewhere in the early centuries of the second millennium B.C.].... To us who live in this late day, the second millennium seems very long ago indeed. We are tempted to think of it as lying near the dawn of time, when man first struggled up from savagery into the light of history, and are prone, therefore, to underestimate its cultural achievements. We are further prone to picture the Hebrew ancestors, tent-dwelling wanderers that

they were, as the most primitive of nomads, cut off by their mode of life from contact with what culture there was, whose religion was the crudest sort of animism or polydaemonism. So, in fact, did many of the older handbooks depict them....

So, I think it can be said, do most otherwise educated adults today depict them!

This, however, is an erroneous notion and a symptom of want of perspective—a carry-over from days when little was known at first hand of the ancient Orient.... Horizons have widened amazingly in the past generation. [written in 1972.] Whatever one says of Israel's origins must be said with full awareness that these lie nowhere near the dawn of history. The earliest decipherable inscriptions both in Egypt and in Mesapotamia reach back to the early centuries of the third millennium B.C.—thus approximately a thousand years before Abraham, fifteen hundred years before Moses. There history, properly speaking, begins. Moreover, in the course of the last few decades discoveries in all parts of the Bible world, and beyond it, have revealed a succession of yet earlier cultures which reach back through the fourth millennium, and fifth, and the sixth, to the seventh and, in some instances, further still. The Hebrews were in fact late comers on history's stage. All across the Bible lands, cultures had come to birth, assumed classical form, and run their course for hundreds and even thousands of years before Abraham was born. Difficult as it is for us to realize, it is actually further in time from the beginnings of civilization in the Near East to the age of Israel's origins than it is from that latter age to our own.[2]

When our eighteenth-century ancestors raised their complaint about the sparsity of historical detail in the earliest sections of the Hebrew Bible, it did not occur to them to ask: "relative to *what*?" Their notions of the historical landscape of the period prior to the Persian

Wars were of necessity extremely vague, depending on the limited and dubious materials in Herodotus and odds-and-ends of even more dubious materials culled from fragments of later Hellenic historians. They had no inkling of the existence of civilizations reaching back several millennia prior to Abraham. They dismissed as pastoral fantasies authentic and historically-valuable materials which are in the Pentateuch, which belong to the beginnings of the patriarchal period and whose true character has only been appreciated since confirmation has been provided from the discoveries of archeology in the last fifty years.[3] We are, however, without their excuse. We are today in a position to marvel at the antiquity of the Jewish practice of historiography and to concede to it priority in the establishment of those standards of integrity which the eighteenth-century would claim for its own critical intelligence. Two testimonies from pre-eminently qualified authorities will perhaps serve our present purpose. The first is from William Foxwell Albright, generally recognized as the dean of Biblical archeologists until his death in 1971:

> The excessive scepticism toward the Bible by important historical schools of the eighteenth and nineteenth century, certain phases of which still appear periodically, has been progressively discredited. Discovery after discovery has established the accuracy of innumerable details, and has brought increased recognition to the value of the Bible as a source of history.[4]

And the other is a rabbi (of the Reform, as distinguished from Conservative and from Orthodox, persuasion) and an archaeologist responsible for much of the reconstruction of the history of the patriarchal period and earlier:

> It may be stated categorically that no archaeological discovery has ever controverted a Bible reference. Scores of archaeological findings have been made which confirm in clear outline or in

exact detail historical statements in the Bible. And, by the same token, proper evaluation of Biblical descriptions has often led to amazing discoveries. They form tesserae in the vast mosaic of the Bible's almost incredibly correct historical memory.[5]

The Historical literature of the Ancient Jews

In Chapter Three we offered some observations about the strengths and weaknesses of the theory and practice of historiography among the Ancient Greeks. Most of our space was devoted to an analysis of one book, the "*Histories*", written by Herodotus. We adopted the view of the most considerable modern scholars of our theme, that Herodotus' work is the best product of the first generation of true Greek historians, and that subsequent generations failed by and large to make advances on either the theory or the practice of historiography—at least as we have come to conceive of this work. The verdict is put more strongly by Denys Hay than by most; but perhaps for just that reason we should quote him and move on: "... most classical historians are bad historians—or perhaps one should rather say that they were attempting to do something completely different from what is now regarded as the historical task."[6]

If we had before us the task of presenting a more thorough survey of Greek or Hellenic historiography, we would follow the example of the master-scholars in this field, offering next a chapter on Thucydides (460/455?–c. 399 B.C.), then others on Xenophon (c. 430–c. 350 B.C.), Polybius (c. 200–118 B.C.), with briefer sections on other individual Greek or Hellenic authors whose work has survived only in fragments; then continuing with a survey of Roman historians: Caesar (c. 100–44 B.C.), Sallust (86–c. 34 B.C.), Livy (c. 60 B.C.–c. 12 A.D.), Tacitus (c. 56 A.D.–120 A.D.), Plutarch (c. 46–c. 120), Suetonius (75–160), and again briefer sections on the Roman authors whose work has survived only in fragments. We would, that is, deal serially and in chronological order with significant authors identified by name and significant books

Ancient Jewish Theory of History 75

identified by title. This is how a survey of Graeco-Roman historiography is always done, and for good reason: this is what is called for in writing a history of history among the Greeks, the Hellenes, and Romans.

When we turn to the Ancient Jews, however, we have to follow an altogether different method. Generalizations about differences between Graeco-Roman historiography and Ancient Jewish historiography are bound to be misleading unless careful attention is first given to the different standing of historiography in the two civilizations.

There are two principal considerations to note in this connection. One is that the Ancient Jewish literature gives to history vastly greater *prestige* than the Greeks knew about or could have guessed at. The second is the fact that on the one hand (the Greek) we are dealing with a distinct vein of literature, a clearly-labelled shelf of particular authors and their books, set apart from all other categories of literature (poetry, philosophy, drama, *etc*.); and that on the other hand (the ancient Jewish) we are dealing with an intact corpus of sacred literature from which it is impossible to select for separate examination the historians and the history books. The "impossibility" of which we speak is both moral and practical.

Our first concern is to get at these two aspects of the question of history's *standing* among the ancient Jews: why history has its extraordinary prestige, and why it requires the whole canon of sacred literature to convey it.

In the case of Graeco-Roman historiography, everything depends upon knowing who is the author of the book you are reading. Subsidiary insights can be gained by putting your author (Xenophon, for example) into the context of the whole tradition of Greek historiography. The fact that these insights are subsidiary is owing to the relative insignificance of speculation about history in the whole Graeco-Roman tradition. It is of primary importance that you are reading Xenophon, and secondarily significant that Xenophon is speaking out of the Greek tradition. This is said (it must be stressed) with respect to our present concern only (namely, the study of the origins of our civilization's theory of history) and does not imply a generalization that I would necessarily want to defend regarding the relative standing of individual authorship *vis-à-vis* the wisdom of the community in the two traditions.

Questions of the identity of the original authority for historical materials in the Jewish Bible are extremely interesting, but generally prove to be of subsidiary importance for determining the reliability of the materials. This is because in the Jewish tradition standards of faithfulness in preserving and perpetuating received accounts of past events were incomparably higher than ever became the case among the Hellenes, and were of longer standing by many centuries. Ingenious scholars have worked for generations at sifting out the "historical texts" from this literature and identifying the responsible, singular authors—searching for traces of persons answering the description of Herodotus or Xenophon, and of monographs resembling the *Histories* or *Anabasis*, so as to make feasible the job of comparing Greek and Ancient Jewish historiography. This sort of exercise is misconceived. It derives from an early-modern prejudice to the effect that the beginnings of our modern historical theory and method lie with the Greeks; and that insofar as there is any "historical content" embedded in the Bible it must have the form and features of Greek works of historiography.

We are not denying that there were ancient Jewish historians of the caliber of Herodotus or Xenophon. On the contrary: we have abundant evidence that the ancient Jewish world produced many more of them than did the Hellenic world, and certainly they must have been of superior quality to the median product of the Greeks. Furthermore, the line of historians goes back several centuries further than it does among the Greeks.[7]

Nor is it the case that the founders of the canon meant to suppress the facts of individual authorship. It is frequently suggested that those who compiled the Biblical canon did not have our modern sense of the

Ancient Jewish Theory of History

importance of historical attestation. This is quite untrue. One of the principal stumbling blocks to popular understanding of this question is the canonical convention of assigning entire books to singular "authors"—*e.g.*, the first five Books to Moses, the *Psalms* to David, *Proverbs* and the other wisdom literature to Solomon—when plain reading of the very texts (let alone external evidence) makes it clearly impossible to assign literal, singular responsibility to these persons.

There is every evidence that the founders of the canon possessed at least as much curiosity as we have about how the first accounts originated and how they were conveyed from one authority to the next. Owing to that trick of perspective of which John Bright speaks (above pp. 71–2), we tend to think of the narratives of "Bible times" in a foreshortened time-frame, and of the men of the fifth century as being so much nearer to Moses' time or Abraham's time than we are that the evidence of those earlier times was all around them. In fact, Ezra is as far removed in time from Abraham as we are from the sixth or seventh century A.D.—from the reign of the Emperor Justinian. If they attributed the whole of the Pentateuch to Moses, it was not because they did not grasp that Moses had had to depend on extant authorities for what he knew about the centuries that preceded; or that they failed (somehow!) to notice that it is incongruous that the report of the circumstances of his death is reported in the book of which he is the "author". It is clear that when Israel became a secure community under the monarchy of the house of David (in the tenth century), enjoying the luxury of archives and houses of scholarship, the Jews worked out a division of labour in historiography not unlike the modern one. Her intellectuals observed traditional practices of attribution in historiography morally if not in detail practically equivalent to our own. This appears from the frequent citation by title of official and possibly extra-official sources which are now long gone. *Inter alia*: there are references in *Numbers* 21:14 to "The Book of the Wars of the LORD"; in I *Kings* 14:19, 15:31, 16:5, *etc.*, to "the annals of the Kings of Israel"; and in I *Kings* 14:29, 15:7, 15:23, *etc.*, to "the annals of the kings of Judah." The authors of *Chronicles* mention twenty-one books and sources, including the books of "Samuel the Seer", "Nathan the Prophet", "Gad the Seer", the "prophecy of Ahijah of Shiloh", the "vision of Iddo the Seer", the "histories of Shemiah the Prophet", the "histories of Jeho the son of Hanani which is included in the annals of the kings of Israel", and "[what is] recorded by the Prophet Isaiah." Typically these references take the form: "The other events of Jeroboam's reign, in war and peace, are recorded in the annals of the kings of Israel" (I *Kings* 14:19)—implying that these sources were extant, and that learned listeners would know how to get behind the present account through archival research.

Frequently, the present text of a single Book in the Jewish Bible offers parallel stories presenting contradictory interpretations of the same event, evidently depending on rival sources. (*E.g.* for the story of the selection of Saul as King, compare I *Samuel* 9:1–10:16, 13:3–15 with I *Samuel* 8, 10:17–27, and 12. And, for the story of how Saul met David, compare I *Samuel* 17:1 to 18:5 with I *Samuel* 17:55–58).[8]

This practice of offering alternative insights on long-past events points to a mature appreciation of the rights of critical intelligence in dealing with evidence. It also makes clear that the primary purposes of the text as we have it is not to provide historical materials as such (these were in the archives for the scholars to study and write about), but to present a theological commentary. Israel's archives were subsequently plundered by her conquerors, and whatever remained was presumably lost forever in the destruction of the Temple.

We can assume that the founders of the canon were depending on certain conventions which governed attribution of literary materials to the proper names of persons who were *known* not to be the literal authors of all so assigned. And it would be unreasonable to expect that we will ever be in a position to fully understand the conventions involved. We have our own conventions in the matter of assigning authorship to public figures and celebrities which make sense to us and are, we assume, generally understood. Those conventions are nowhere committed to writing for record, but are a great deal less defensible than the convention which assigns all "Psalms" to David and all "Wisdom" to Solomon. Do we expect that historians twenty-five centuries from now will be able to duplicate the reasoning that assigns authorship to tens of thousands of *pages* of public documents to the personal authorship of Ronald Reagan? Will they understand that his actual creative contribution to these materials extends to no more than a few thousand *words* spoken into a dictation machine? Will they really assume that the movie stars and heroes of business all literally "wrote" the literate and witty autobiographies (which will surface some day as the major literary deposit of American civilization of the 1980's)? Or, more likely, will they penetrate, through ingenious research, to the "secret" of ghost authorship, and proclaim that their higher criticism has uncovered the truth that was somehow withheld from us?

We assign nominal authorship to ghost-written materials because we are caught up in certain conventions which amuse without deceiving us. The founders of the canon sometimes assigned nominal authorship to materials whose true, literal authors they frequently did no know; and we shall never know them either because they go back so far—in some cases to oral traditions. But they did not make these assignments with intent to deceive. And they certainly could not have tolerated the modern frivolity of assigning false authorship to satisfy the vanity of living people. If they knew who was the original author of a source, they said so.

What would a fifth century B.C. Jew assume was meant by Moses' "Authorship" of *Genesis*? I start by assuming that we can never know exactly. But I guess that he believed that Moses was responsible for bringing up to his own date and into one account fit for recital by the whole community in public ceremony, and for commitment to memory by the priests—all written or recited material that shed light on the meaning of the existence of the People of Israel; and that, after he was gone, this task was continued in the tradition established by him.

Prima facie, there is no good reason why Moses should not have been the literal, singular author of most of the present form of the text of what we find in *Genesis*—through *Deuteronomy*.[9] It is unthinkable that Moses, brought up within the nobility of Egypt, would lack the literary skill involved in overseeing the collocation of extant literary and/or oral materials as they bore on the historical traditions (as, for instance, Eusebius did with the sources for the early history of the Church in the first quarter of the fourth century A.D.) And as for the possibility of Moses' drawing upon ancient *written* materials, archaeological discovery throughout the Near East over the past half-century has made clear that written language and literate learning go back much further than was assumed when Wellhausen and his epigones made their entirely conjectural assignments of the materials in the Pentateuch to "oral" and "written" categories:

> The earliest texts known to us anywhere come from the closing centuries of the fourth millennium. Though they cannot as yet be read with assurance, they seem to be chiefly inventories and business documents, and thus witnesses to the growing complexity of economic life. Since economic life centered about the temple, we may assume that the characteristic organization of the city-state about the shrine, familiar to us from the third millennium, had already been developed. In any case, we can record the fact that the threshold of literacy had been crossed some two thousand years before Israel emerged as a people. Nor are we to suppose that this cultural flowering was a thing done in a corner, exerting no influence beyond Mesopotamia. On the contrary...there is indisputable evidence that before the end of this period there were links of trade and cultural intercourse with Palestine and predynastic Egypt.[10]

The fact is, therefore, that no one knows where to draw the line and say: beyond this it is all "oral tradition". We know nothing of the process by which, for example, the lists of nations of the world found in *Genesis* 10 (see below, pp. 95–96), were retained and conveyed, nor who first devised them, nor when; nor do we know whether they appeared first in writing or as items or oral recital. We can be sure that there is no point where the practice of oral recitation of traditional materials was discontinued in favour of the written medium. Oral recital persisted throughout the whole Biblical period as a check on written literature, as indeed it still does in the Jewish tradition of learning.

Even if we set aside the possibility of Moses' own authorship (in the full literal sense) of any or all of the Pentateuch, and go along quietly with the conventional textbook distinction of an earliest written text to be called "J", which makes up only part of the Pentateuch and is written c. 900 B.C.—we have still got a written text containing much historical narrative of the highest quality, and whose historical reliability has been vindicated in detail after detail by archaeological discoveries over the past century. Whoever were the individuals who put together the original narratives (written or oral) out of which came the *Genesis* account of the patriarchal period, the variety of psychological and moral observation that we find there shows them to be Herodotus' equals in the matter of literary sophistication; and the recurring vindications in modern archaeological discovery of details of geography, ethnology and so on, prove them to be consistently superior in critical judgement.

In Greek literature, there is nothing at all of use to historians for the history of the Greeks dating back within several centuries of the time of Abraham.[11] Nor is there any other literature anywhere in the world that gives us anything at all of an authentic, historical character regarding that period that precedes the stage of city-based civilization.

> Hebrew national tradition excels all others in its clear picture of tribal and family origins. In Egypt and Babylonia, in Assyria and Phoenicia, in Greece and Rome, we look in vain for anything comparable. There is nothing like it in the tradition of the

Germanic peoples. Neither India nor China can produce anything similar, since their earliest historical memories are literary deposits of distorted dynastic tradition, with no trace of the herdsman or peasant behind the demigod or king with whom their records begin. Neither in the oldest Indic historical writings (the Puranas) nor in the earliest Greek historians is there a hint of the fact that both Indo-Aryans and Hellenes were once nomads who immigrated into their later abodes from the north. The Assyrians, to be sure, remembered vaguely that their earliest rulers, whose names they recalled without any details about their deeds, were tent dwellers, but whence they came had long been forgotten.[12]

The prestige of history among the Ancient Jews

> Biblical theology ... is a recital or proclamation of the acts of God, together with the inferences drawn therefrom. These acts are themselves interpretations of historical events, or projections from known events to past and future all described within the conceptual frame of one people in a certain historical continuum.... Biblical theology is the confessional recital of the redemptive acts of God in a particular history because history is the chief medium of revelation.
>
> George Ernest Wright[13]

> To say "man" is to say "history".
>
> Karl Barth[14]

Consideration of the prestige of history in ancient Jewish faith must begin with the account of the Creation. Fundamentalist scholars, both Jewish and Christian, insist that we must think of the whole of the content of the Pentateuch, from *Genesis* 1:1 forward, as historical documentation. The account of Creation (they say) was given face-to-face by the Creator to Adam, who is thus the author or at least the recorder of the first four chapters. *Genesis* 5:1, which reads "This is the record of the descendants of Adam" ("This is the book of the genealogy of Adam," in *New King James Version*), thus really means something like: "the above is the account or the history of things down to the time of Adam." Similarly, *Genesis* 10:1 means "the above is the account or the history of things down to the time of Noah and his sons," and Noah is the author of the above. Whatever the theological wisdom of this approach, it cannot be relevant to a study of the *method* of history, assuming as it does an order of reality in which God directly addresses the historian, dictating the contents of historical texts. But insofar as *theory* of history is concerned, we cannot avoid certain implications of the way in which the *Book of Genesis* links our knowledge of created reality with the authority of history.

Everything depends on our being open to the possibility that this story tells us some things that cannot be told in any other form than as a story (narrative) whose authority traces to its telling by the first man that ever was. We were not there when order was created. It is important for us to know that the present order of reality is not the reality for which we were made "in God's beginning" (*Genesis* 1:1.)

> [T]he Bible does not begin by saying, "God created heaven and earth;" it begins by saying, "*In the beginning*." The essential message is not that the world has a cause, but rather that the world is not the ultimate. The phrase "in the beginning" is decisive. It sets a limit to being as it sets a limit to the mind.
>
> The supreme question is not, "Who made the world?" but rather, "Who transcends the world?" The biblical answer is, "He Who created the heaven and earth transcends the world."[15]

The message of the Bible (this "confessional recital of the redemptive acts of God"—in Wright's formulation) is that we are being remade for life in an eternal reality by God's direction in the realm of this life. The intimation of our need to be *remade* in order to be really human; and the related intimation that to be really human is to have an eternal life, is *basically* human: that is, it traces to an original ("Edenic") time when we (Adam) were (was) without knowledge of death; for death, if not contradicted, frustrates all efforts at finding meaning in reality. This double-intimation is what disposes us to look to history for the largest meanings we can have: meanings with the authority to contradict death.

History's authority is inseparable from the fact that it does *not* describe, as science *does*, the given order; and therefore it does not derive its authority from any ability to generate laws about our life in this present reality. History is either about nothing at all worth knowing, or it is about new realities entering this life as the result of a power which transcends the laws that we know from our science and philosophy. If history does tell us anything at all about that decisive power, it has necessarily the authority to contradict the perfectly-accurate descriptions of reality which result from our application of disciplined intelligence (philosophy and science) to this life.

The authority that history has is, from one angle, the most frail, the most vulnerable of all authorities, because it depends finally on what we are told by human witnesses now long-gone, and not available for cross-examination, about a state of affairs that is likewise gone beyond reach of present touching and tasting and seeing. Absolutely everything depends upon the faithfulness of that testimony. The circumstances cannot be recreated so that we can test the facts for ourselves. It is always finally possible that we are being lied to. Undaunted by this, the ancient Jews believed in the paradox that historical testimony was the only kind really worth having! It may be that we cannot finally trust our fellow-men. All we can do is cling to the fact that they are our "fellows"—that is, we are like them; and counting upon our likeness to them, we judge whether we should "trust in" them. It is the same with respect to our fundamental attitude toward this life in which we find ourselves. "Trust in" life's ultimate reliability is risky, in the same sense as is historical knowledge. If we believe in *any* message about a meaning in life which contradicts the meanings which describe nature as it is (all of which meanings end by affirming death), we do so in confidence that there is something in us capable of recognizing its own likeness in that meaning (God) of which such messages (the religions) speak. *HE* would not lie to us. We can "trust in" Him. We would recognize it if we were being lied to. This is precisely the kind of confidence required for believing historical testimony. It has the same kind of vulnerability, and the same power to contradict all other testimony *if it is true*.

By contrast, we cannot "trust in" nature. That is, we could never expect that the largest meanings we need to make our life meaningful would emerge from the study of nature. Nature does not tell us anything about any possibilities that contradict the fact of death-in-time.

By the Bible's logic, we must believe that if there is a largest-of-all-meanings it must be about the redemption of men from the realm of nature, wherein the last word belongs to death. And this largest meaning must be about something yet to come, since clearly death is the present governing reality in our midst. But if this largest meaning is of greater force than nature's reality, it must be always and everywhere at work. And so it must have been at the beginning of reality (if we can think such a thought.) But since we were not at this beginning—we cannot think our way to the beginning of anything, let alone the beginning of All!—we must have someone to tell us about it. Scripture proclaims that an authoritative testimony to the work of the redemption of this present reality began with human time itself (with the "sixth day" of creation.) This testimony begins with "the first man", and its authority is the same as that of all historical testimony.

I have said that these insights belong to "the Bible's logic". But of course the whole authority of the Bible depends on its claim to know these things because they are "the Word of God", and not because they are "logical". The Bible tells us these things in the form of narrative, because they have the authority to contradict logic, and because (as the other side of the coin) they have no more than the authority of the men who tell the story—which authority is bound up with the risk that they are lying to us. The voices that speak to us in the Bible say that they know the stories that they tell on the authority of a chain of human witness reaching as far back as man is to be found; and (the other side of the coin), that this is the Word of God. There is no possibility of thinking our way out of this circle.

Creation-in-time: the foundation-principle of Jewish theory of history

The creation account expresses commitment to certain principles which are vital for our theory of history:

(1) *the principle of creation-in-time*

We recall (above, pp. 25–34), that Greek historians based the possibility of telling the whole story of mankind as a single story having a single direction on the dogmatic-theological principle that the material and moral basis of human society was laid down globally during a period when the generation of gods known to the Greeks began their withdrawal from this world of men, leaving the gift of human government behind. (This is the generation of gods whose chief is Zeus, son of "Chronos", that is, of *Time*.) They saw no possibility of giving historical order to what lies beyond that foundation-generation of the historical aeon. The thought that we could account for anything like a process leading back to "the beginning of things" was to them unthinkable. In fact, what suggested itself to those Greeks who searched back beyond the foundation-generation when universal history can be said to begin was not a beginning of anything, but rather another aeon of reality, presided over by different powers. Perhaps these powers are "gods", perhaps they are not; but certainly there is nothing human on that scene. Beyond that aeon in turn is a previous one; and so on and on. To resist this logic is, on the Greek view, blasphemous. We are not allowed to identify an order of reality that has man in it—or more shocking still, that has man at its centre!—with the whole cosmos of possibility.

On Greek-philosophical or Greek-scientific premises the notion of the beginning-of-all-things (creation) cannot be thought. The object of thought is the sum-total of reality—everything that is in the cosmos, which must in principle be allowed to include all the things we know and all the alternatives to those things, including their opposites.

> The Greek concept of being represents a sharp antithesis to the fundamental categories of biblical thinking.... Indeed, the very theme of ontology, being as being, "can neither be thought nor uttered" [on Biblical premises].
>
> [To the Biblical mind:] The acceptance of the ultimacy of being is a *petitio principii*; it mistakes a problem for a solution. The supreme and ultimate issue is not *being* but the *mystery of being*. Why is there being at all instead of nothing? ...The biblical man does not begin with being, but with the surprise of being.... To Parmenides, not being is inconceivable ("nothingness is not possible"); to the biblical mind, nothingness or the end of being is not impossible. Realizing the contingency of being, it could never identify being with ultimate reality. Being is neither self-evident nor self-explanatory. Being points to the question of how being is possible. The act of bringing into being, creation, stands higher in the ladder of problems than being. Creation is not a transparent concept. But is the concept of being as being distinguished by lucidity? Creation is a mystery; being as being an abstraction.[16]

In contrast, Jewish reflection on the question of meaning begins with Creation *ex nihilo* at the beginning of time. God decides in favour of a certain set of realities as a fit order for men to live in. Alternatives to this order have no standing in reality. He sets a greater light by day (the sun) and a lesser light by night (the moon) (*Genesis* 1:16). He provides appropriate settings: an order of nature, including a fitting range of plants, trees, grass, animals, and so on. He creates man in his own image: "...in the image of God he created him; male and female created he them." (*Genesis* 1:27.) This creation account has the effect of forbidding us from speculating on why there are not three sexes rather than two; why trees and all the rest of the given order of flora are appropriate, and not something else. Alternatives to what is created have no standing anywhere in reality, and therefore none in thought. We know this because we are told of God's beginning in time with the creation of an order of reality appropriate for man. There is a logic to God's plan. But it is not immanent in nature, and not susceptible to discovery by scientific inquiry. The plan for mankind's eternal destiny is prior to creation. Likewise, the logic of that plan (the plan of man's deliverance) is prior to the logic of nature. If we have any access to that prior logic of deliverance (which is to be accomplished in history) we have access to something which necessarily contradicts anything we may discover about the logic of nature.

(2) *the principle of the original unity of mankind*

If we are going to undertake to tell the whole story of mankind as a single story having a single direction we must have the prior confidence that there is a human nature that is always and everywhere recognizable, so that we will know what to include and what to exclude. Or so one would assume *a priori*. In fact, Herodotus nowhere takes time out from his narrative and his speculations about the ways of the gods with men and of men with other men to define what qualifies as human. He simply insists that every community of men requiring consideration has been brought into his story. He takes as proven that, along the whole line of history to the point where he takes up his story, all nations of men have come within the orbit of either the Persian Empire or the Greek city-states, making it possible for a recital of the evolution of the conflict between these two hemispheres

Ancient Jewish Theory of History

to serve as the matrix of universal history. As we have seen (above, pp. 49–50) Herodotus simply shouts down speculation about vast stretches of unexplored geography and undiscovered human population—a telling exception to his generally tolerant policy towards contrary evidence. The painful fact is that if a community of men were to appear which had never yet crossed the path of either of his two protagonist-Empires, the structural assumptions upon which his world-history is based would be scuttled.

But suppose there are populations whose destinies have never been linked to this unifying story: the emergence of the Graeco-Persian conflict, with its corollary theme of liberty *vs* tyranny? If there are other human destinies, are there other *themes* to human life? Are there *other* human stories?

If there is one of Herodotus' intellectual inventions that could be called fundamental it would surely be the discovery that historical narrative requires a unilinear direction. He was absolutely commited to the conviction that all the prior adventures of men tended toward a point of focus in the Graeco-Persian conflict. How can you tell any story unless all events are tending towards some outcome, which is the point of the story? If there is a global human story, what is the point toward which it is tending? If there are many human stories, tending towards different points, then there must be different human destinies. And if there are different destinies there must be different meanings emerging. And if human meaning is even hypothetically various (corresponding to a variety of human destinies), do we not then have to abandon all hope for philosophical knowledge of man?

The Biblical view is that absolute confidence in the unity of human destiny depends on dogmatic confidence in the unity of human *beginning,* expressed in the story of our common derivation from the one human couple. Philosophical speculation does not lead to this knowledge: there is nothing at all *necessary* about it, in the philosopher's sense of the word. It is something we are given as the testimony of a chain of witnesses purporting to be intact, leading from the present Word of God, which is Scripture, to the first man that ever was. But if theory of history is bold enough to base itself on this ground, then in practice historians can pick up any and all evidence of human history wherever on the face of the earth and whenever in time documentation presents itself, and *know* that it is dealing with evidences of the one human destiny. The alternative possibility of a variety of human destinies and a variety of human meanings is ruled out in advance. Philosophy and science may agonize about these possibilities all they wish. For the Biblically-based historian the practical task of history is clear: to search back in time toward the common human beginning, looking forward toward the common global outcome. We do not need philosophy's approval for this. Which is well, as we shall never get it!

The redemptive work in time

> I am the LORD your God, the LORD of Hosts is my name. I cleft the sea and its waves roared, that I might fix the heavens in place and form the earth and say to Zion, "you are my people." (*Isaiah* 51:15-16.)

The unique message of "Jewish monotheism" is not the proposition that there is one God (rather than a plurality of "Gods") but that God is One. The "Shema", "the creed of Judaism," reads "Hear O Israel, the LORD is our God, one LORD". (*Deuteronomy* 6:4.) There is nothing else to be taken into account as we look for meaning than God, ourselves, and God's dealings with ourselves.

> To Greek philosophy, being is the ultimate; to the Bible, God is the ultimate.... The God of Israel is a God who acts, a God of mighty deeds. The Bible does not say how He is, but how He acts.... It is not as "true being" that God is conceived, but as the *semper agens*. Here the basic category is action rather than im-

mobility [as it is in Greek philosophy.] Movement, creation of nature, acts within history rather than absolute transcendence and detachment from the events of history, are the attributes of the Supreme Being....[17]

Greek theory of history has to find its place in a setting of ultimate, cosmic laws, whose authority is superior to the authority of the gods themselves. "Not God himself could escape destiny," Herodotus tells his readers. (*Histories* 1:91.) Because these largest of all laws are cosmic, they are also eternal. The notion of a creation of all things in time was thus outside the ken of the Greeks. It did, however, have a place in speculation of other Near Eastern civilizations,[18] and seems to figure in the speculations of most other peoples.[19] As is well-known, elements of the Biblical Creation account are to be found in the oldest Mesapotamian sources, and can be presumed to borrow from what Theodore Gaster calls, "the oldest stories in the world." But,

> In Israel, all of this cosmogonic material was demythologized. All the polytheistic divinities of the earlier accounts were erased, leaving only one Creator, and all strictly mythological allusions were deleted. In the Hebrew version of Genesis, no reference remains to the battle between the gods and the primordial monsters of chaos. As far as the Hebrews were concerned, Yahweh had always existed; before Him, there was no existence at all—much less any philosophic notion of "pure being."[20]

Inseparably linked to the Bible's acknowledgement of God as the Lord of History is its positive attitude toward time. "On the sixth day God completed all the work he had been doing, and on the seventh day he ceased from all his work. God blessed the seventh day and made it holy [*kadosh*] because on that day he ceased from all the work he had set himself to do." (*Genesis* 2:2-3a). This, Abraham Heschel notes, is the first use of the word "holy" in scripture.[21] Similarly "in the Ten Commandments the term "Holy" is applied to one word only, the Sabbath".[22] "Now what was the first holy object in the history of the world? Was it a mountain? Was it an altar?... How extremely significant is the fact [that the first application of the word holy [kadosh] is] to time."[23]

Biblical man does not take for granted the existence of the cosmos, nor the existence of the least thing in it. He does not regard "non-being" as a non-problem. It is not unthinkable that all being could give way to non-being. (This possibility is a part of everyone's calculation in the nuclear age—an instance of the historical process turning into inescapable event what the religious mind has always known.) The biblical man believes that the existence of every thing and all things requires the constant sustaining action of the original Creator of all. It is because God is constantly active that anything *is*. By this logic it follows that the possibility that anything will continue to be is no more and no less problematical than that anything has been or is now. There are fearful possibilities in everything in life. Any one of the processes that sustain me individually or that sustain the whole cosmos entirely might, in principle, fail in the next instant. The fact that anything at all *is* in this instant is not more or less problematical than the fact that all was once created. And the expectation of anything or everything continuing to be in the next instant is not better or worse founded. If we lack confidence in reality's foundation, we must not make a special case of the future.

But of course, everyone does! If we feel more comfortable with the past than with the future it is because there are no more surprises in the past. For all that there is in the past that we should prefer had not been, at least what did happen, good and bad, was allowed to happen and has some standing in our thought. The Biblical view is that God sustains all that is for a purpose. The purpose is accomplished in time. If we think we see any meaning whatever in what has been in time we must believe that the source or guarantor of that meaning will be able to sustain that same meaning through subsequent events in time.

Ancient Jewish Theory of History   93

Confidence in previous meanings and confidence in subsequent meanings are grounded in the same author of meaning, or they are not grounded at all—that is, they are not "meanings" but only apparent "meanings". Thus the very possibility of *meaning* requires confidence in time.

But to have confidence in time runs against man's natural inclination. This *entirely unique* confidence in the redeeming work of God in time undergirds the Jews' *unique* sense of seriousness about history. "Judaism is a *religion of time* aiming at *the sanctification of time*" (Heschel).[24]

The Creation account describes God purposefully establishing the whole setting for man's living of his life; then He sets the example for man's own purposeful life by establishing the calendar. Man is not to take the cues for his own purposive behaviour from nature. He will establish his own human agenda in the midst of nature. The keeping of every seventh day is a holy duty because it marks off an interval of time—always the same interval of time, however "eventful" or "uneventful", however "productive" or "unproductive"—in acknowledgment that some distance has been gone in time. Although nothing new has been reflected in nature, we know that God's work of redemption is a week further along. Superimposed on this regular weekly-reckoning of time—not diminishing its significance but in fact making its significance clearer—is another set of occasional days that the Jews will observe, which acknowledge extraordinary events in the history of the nation—certain actions of God which revealed his purpose for history as a whole. The *annual* celebration of these events served to mark out the passage of seasons, and thus entailed a positive acknowledgment of the regime of nature. The Jews superimposed upon the solar and mensuel rhythms (necessarily reminiscent as these are of the natural laws which govern agriculture, the basis for our physical sustenance), the recollection of God's actions in previous history. Thus they affirm their confidence in the redeeming purpose of

God in the present and in the future. Here is the uniqueness of Biblical faith in a nutshell:

> The festivals of ancient peoples were intimately linked with nature's seasons. Thus the value of the festive day was determined by the things nature did or did not bring forth. In Judaism, Passover, originally a spring festival, became a celebration of the exodus from Egypt; the Feast of Weeks, an old harvest festival at the end of the wheat harvest (ḥag hakatzir, Exodus 23:16, 34:22), became the celebration of the day on which the Torah was given at Sinai; the Feast of the Booths, an old festival of vintage (ḥag hassif, Exodus 23:16), commemorates the dwelling of the Israelites in booths during their sojourn in the wilderness (Leviticus 23:42 f). To Israel, the unique events of historic time were spiritually more significant than the repetitive processes in the cycle of nature, even though physical sustenance depended on the latter. While the deities of other peoples were associated with places or things, the God of Israel was the God of events; the Redeemer from slavery, the Revealer of the Torah, manifesting Himself in events of history rather than in things or places.[25]

Human character and human history

The Creation account (*Genesis* 1 to 2:4) establishes the assumptions necessary for the autonomous authority of history. The next few chapters reveal something of the human forces at work in history, anticipating lessons that become more explicit when the text sharpens its focus (with *Genesis* 11:10) to deal with the history of Israel itself. In Chapter 2, beginning at verse 15 and through to the conclusion of Chapter 5, we are told a number of stories about the first generations of mankind, which establish the Bible's assumptions about human behaviour and about God's response to men's exercise of the radically free will he has been given.

Chapters 6 through 10 take account of the mystery of the presence of many races of men in the world, preparing us for the discovery of a variety of populations lying beyond the ken of the readers of this history. The possibility of a variety of human destinies and therefore of various meanings to human life is (as already noted, pp. 28f) ruled out *ab initio* by the Bible's assumption that all the races of men are accounted for as descendants of Noah. There appears in *Genesis* 10 a record of the races of men as they were at the time of their ancestors' beginnings as citizens of some early Mesapotamian empire. It is not claimed that this is an exhaustive list of all nations, extant now or then, but rather that all nations, even those in the remotest corners of the world and whose names and very existence were not presently known to the authors of the Biblical books were not exempt from the common human destiny and would not turn out to be alien, when encountered. ("[From the sons of Japheth] ...the peoples of the coasts and islands separated into their own countries, each with their own language, family by family, nation by language." (*Genesis* 10:2-5).)

Who would deny that these accounts present great difficulties for historical understanding? But again, the proper question is: relative to *what*? There is nothing having anything like historical authority that improves on these as records of the third millennium B.C. On monuments uncovered in recent archaeological digs in the Near East, the scholars have found names matching several of the nations listed in *Genesis* 10, previously unknown to the historians and not attested in the Bible's references to later history of Israel nor in any other sources after the patriarchal period.[26]

It would be reckless to assume that archaeology is done shedding light on the historical substance behind the materials of these chapters. It is a striking testimony to the unparalleled commitments of the ancient Jews to the value of historical memory that they provided for retaining, reciting and conveying to each new generation proper names, topographical details, details of customary behaviour, and so on, which came eventually to correspond to nothing that later generations knew of in their own experience. If some of this material still resists our historical inquiry, enough has found recent illumination through archaeological discovery that we know we are dealing with witnesses who cared for historical accuracy and would, we are sure, be incapable of willfully misrepresenting historical truth.

Our concern in this place is not primarily with the Bible as an historical source. Our concern is theory of history. But enough has been said here to meet any insinuation that the Bible's high-toned *speculations* about history were not matched by the same level of seriousness about the method and practice of history. We do not know enough to satisfy our curiosity about the original practice of history among the ancient Jews. But we are today in a position to confirm the presence of critical-historical intelligence (in the company, of course, of many other kinds of interests and spirits) in the earliest sources of *Genesis*. Nothing so far discovered anywhere even hints at the existence of the same spirit in any contemporary people.

• • •

One of the most insistent lessons of these chapters (*Genesis* 1 to 10) is that man's commitment to history is not something that he has sought. Indeed, he is shown being carried kicking and screaming into history. Men are, in the Biblical view, doomed to history.

Without exception, the noblest characters in the Jewish Bible are described as initially resisting the part which they are called to play in history. And invariably also, it is hinted that this reluctance to enter onto the necessary work of history traces to the nobler side of human nature, which, because of Adam's rebellion, cannot be purely expressed in a fallen world. In contrast, Greek and especially Graeco-Roman apologists for history base their best case for history on its being a stage that naturally draws to it the noblest natures. (see above, pp. 63–6)

The Jewish Bible does not lead us to history for entertainment, nor for vicarious fulfillment of our need for adventure. On the path of history, God and man together are commited to a long and often dark work. God's repetition of the injunction to "increase, and fill the earth" (*Genesis* 9:1), "swarm throughout the earth and rule over it" (*Genesis* 9:7; *cf* 35:11) implies man's inclination to resist the course of action within history. In the story of the Tower Babel (*Genesis* 11: 1-9), the whole community of men stands together, apparently within one polity, speaking one language, and having just taken a vote in favour of making this place (Babel, i.e. "Babylon") their permanent home— "or we shall be dispersed all over the earth." (11:4) From this secure place, they will directly reach up into heaven, "and make a name for ourselves." But Israel's God will have none of this. God has covenanted with man to accomplish a definite work in history. Man's inclination (this story tells us) is to set limits. In his daily life he wants routine; in his philosophy he wants "ontological certainty" (in Reinhold Niebuhr's phrase.) His instinct for happiness cries out for *no more history*.

Immanuel Kant was expressing a philosopher's gloss on this truth when he wrote: "Man wants concord... but nature knows better what is good for his kind; nature wants discord.... To be happy is necessarily the desire of every rational but finite being... [but] it lies in the nature of human desires that they can never be wholly satisfied.... The infinitely manifold and unstable world of happiness, in itself without foundation or ultimate aim, is the medium of a realization which is subject to other conditions and other guidance."[27]

We note that both in the Bible's story about Babel and in Kant's thoughts on the interaction between "happiness" and "Nature", civilization presents certain impediments to the Purpose which God (or Nature) has for history. Civilization amounts to a certain way of organizing and aligning the many individual impulses to "happiness". In the Biblical account, the striving for stability ("[lest we] be dispersed all over the earth") is paradoxically linked with ambition (let us "make a name for ourselves") as impulses for avoiding history. The question occurs: are we being condemned for inertia or for ambition? But a little reflection will suggest how these apparently contrary "drives" (as the psychologists say) are in fact paradoxically related in real life. The sorts of ambition that serve the purposes of advancing civilization (making life more complex) are soon at war with that simple trust in God that would risk all that civilization itself has given us in order to obey Him. Civilization ("Babel") is condemned in this story for fostering inertia. Inertia (as the later story of Sodom and Gomorrah is meant to show) fosters degeneration. But, paradoxically, degeneration expresses itself as experimentation (i.e., "sodomy"), that is, deviation from nature.

The course of history must be run, and therefore we are not permitted to make our lives secure against change. Resistance to the path of adventure which is history is linked in the Bible to our preference for security. But this preference for security somehow irresistibly leads to impatience with the limitations of nature. The goal of God in his covenant with man is a redeemed nature; and, paradoxically, to reach this goal requires our fidelity to the limits of our original (given, created) nature and the ethical behaviour implicit in it. For example, homosexuality (the characteristic vice of Sodom [*Genesis* 19:1-5]) is condemned as a violation of limitations implied when the statement that man was made "in the image of God" is coupled with the statement that "He created them male and female" (*Genesis* 5:1-2). The call to enter onto the path of history is therefore not a call to unqualified adventure. Man is not to undertake to re-create himself. But, as the story of Babel shows—"Babel" (Babylon) typifying advanced civilization, its arts, and its collective ambition—man is called away from sufficiency and routine, so as to be available for God's re-creative use of him.

The recital of world history centered on the story of the line of Abram/Abraham

In Chapter 12 of *Genesis* we find the principle upon which this recital of world history is to be based:

> The LORD said to Abram, "Leave your own country, your kinsmen, and your father's house, and go to a country that I will show you. I will make you into a great nation, I will bless you and make your name so great that it shall be used in blessings:
> Those that bless you I will bless, those that curse you, I will execrate. All the families on earth will pray to be blessed as you are blessed". (*Genesis* 12:1-3).

At this place, the narrative focus of the Bible narrows to describe the adventures of one man and his descendants. It is at this very point of "narrowing" that the text declares the unifying theme of global history. Abram/Abraham is at once the father of the Jewish race and the type of all men who respond to the call to partnership and God in history. (Abram's name—which meant father of Aram, that is of one branch of the Semitic race [see *Genesis* 10:22]—is changed by God to Abraham, that is father of a multitude, "for I make you father of a host of nations". (17:5).

We recall that for Herodotus the recital of world history was organized upon the story of encounter between Persia and the Greeks —an event from the recent past (indeed, probably within his lifetime). In an equivalent sense, world history was organized by the ancient Jews around the story of the calling of Abraham out of Mesopotamian civilization—an event many centuries previous to the commitment of *Genesis* to its present form. This singular *event* has made possible— that is both morally, and practically possible—the telling of the history of all nations as a single story, having a single direction, and governed by the set of themes which have been elaborated in the previous eleven chapters of *Genesis*.

Perhaps the most striking point of contrast between these two principles of organization (Herodotus' and the Bible's) is that the legitimacy of the first is supposed to be manifest in contemporary political realities, while the legitimacy of the Bible's organizing principle is not. We recall that in order to prove that the Graeco-Persian conflict was the event toward which all history tended, it was necessary for Herodotus to show that all communities of men were, in principle, accounted for in the story leading up to that struggle (Above, pp. 49-50). Furthermore, it had to be shown that this event truly brought into focus the major issues that bear on men's destiny everywhere. These were for Herodotus summed up in one over-riding issue: that between freedom and tyranny. The vulnerability of this device is obvious. If it should later be discovered that some communities of men have been over-looked in Herodotus' account, it would then become possible to believe that he was mistaken regarding the real issues in human destiny; or it might mean that there is a variety of human destinies in the world, and therefore no legitimate organizing principle for world history. And even if research should never uncover any communities of man unknown to Herodotus, what shall we do for an organizing principle if these two principals (Greece and Persia) should ever vanish from the scene, or lose their pre-eminence?

Of course, there is a real sense in which Herodotus' organizing principle has outlasted the ancient Persian and ancient Greek nations, and survived the discovery of the hosts of nations beyond Herodotus' world. Roman historians were fond of portraying themselves as the legatees of the struggle between Greece and Persia, West and East. Medieval historians were drawn to the notion of Christian Europe as the successor of pagan Rome, and offered a baptized version of Herodotus' original East-West hinge-of-history. Hegel made Herodotus' notion of a basic East/West polarization of values the starting point of his theory of history. The seed of all dialectical philosophy of history is here in Herodotus' original organizing principle. Is there not, after all, a certain logic that requires us to tell history dialectically? If we tell it as a single story having a single direction, is there not something in the imperatives of narrative that disposes us to look for opposing principles at work? And when history is told as a story of political forces, will not the tendency be to assign the actors in the story to opposite corners as embodiments of opposite principles?

In contrast to Herodotus' principle of organization of world history, based on a given, present, and manifest configuration of world politics, the Bible offers the story of the man Abraham, who makes *the first act of human decision within the Covenant*, from which follows a chain of decisions which ultimately will involve all of mankind in the one global destiny. Abram/Abraham is the father of the Jews, and he is also the type of all men who enter positively and self-consciously into active participation in the covenant by which God is accomplishing His historical purpose. The history of the Jews is at once the paradigm of the history of all communities of men and the centre from which the Purpose for the history of all mankind is carried forward.

The relation between the adventures of Israel on the one hand and the adventures of all other nations on the other, is not in any sense dialectical. It is not that one "side" represents one principle and the other side its opposite (Tyranny *vs* freedom, for example). The claim is rather that a sequence of decisions derives from one centre—one event in time, that is Abraham's response to God's call to him, to leave Mesapotamia and to go beyond the river to make a new beginning, for himself, for his family, with ultimate consequences in history for all nations, in "a country that I will show you". The effects of that single decision, accumulate along the line of subsequent human history and will issue in an eventual global result, which will be history's decisive and global outcome.

The Bible does not suggest that it was manifest to anyone other than Abraham himself that this was the significance of his decision. On the contrary, what was immediately manifest was a decline of Abram's stature *vis-à-vis* all that was counted as significant in the civilized world. It is claimed however, that ultimately the significance of Abraham's decision will be universally conceded, because its *end-result* will be inescapable: "All the families on earth will pray to be blessed as you are blessed". To see the global significance of the story so far requires Abraham's sort of faith in the eye of the observer. Once received, it can then be seen in part with the eye of disciplined intelligence and can be up-to-a-point defended in terms of ostensible historical results, even though the better part of its meaning will always remain mysterious till the end.

Before we deal with the various expressions of this theory, let us note one ostensible advantage over Herodotus' theory and its dialectical successors. That advantage (perhaps strangely, at first blush) is its *efficiency*. On the Biblical view, history is *centered*. Everything that happens everywhere on the canvas of human history can be located in time *vis-à-vis* the comparatively sparse details of this story. If there were nothing else to be said for it, the Biblical theory of history has given us the inestimable boon of a single chronology, which in fact, locates all historical events everywhere in terms of the internal history of the Jewish people.

This proposition, I believe, would be equally acceptable to Jews, though it is made by a Christian and, it does not overlook the fact that orthodox Judaism has its own system of chronology, under which the year 5743 began on September 18, of 1982 A.D. Christians, non-Christians and post-Christians, when they address each other and the rest of the world, use the framework B.C./A.D., or B.C.E./C.E. ("Before the Common Era"/"Common Era"). The Year One is not by anybody's reckoning the actual year of the birth of Jesus of Nazareth. But practically speaking every serious student of history accepts that the events that took place during Jesus' lifetime brought about a decisive confrontation between Rome and Jerusalem, from which followed the destruction of the Temple, the Diaspora, the Christianization of Europe, and by stages the process which I have called the globalization of human destiny, the central theme of history. We date all these events, as well as all known events prior to them, by a benchmark drawn from the internal history of Judaea, marking roughly the birth of Jesus, and which (no matter what one's attitude to it otherwise) is *practically speaking* the hinge in the story of Abraham's seed and their place in the destiny of all nations. This same event (we believe not coincidentally) has come to serve as the universal benchmark for locating all historical events *vis-à-vis* one another—just as Greenwich, England, served, to the convenience of all, as the universal hinge for reckoning the passage of the hours of the day, locating all the daily activities of all of us, all over the globe.

The radicality of human choice/the irreversibility of human decision

"*And so Abram set out as the Lord had bidden him*" (*Genesis* 12:4 a).

Abraham is presented as the type of the man of faith. Everything in this account depends on our believing that Abraham's decision is authentically free. This stands in stark contrast to Herodotus' view that men are essentially interchangeable instruments of Destiny's purposes. On the Greek view, a slight modification of the pace of events would have given Abraham's task to someone earlier (his father or grandfather, or great-grandfather perhaps, all of whom are named in the account [*Genesis* 11:22-26]), or to someone in the following generation or two. We miss everything if we do not understand that the option of not accepting God's call was open to Abraham, and that everything that follows from Abraham's decision is part of the cumulative result of a single, *radically free* human decision. On the other hand, we are *not* invited to reflect on the "alternative model" which follows if Abraham "*does not*" obey God; for only what Abraham did, and not what he did not do, has any standing in reality. We are told to think of every historical fact in our present world as being in place as a consequence of Abraham's decision. The name of Abraham and recollection of the decision he took in faith are constantly being evoked in the Jewish Bible and no less in the *New Testament,* and the lesson is always the same: that questions that fall to us in this moment of time and about which *we* must decide are determined—not our decisions, but the questions!—by Abraham's first decision.

For some reason, it is difficult to persuade people of the *practical* fact that the decisions men make in history have not only irreversible but also cumulative consequences. For illustration: Solomon Grayzel, in justification of his decision to exclude the Biblical period from his *History of the Jews,* writes:

> [T]he further back one goes, the less direct is the influence of historical events on modern times. The Bible and its characters of course, have affected and still affect Jewish life. But the historical events of biblical times have not had and do not have any such influence. More significant and influential than the events recorded in the Bible have been the interpretations of these events by men who have lived during later periods.[28]

Quite the opposite is the case, as a moment's reflection should tell us. Let us set aside for the moment the dogmatic-theological statement (which is the premise of the distinctively Jewish theory of history) that Abraham's decision was the first in the series of decisions made in Covenant with God, and that determine the outcome of history. Let us simply compare the practical effects of the decision taken by Abraham about four thousand years ago and those following a decision taken by some political leader last week. There are extant in the world this week many fewer consequences of the latter than of the former. Furthermore, each new consequence adds momentum to the whole agglomeration, so that all the consequences of Abraham's decision carry much more weight, that is, they will have more tendency to elicit even more new responses this week than will the recent decision of the contemporary politician.

To choose a different example: it is *not* true that the effects of Caesar's decision to cross the Rubicon is "less direct" in our own time than in 49 B.C. It strikes people that this influence is less "direct" only because the event is further away from their daily consciousness, and their opinions about it are less strong than their opinions about this week's news. But its impact is every bit as "direct", and furthermore greater, because its effects have been accumulating for centuries.

Neither is it true to say that the newest consequences of Abraham's (or Caesar's) decision are merely the latest *mediations* of his once fresh decision. These are still *his* effects—the effects of his decision. It would be exhausting—in fact, it would be utterly impossible—to think through all the consequences of Abraham's decision every time we mention his name. But as for the new figure of action this week and his latest action, that is still small enough that we can mentally deal with its consequences. It is easier to see its impact, because it is a new item in our reckoning, and therefore we think of it as "direct", or "immediate" (in contrast to "indirect", or "mediate").

Before we turn to examine the concept of the Covenant, more should be said about this issue of the radical freedom of the human will, because many people find logical difficulties at this point (as well they should!).

There are at least two aspects to this problem:

(1) *how can the individual will be radically free, if God's will is sovereign over history?*

A good test of our readiness for the Bible's paradoxical treatment of this issue is in the story of God's dealings (through Moses and Aaron) with Pharaoh at the time of the Exodus. The Lord presents Himself to Moses with this announcement: "I have heard the groaning of the Israelites, enslaved by the Egyptians, and I have called my covenant to mind. Say therefore to the Israelites, 'I am the LORD. I will release you from your labours in Egypt. I will rescue you from your slavery there... Tell Pharaoh king of Egypt all that I say to you... You must tell your brother Aaron all I bid you say, and he will tell Pharaoh and Pharaoh will let the Israelites go out of his country; but I will make him stubborn. Then will I show sign after sign and portent after portent in the land of Egypt. But Pharaoh will not listen to you, so I will assert my power in Egypt, [etc.]...'" (*Exodus* 6:5-6, 29b; 7:2–4.) The pattern is repeated several times in this story. God is determined that Israel will go. He rehearses (6:2-6) the history of Israel to this point, and foretells its next chapter, the conquest of Canaan (6: 7–8).

In the light of God's sovereign determination, what is the point of talking about what Pharaoh will or will not do? In the event, Pharaoh really does resist—really does exercise his real (not apparent) free will. But in the same breath we are told that "I (the Lord) will make him stubborn" (7:3, and again 14:4). Is a man's will his own or is it not?

There are ways of thinking through these difficulties—provided one is prepared to think *religiously*. All religions insist that there are realms of a larger reality that enclose this world we know. Both Judaism and Christianity speak of God as living in that larger reality, and they call it "eternity". From this perspective of eternity, all that will happen in history is over and done with; and God sees things from that perspective. From our perspective in time, there are decisions yet to be taken; but God knows eternally all that we do. In the instant case of Pharaoh and the Israelites, God knows eternally that Pharaoh has refused. And He has already, in eternity, dealt with it. He has already taken it into account (even now as He talks to Moses, for whom it is a future possibility) and He has added new decisions of His own that will deal with that real, *free* refusal.

As Moses hears these things, neither Pharaoh's refusal nor God's subsequent response to that refusal is a fact in history. Pharaoh is still radically free to agree or disagree. But God is likewise still free to act. What God will do and what Pharaoh will do are both future events to Moses. From God's eternal perspective, it can be said now (as He speaks to Moses) that He has already dealt with Pharaoh's decision. Moses is being told something that is true from the perspective of eternity. At Moses' place in human time, this privileged knowledge of God's action in response to Pharaoh's resistance is knowledge of the combined future outcome of Pharaoh's deed and God's deed—namely, the frustration of Pharaoh's resistance. As God's will is the first item in the account, and as His free response to man's free decision is likewise always the last item in the account, it has to be said that even in the "hardening of his [Pharaoh's] heart" it is God's will that is done.

At least: it is along these lines perhaps that religious thought may "interpret" this paradox. But it may well be that in religious thought there are other sorts of interpretation that are just as pious and just as ingenious—*not wrong*, but not *really explaining* either! It is not something we can *explain*. It remains something we must *"tell"*. The Biblical way was to *tell* the largest meanings, not to explain them.

One might divide up the jurisdictions of the historian and the theologian in regard to this story—which is not to say that one person should not be both, but that we should distinguish between what is required for historical understanding of this account and what is required for theological interpretation of this account. The separation is not difficult (and the fact that it is not difficult makes clear that the ancient Jewish mind was fully appreciative of these different intellectual needs and how they were to be served).

The historian says: Moses and Aaron presented themselves under God's instruction, to Pharaoh. They were confident that God would compel Pharaoh to let the people go. Pharaoh refused. A number of terrible calamities came upon Pharaoh's people, which he ultimately accepted as evidences of the power of the God of the Hebrews. He submitted to these evidences, and let the people go. *Et cetera.*

The theologian says: God had a purpose for Egypt and for the Israelites in which He would not be thwarted. This is in fulfillment of the purpose that he has for the whole of human history, and which we find expressed in his covenant with Abraham. Pharaoh had the regulation human issue of free will, which he used to defy God. In view of the consistent testimony in the Word of God, to the effect that

God is sovereign in history, we say confidently that God caused both Pharaoh's refusal and his ultimate repentance. *Et cetera.*

The historian deals in sentences like these: "When the king of Egypt was told that the Israelites had slipped away, he and his courtiers changed their minds completely, and said, 'What have we done? We have let our Israelite slaves go free!' So Pharaoh put horses to his chariot, and took his troops with him.... (*et cetera*)" (14: 5-6). The sentences: "the Lord will make him stubborn" and "the Lord hardened his heart" belong to the theologian.

In other words: the historian as historian can deal only with the evidences of free human decision. The mystery of the relation between human freedom and divine sovereignty is honoured by the Christian historian by being left to the province of the theologian.

Theological explication of these mysteries leads the theorist of history back to the terrain of paradox. These largest meanings cannot be explained, but can only be *told*, and told again. That is why it never occurs to the ancient Jews (as it does immediately to philosophers) to attempt to "rise above" narrative for the sake of explanation.[29] It is this fundamental orientation towards narrative as the most authoritative mode for conveying the truth that makes the ancient Jewish mind so congenial to the historian. Christian historians suspect that something more serious than the relative prestige of our academic discipline is at stake when we observe the current denigration of narrative as the basis of history.[30] "The bible narrative" (one theologian claims) "is the basis of our culture... [W]ithout it we shall surrender to the repetitive clichés of mass media or to the chaotic flashes and meaningless signals of discontinuous sights. The narrative, and the faith associated with it, stands in direct opposition to cybernetic control and irrational psychedelic jabs on our senses".[31]

There is no way of proving that humans have the possibility of acting with radical freedom. Nor is there any way of explaining satisfactorily how God could "require" human cooperation in accomplishing His sovereign purposes. Radical human freedom and the radical sovereignty of the God of history would appear to be related as mutually exclusive principles. Systematic speculation leads to the eclipse of the one possibility in the other. Or it leads nowhere:

> It is a commonplace to say that biblical religion knows of no speculative proofs for God's existence. It is one of the surprising features of the Bible that nowhere does it make the slightest attempt to prove rationally that there is a God. Now, this is not all due to the naive piety of the biblical narrative—the Bible is anything but a book of naivety—but to the very essence of religion. Whether God's existence may be proved rationally or not is of little interest to religion.... [I]t is possible for man to entertain extremely exalted philosophical opinions concerning God and yet—just because of such opinions—reject religion proper.... The foundation of religion is not the affirmation that God is, but that God is concerned with man and the world; that, having created this world, He has not abandoned it.... The foundation of biblical religion, therefore, is not an idea but an event which may be called the encounter between God and man.32

If we accept the authority of the Bible on the terms it demands; and if we are willing to make our own its assumptions about the possibilities of history, we must give up on the possibility of a theory of history that *explains* without remainder what is happening in history. There is no possibility of reaching the logic by which the sovereign God, Creator of all reality apart from Himself, *requires* the cooperation of men. It should be already clear that the Jewish Bible rules out all possibility of telling history as "theodicy". Herodotus (not to mention later Graeco-Roman historians in the mold of Livy) comes much closer to presenting history as theodicy. But, paradoxically, it does prove possible to take a much more radical view of human freedom on the Biblical than on the Greek premises—provided that we do not qualify the absoluteness of God's sovereignty. This simply means that we must abandon the temptation to *explain* (*i.e.*, to state in the form of logical propositions) how these two realities co-exist in the real world.

The "offense" of God's covenant with Israel

In agreeing to obey God, Abraham entered into "covenant" with Him. Responsibility for continuing this covenant belongs to "Abraham's seed". And lest there be any doubt that this means biological descent, we are given immediately several stories that make clear the urgency of Abraham's having legitimate heirs of his body. These include the story of the extraordinary circumstances surrounding the birth of Isaac (*Genesis* 15 to 21); the stories regarding the consistent frustrations of Ishmael's claims (*Genesis* 16, 17 and 21); and the story of God's test of Abraham's faith in the call for Isaac's sacrifice (*Genesis* 22).

There are many insights for our theme in these stories; but we will deal only with the first story. This is the story of how Sarah conceived when her age seemed to rule out this possibility, and bore Isaac. Abraham already had another son, "legitimate" by the laws of the time of place, but borne by Sarah's Egyptian slave girl, Hagar. This was Ishmael (from whom the Moslem religion claims that the faithful Arabs descend). Protesting his own advanced age and that of Sarah, Abraham declaims: "If only Ishmael might live under thy special care" (*Genesis* 17:18.) But God's reply is: "I have heard your prayer for Ishmael. I have blessed him and I will make him fruitful.... But my covenant I will fulfill with Isaac" (17:20-21.)

It seems that each generation has to discover all by itself the "offensiveness" of this procedure. For vintage expressions of modern reflection on this theme, readers should go to the French Enlightenment—*inter alia*, to Voltaire's entries in the *Philosophical Dictionary* and to his *Philosophy of History*.[33] A twentieth-century elaboration is in Arnold Toynbee's handling of the theme of Israel in his *Study of History*, where we find that "the most notorious historical example of... idolization of an ephemeral self" is the Biblical belief in the chosenness of Israel.[34] Beginning with the Eighteenth-century (as philosophy increasingly set its face against the Judaeo-Christian premises of Western thought, and as popular knowledge of the content of the Bible declined from the high general levels achieved in the two centuries following the Protestant Reformation), the notion took hold among intellectuals and has since been popularized, that the ancient Jews were insensitive to the possibilities of offense in their notion of God's covenant with Israel. Ludwig Feuerbach speaks for the emancipated mind of the late nineteenth-century: "Jehovah is the ego of Israel, which regards itself as the end and aim, the Lord of nature.... If, in the course of time, the idea of Jehovah expanded itself in individual minds, and his love was extended, as by the writer of the book of Jonah, to men in general, this does not belong to the essential character of the Israelitish religion."[35]

In fact, the notion of Jehovah as "the ego of Israel" is light years removed from anything we find in the Bible. The Bible does *not* claim to be able to defend the necessity of God's choice of the Jews. The beginning of wisdom on this theme is to go to the Bible's own reflections on God's choosing of the Jews. If moral sensitivity is what we prize, there is no improving on these. Again and again, the Bible opens the issue of the ostensible "unfairness" of the covenant choice, and ventilates it thoroughly. The conclusion of this recurring reflection is always the same: in the interest of realism we are told not to invest our intellectual energies or our moral sensitivity where both are incompetent. There is, for example, no thought of justifying the cruel behaviour of Sarah towards Ishmael (21:8-10). Ishmael, rejected for Isaac's role, is blessed in such generous terms, and promised so great a future that centuries later Mohammed would insist on attaching the destinies of his people to these promises from the Jewish scriptures (in *Genesis* 16:11-16, 17:20-22, 21:13). Similarly, there is no thought of justifying the low deceits carried off by Jacob against his twin brother Esau—and which, moreover, began in the womb! (*Genesis* 25:19-34, and chapter 27). The Bible stresses that all of Jacob's frustrating labours in "the land of the eastern tribes" (*Genesis* 27 to 31) are a foretaste of the price that Jacob (Israel) and his descendants would pay for "their iniquities".

The "end and aim" of the Lord of Israel in summoning Abram/Abraham (*Genesis* 12: 1-3) is not the seed of Abraham but a new heaven and a new earth, the blessings of which belong to all nations according as they have blessed Abraham, the father of all faith, and his seed. Nor is it true (as Feuerbach claims) that, in the case of certain individual minds (like Jonah) "in the course of time the idea of Jehovah expanded itself"! This notion of the Jewish vision *evolving* from tribal particularism to ethical universalism is utterly unfounded —a notorious "red herring". The covenant with Abraham is for the sake of the *prior* covenant with Noah (*Genesis*, Chapters 6 to 9), identified as the father of all men now alive (that is, whether within or without the community of "Abraham's seed"). This prior covenant is the basis of all the blessings that derive from nature: "Never again will I curse the ground because of man, however evil his inclinations may be from his youth upwards.... While the earth lasts, seedtime and harvest, cold and heat, summer and winter, day and night, shall never cease" (8: 21-22).

The Book of *Jonah* entered fairly late into the canon and belongs to the section called "minor prophets". It tells the story of a man who has persuaded himself that the blessings being accomplished by God under the covenant are to be kept within the family of the Jews, and who is, *for this very reason*, singled out by God for the uncongenial task of being a missionary to the gentiles! He is directed by God to "the great city of Ninevah" (*Jonah* 1: 1-2) whose fortunate people have been the conquerors of the whole world known to the Jews. (The Jews had, by this point, suffered several centuries of routine humiliation under the heel of a succession of empires, with many more centuries of the same to come). Jonah seeks to hide. God obliges him by hiding him as deeply and as far from the eye and ear of the Ninevites and all other men on earth as it is possible to be. (To think that the mentality of publicly-educated grownups has sunk during the last century to the point that the ordinary man's access to this marvelous message is blocked by the "problem" of the probability of being swallowed by a whale! This, to his credit, was not Feuerbach's "problem" with the story of Jonah). That lesson learned, Jonah is dragged, kicking and screaming to his task. His worst fears are realized: the Ninevites repent! Jonah, in his own words "should be better dead" (4: 9) than live with the implications of the repentance of the Ninevites. He sulks away to brood, finds a tree to lean against, and falls asleep. God provides a gourd to grow over his head and give shade. Jonah, not thinking who has provided the gourd—namely, He who is creator of all, including the Jews, and all the other nations—is carelessly "*grateful* for the gourd" (4: 6)! Then God provides a worm to eat the gourd, and a scorching wind to blow from the east. The God of nature is no more partial to Jonah than the God of Israel is to the Jews!

> The sun beat down on Jonah's head till he grew faint. Then he prayed for death and said, "I should be better dead than alive". At this God said to Jonah, "Are you so angry over the gourd"? "Yes", he answered, "mortally angry". The LORD said, "You are sorry for the gourd, though you did not have the trouble of growing it, a plant which came up in a night and withered in a night. And should not I be sorry for the great city of Ninevah, with its hundred and twenty thousand who cannot tell their right hand from their left, and cattle without number"? (4:8a-11)

The whole point is that this *lesson* that the Lord teaches Jonah—in giving him his original assignment, in thwarting his escape by sea to Europe, in hiding him away inside the great fish, in rescuing him from the fish, in giving him success in his mission to the Ninevites, in the episode of the gourd—is an old, old lesson. It is the original lesson of the blessing to Abraham—and Jonah knew it all along. "This, O Lord, is what I feared when I was in my own country, and to forestall it I tried to escape to Tarshish" (4: 2). In Israel, they know (for their pains!) that Jehovah is God of all nations, and means to redeem them all. Hopefully, they don't know this yet in Tarshish! (The episode of the gentile sailors [1: 3-16] shows that *they* know nothing of this sort of God). Nothing better illustrates the integrity of this theme in Jewish religion, and the characteristic misrepresentation of it in liberalism, than the way in which the Book of *Jonah* points us *back* to the premises of the covenant for the case against the notion of Jehovah as "the ego of Israel".

There is no way to reduce to propositions the myriad implications of this notion of the covenant between Abram/Abraham (the type of all men of faith, and the father of Israel) and God. Its meanings are not finally conveyable in propositions but must be *told*, as the Bible tells them. Beginning with Abraham, we have a sequence of figures, descendants of Abraham, who with imperfect faithfulness and consistency appear as witnesses of the covenant with God. We are told that along the track of this history God is accomplishing the reconciliation of man to man, of man to nature, and of man-and-nature-together with God.

There is an inside and an outside to this process. Inside the community of Israel, God has been at work overcoming that people's resistance to his will for them, so that Israel would some day experience the blessing of living at peace with Him. The outside of the process is the story of Israel's role as the bearer of the blessings of the covenant to all nations.

Israel's entire history is the medium of God's purpose:

As in its particularity it takes place in the unity of Yahweh's action with that of his people, it also takes place in the centre between the will and plan of Yahweh and the rest of human history.... It is the indispensable link between God and earthly history in general. In its particularity it has a microcosmic character. What the one God wills and plans and has done and does and will do with the human world as a whole, He causes to take place on a small scale, but in a way which recapitulates or pre-figures the whole, in His history with this one people Israel. The election and rejection of this people, the disclosure of its transgressions and forgiveness of its sins, the fulness of the benefits with which He provides for it and the severity of the judgments in which it is overtaken by His chastisement, the incomparable distinction yet also the contemptible littleness with which He causes it to exist among other nations, the whole *doxa* of the covenant with which He invests it—these are *in nuce*, in compendious form, His action with all humanity. In all these things the history of Israel is a paradigm or model for the history of all nations, and to the extent that it is prophecy, and is known as such, it is the key to the understanding of world history. Hence it is mediatorial history in the sense of exemplary and therefore representative history. It takes place among all other histories, but in such a way that it implies, comprehends, repeats and anticipates their origin, content and goal.[36]

Somehow, the story of Israel's relations with the world of nations discloses and accomplishes the reconciliation of all nations with each other, which (we are repeatedly told in the Jewish Bible) is a precondition of the world's reconciliation to God, and of man's reconciliation with nature. This proposition is summed up for Christians in Christ's own words: "It is from the Jews that salvation comes". (*John* 4:22b)

Chapter 5:

The God of Israel and the History of World Empires

"I have a plan to carry out, and carry it out I will." (Isaiah 46:11b)

The historical wisdom of a humiliated nation

We have already noted (in the first paragraphs of the previous chapter) the points of synchronism between the story told by Herodotus and the history of the Jews. We noted there the destruction of Jerusalem and its Temple and the beginning of Babylonian exile (587), which had put an end, ostensibly forever, to the separate national existence of the Jews. We noted that the first canon of Hebrew scripture was set out during this period of humiliation. The Jews expected to find, in their reading of this literature in regular assembly, (a) the explanation for the situation in which they found themselves; and (b) the basis of their hope for the new order of reality which God was preparing to replace the present world-reality. The *hope* was founded on the *history*. That is, it followed from it.

Here we come to the most conspicuous point of contrast between the theory of history implicit in Herodotus' book, *The Histories*, and that of these many books combined into one book, the Jewish Bible. Herodotus started from an assessment of ostensible political realities in his present world, and told the story that seemed to be required to make an orderly evaluation of the past and present fortunes of the great powers of his time. His theory of history amounts to conclusions, following in a compelling, realistic way from those present, political conditions; and we have little difficulty following him, provided we are prepared to think dialectically. The case is quite different with the authority of the Biblical theory of history. That theory allegedly derives from the whole course of the history of the Jews, beginning in the far-off singular decision of Abram/Abraham. And it is presently (that is, in the Fifth-century B.C.) proposed against the background of the conspicuous political insignificance, in fact, the humiliation of the Jewish people. A dispassionate verdict on this (if one is imaginable) might be that it is *ironical*. Many have called it *perverse*. But Jewish and Christian believers have seen in this situation its authentic authority, drawing from it not only their theory of history but their model for faithful religious behaviour.

This "Babylonian" Empire into which the Jewish people had been exiled turns out to be exceptionally short-lived by comparison with previous and subsequent Eastern Empires, and is nowadays usually called the Neo-Babylonian Empire, to make the point that among the earliest-known Empires of Mesapotamia at least one and perhaps several earlier empires had already centered on that same city; and of these the earliest goes back somewhere toward the middle of the third millennium B.C. Since then, there had been a complex succession of Mesapotamian Empires, some of which extended as far as the frontiers of Egypt, and thus included Palestine either as a client territory or as a subject territory. The other great centre of empire which throughout this period dominated Palestine when one or another Mesapotamian Empire did not was of course Egypt.

There is only one brief period during which Palestine was not dominated by an Empire based either on the Euphrates or the Nile, and that was for roughly five hundred years, beginning *circa* 1200. It was a time when Egypt was relatively weak, owing to internal power struggles and the distractions of her wars against the "sea peoples". And it was a time when Mesapotamia was divided between two or more centres of power. This situation ended with the intrusion into Palestine of the greatest of all the empires to date, the Assyrian. The beginnings of that Empire are in the early fourteenth century, and its intrusions into Palestine become serious early in the ninth century. The northern portion of the divided Jewish state was defeated in war, and its population dispersed in 722. The southern portion, the

The God of Israel and the History of World Empires

Kingdom of Judah, barely escaped defeat, but lived under constant threat from this empire, and for a while under semi-tutelage to it, until Assyria's defeat by the "Neo-Babylonian Empire" in the seventh century. The end came with the conquest of Judah and the destruction of the Temple in 586.

For about five hundred years following 1200 B.C. circumstances permitted a people with a mature political system and a strong ideological unity to ward off absorption into the empire-system of the brutal warrior civilizations centered in Mesapotamia and the Nile. Here we must stress the relativity of the security enjoyed by the ancient Jews in this brief period. The fact is that this was, practically speaking, the only period (with the brief exception of the Maccabean kingdom (166-63 B.C.) and the present open-ended period beginning with the establishment of the State of Israel in 1948 A.D.) when the history of the Jews is not told as a story of political humiliation.

The nadir of the political fortunes of the ancient Jews undoubtedly belongs during the generation that saw the actual fall of the kingdom of Judah, the destruction of the Temple, and the enforced exile of the King and the entire leadership of the kingdom to Babylon. Preceding the actual conquest of Jerusalem (586) there was a period of about a quarter-century, beginning with Babylon's unexpectedly sudden overthrow of the Assyrian Empire, (612) when the kings of Judah sought through defensive preparations and diplomatic alliance with Egypt and other potential fellow-victims of the new Empire, to ward off the fatal day. One after another, all the devices of her soldiers and her politicians failed. As the drift of political realities became unmistakable, the awful thought began to take hold in some minds that the domain of great power politics is subject to other laws than the Torah (which is the Law of the God of Abraham, Isaac and Jacob, and of Moses).

Towards the end of this period, in the reign of King Josiah (640-609), there was a great upsurge of national piety, provoked by the perception that in the Northern Kingdom of Israel a decline of public morality and religious cult had preceded its conquest by the Assyrians. God punished the evil behaviour of nations with military defeat. At intervals in the past, there had been moments of spiritual awakening, when the people as a whole had re-confirmed their fidelity to the original covenant. (Joshua had shown them how to do this, as the last act of his life: *Joshua*, chapters 23 and 24). And it was in one of these moods that the people had followed the example of King Josiah. (See *II Kings*, Chapters 22 and 23).

Josiah's reign and his work as a purifier of the national cult had been foretold (*I Kings* 13: 1-4) in the reign of Jeroboam (c. 922-901), the first King of the schismatic northern Kingdom of Israel, the man invariably blamed thereafter in Judah as the author of disunity, of religious innovations, and all the troubles that followed therefrom. (*I Kings* 12:25 to 14:20). Now Josiah (whose name means, "the LORD heals") himself took the initiative in driving paganism and immorality out of the Temple. He inspired a rigorous purification of the religious cult, its centralization in Jerusalem, and codification of the Laws. In fact, public and private morality improved, and the nation prospered. So striking was Josiah's success in associating high ethical standards, rigorous cultic standards and civic responsibility, that his name was always involved thereafter as the paragon of Jewish statecraft. ("No king before him had turned to the LORD as he did, with all his heart and soul and strength, following the whole law of Moses; nor did any king like him appear again") (*II Kings* 23:25).

But the story has a disastrous conclusion. When the Egyptian Pharaoh Necho sent an army through Palestine intending to lead an alliance of the lesser states on Judah's borders against Assyria, Josiah perceived this as a threat to his kingdom's peace. Proceeding to the defense of the kingdom at Megiddo, he there died in battle against the Egyptians. His death under these circumstances posed appalling difficulties for the people's understanding of God's ways. The explanation offered by the Book of *Kings* (*II Kings*: 23: 26-27) is that the Lord was still exacting punishment for the people's sins outstanding since the reign of Josiah's predecessor Manasseh (687–642), considered the most

The God of Israel and the History of World Empires 121

wicked king of Judah. Now God had taken away Judah's champion, Josiah, and *willfully* exposed the nation by leaving a totally incompetent successor! How was it possible to make sense of history and affirm the sovereignty of the God of Israel in the face of trials like these?

Given the reputation of both the Assyrians and their Babylonian successors for cruelty as military adversaries and as masters; and given the appalling character of their religious cult and their ethics—was it possible to believe that the God of Israel (who had led Israel out of slavery in Egypt, through the trials in the wilderness, to victory against apparently hopeless odds against the Canaanite populations, to national unity under the Davidic dynasty, to civilized dignity and prosperity under Solomon) had permitted Israel to be led off that path of fulfillment (through the division of the kingdom, the decline of the religious cult and of the morality in the Northern kingdom, to defeat of that kingdom by the Assyrians and the scattering of her population)—and that he intended now, finally, after a series of terrifying and humiliating harassments by the Assyrian empire and other enemies, to abandon Judah, and mock her for her trust in His covenant with them, sending them down the same path to oblivion followed by the Israelite tribes of the north, not to speak of the Philistines, the Hittites, the Horites, and all the other now-forgotten nations who once thought "that they would live forever"?

In fact, only a quarter-century of life remained for the kingdom of Judah after the death of Josiah. The political leaders and the priests insisted that God was committed to prove Himself Israel's champion. Setbacks, like Josiah's death, were explained as divine tests of the national will, calling for renewed efforts at cultic purification, which were pursued half-heartedly at best. The keystone of the people's faith now was that Jehovah could not, for the sake of his own reputation, permit the conquest of Judah. A distinctly hard-boiled mentality had set in. The effect was strangely circular: confidence that God *could not* (for the sake of his own reputation) let Jerusalem fall justified a policy of alliance with Egypt against Babylon *so that* Jerusalem should not fall!

The alliance with Egypt was undertaken in apparent forgetfulness of the history of Egypt's oppression of the Israelites and her long ill-concealed ambition to restore her own empire in this area. The pattern of the past was clear: diplomatic dealings with Egypt always led to extra-territorial concessions to the Egyptian religious cult in Jerusalem, and this ultimately to the infection of Israel's own cult at the Temple. The logic of all of this was that the statesmen and the priests were blindly leading Judah to resistance against the power of Babylon—which, if it succeeded, would result in subjection to Egypt and degradation of the national cult; and, if it failed, would provoke Babylon to terrible acts of revenge.

The fatal underestimation of Babylon's power and will to destroy Jerusalem was owing to the ingrained notion that Jehovah's concern for His own prestige *required* him to champion Judah against the false gods of Babylon. Paradoxically, this attitude amounted to affirming those other gods—for why should God be jealous of his standing relative to nonentities? And (the other side of the same coin) it meant behaving as though God's jurisdiction did not extend to the history of other nations.

This is the immediate background to the prophetic mission of Jeremiah (c. 640-587). He attacked the central fallacy in the propaganda of the statesmen (the official religious leaders, and the "false" (the "comforting") prophets): namely that Jehovah's prestige began and ended with the matter of His championship of the Jews. They had forgotten the original premise of the covenant with Abraham: that it was for the sake of the establishment of a new world order of peace involving all nations. God's relationship with Abraham's seed was not for its own sake. The preservation of the Temple was not the goal of all history: "You keep saying, 'This place is the temple of the LORD, the temple of the LORD, the temple of the LORD'! This catchword of yours is a lie; put no trust in it" (*Jeremiah* 7: 4). Neither as a building, nor as the seat of God's presence (his *shekinah*), nor as the headquarters of the cult, nor as the focus of national identity is the Temple the *reason why* there is history. The ceremonies and sacrifices that took place in the Temple had developed beyond the original intention of expressing gratitude for God's presence with the Jews, taking on the character of ceremonies intended to *bind* God to the Temple:

> These are the words of the Lord of Hosts the God of Israel. Add whole-offerings to sacrifices and eat the flesh if you will. But when I brought your forefathers out of Egypt, I gave them no command about whole-offering and sacrifice; I said not a word about them. What I did command them was this: If you obey me, I will be your God and you shall be my people. You must conform to all my commands, if you would prosper. But they did not listen; they paid no heed, and persisted in disobedience with evil and stubborn hearts; they looked backwards and not forwards, from the day when your forefathers left Egypt until now (*Jeremiah* 7: 21-25).

The people had sunk so far from their previous understanding of God's sovereign freedom that they were now emulating the worst pagans in seeking to bind God to defense of his city by sacrificing their own children, on altars established in the valley that surrounds the exposed eastern flank of the city (7:31-32). Ironically, all the official declarations of confidence about Jerusalem's safety, coupled with all these efforts to bind Jehovah's honour to the defence of the city, betrayed a growing anxiety about the future.

> But I [Jeremiah] said, O Lord GOD, the prophets tell them that they shall see no sword and suffer no famine; for thou wilt give them lasting prosperity in this place. The Lord answered me, The prophets are prophesying lies in my name. I have not sent them; I have given them no charge; I have not spoken to them.

The prophets offer them false visions, worthless augury, and their own deluding fancies (14: 13-14).

All of these efforts to fix the course of history by binding Jehovah forever to the defense of Jerusalem recapitulate the lesson of the Tower of Babel (see above pp. 96–8) in the light of the covenant. In fact, Judah had lost confidence in the universal character of the covenant. Put somewhat differently: they had lost faith in the universal jurisdiction of the God of history.

This insight of Jeremiah was not a new one. During the parallel period in the history of the Northern Kingdom (that is, in the reign of Jeroboam II [c. 793-753], just prior to the conquest and destruction of the Kingdom of Israel [722], the prophet Amos had denounced the complacency of the Israelites. They too had preferred to look down with contempt on the ugly characters who were the movers and shakers of history in those times, refusing to acknowledge that they had to be taken seriously in a world where God had covenanted to protect His chosen people. Amos' message was that Jehovah was the God of universal history. He had His purposes for all nations, which in no way contradicted the promises made to "Abraham's seed". The history of Israel's relationship with other nations is the key to universal history. And her own individual history is paradigm of the individual histories of other nations: "Are not you Israelites like Cushites to me? says the LORD. Did I not bring Israel up from Egypt, the Philistines from Caphtor, the Aramaeans from Kir"? (*Amos* 9: 7-8.)

Like Amos before him, Jeremiah commends ethical behaviour as the true worship of God (c.f. *Amos* 8:1f and *Jeremiah*: 5:1f); he identifies the tendency to escape from plain humane obligation into cult as the cause of a hardened public conscience, and further identifies this moral hardness as the true cause of God's displeasure. (*cf Amos* 5:21f. ("I hate, I spurn your pilgrim-feasts.... Spare me the sound of your songs.... Let justice roll on like a river and righteousness as an ever-flowing stream") and *Jeremiah*, Chapter 5). Like Amos, Jeremiah predicts that

God will deliver the people over to the enemy in His despair over their refusal to learn from their true (i.e., the "uncomfortable") prophets. (*cf. Amos*: 5:27: "I will drive you into exile beyond Damascus. So says the LORD; the god of Hosts is his name"), and *Jeremiah* 14:15f, and Chapters 20 and 21.) Like Amos, Jeremiah insists that the covenant of God with Abraham's seed will not be broken in all of this. (*Amos* 9:9-15: "No, I will give my orders, I will shake Israel to and fro through all the nations as a sieve is shaken to and fro and not one pebble falls to the ground. They shall die by the sword, all the sinners of my people, who say, 'Thou wilt not let disaster come near us or overtake us.' On that day I will restore David's fallen house; I will repair its gaping walls and restore its ruins.... I will restore the fortunes of my people Israel; they shall rebuild deserted cities and live by them, they shall plant vineyards and drink their wine, make gardens and eat the fruit. Once more I will plant them on their own soil, and they shall never again be uprooted from the soil I have given them. It is the word of the LORD your God") and *Jeremiah*, Chapters 30 to 33: ("... These are the words of the LORD: If I had not made my law for day and night nor established a fixed order in heaven and earth, then I would spurn the descendants of Jacob and of my servant David, and would not take any of David's line to be rulers over the descendants of Abrahams, Isaac and Jacob. But now I will restore their fortune and have compassion on them". (33:25–6)

The gentile empires as the instruments of God's purpose

The enduring lesson in these reflections of the prophets on the course of history is that we must take with full seriousness the world of great-power politics as the realm in which the God of Israel is master. Human affairs are evidently not meant to be stable on this side of eternity. In striking contrast (again) to the best advice of the noblest vein of Greek philosophy, we are told not to invest anything at all in the vision of a stable world order in the realm of this historical life.

(This, incidentally, frees us from the temptation to identify any present political force as the present or potential guarantor of that stability.) The world order we should have in view is that which comes at the end of history, which will follow after the purpose for which God covenanted with Abraham is accomplished within history. The centrepiece of that purpose is the return of Israel from captivity, the restoration of the former life of the Israelites in their former home: "They shall rebuild deserted cities and live in them ...plant vineyards ...drink their wine ...make gardens ...eat, drink, *etc.*"—that is, live the life of a community of men on the pattern of all ordinary communities of men, within this present historical dispensation. History's complex gyrations are centered on this theme of Israel's restoration—and this not metaphorically, but really.

In Amos' and Jeremiah's prophecies regarding the course of history, the emphasis is on making sense (in the terms of the covenant) of the coming military and political humiliation of the people of Israel. In the light of the absolutely irresistible power of Babylon, it is not loyalty to Jehovah but disloyalty to Him to resist that Empire; and the fact that the champions of such resistance are delivering Judah into an alliance with Egypt is the best measure of the madness that follows upon such disloyalty. Therefore, true piety in this context is to deal realistically with power realities; and true realism amounts to choosing life over death: "I offer you now a choice between the way of life and the way of death. Whoever remains in this city [i.e., resisting the Babylonians] shall die by the sword, by famine or by pestilence, but whoever goes out to surrender to the Chaldeans who are now besieging you, shall survive" (*Jeremiah* 21: 8-9). In keeping as always with the premise of the radical freedom of the human will, Jeremiah as Amos before him, insists that the people had always had it in their power to choose good over evil and thus to have prevented this outcome. And right up to the end, the prophets, in certain moods, speak as though a radical conversion of heart and mind could yet bring on a different outcome than the one which they report (as a message delivered from God) consistently in the past tense: "I have set my face against this city, meaning to do them harm, not good, says the LORD. It shall be handed over to the king of Babylon, and he shall burn it to the ground. To the royal house of Judah. Listen to the word of the LORD. O house of David, these are the words of the LORD: Administer justice betimes, rescue the victim from his oppressor, lest the fire of my fury blaze up and burn unquenched because of your evil doings" ((*Jeremiah* 21: 10-12). "Mend your ways and your doings, deal fairly with one another, do not oppress the alien, the orphan, and the widow, shed no innocent blood in this place, do not run after other gods to your own ruin. Then will I let you live in this place, in the land which I gave long ago to your forefathers for all time" (7: 5-7).

• • •

The city of Jerusalem was devastated and the Temple destroyed and the best part of the people themselves carried into captivity in Babylon. During the captivity, faith in the sovereignty of the God of Israel as the God of History continued on the promise consistently given by God through Isaiah, Jeremiah and Ezekiel that Israel would return to its holy land. As consistently predicted by these same prophets, the Babylonian Empire collapsed suddenly (539 B.C.). It fell to the Persian conqueror Cyrus II ("the Great"), who quickly became the ruler of the largest empire to that date in the history of the world. Here the story of the ancient Jews links up with *The Histories* as told by Herodotus. We should remind ourselves, however, that Herodotus makes no explicit mention of the Jews. We do know from Herodotus that Cyrus made a policy of encouraging the free exercise of the cults of all subject peoples; and indeed we have Cyrus' own declaration of this policy preserved on a clay cylinder.[1]

As we noted at the outset of Chapter Four, the reign of Cyrus the Great of Persia (548-529) marks the beginning of a period of renewed hope for the people of Israel. Cyrus allowed the return of the Jews, transported a generation previously under the Babylonians, to Judaea; and he not merely authorized but actually subsidized the project of rebuilding the Temple (*Ezra* 1 and 6: 3-5, and II *Chronicles* 36: 22-23).[2] A small province was established, with Jerusalem at its centre. The first contingent of zealots—probably a meagre few hundred—set out for Jerusalem under one Shesh-bazzar (presumably a member of the Davidic family exiled in Babylon). A few years later, a larger contingent followed under Shesh-bazzar's successor as "Governor of Judah", Zerubbabel. Most scholars doubt that anything like the majority of the exiled Jews did in fact return to the barrenness of Israel (as it now must have seemed to them in civilized Babylon, on the banks of the fertile Euphrates, their new community life focused on a district of their own named, interestingly, Tel Aviv (*Ezekiel* 3:15). Josephus (who usually puts the best face on things that touch the prestige of his ancestors) admits: "yet did many of them stay at Babylon, as not willing to leave their possessions"[3] A standard work estimates the population of Judah by 522 as 20,000.[4]

Re-examining the promise of restoration in the light of the return to Jerusalem

This is the last period of history for which the present canonical Bible provides evidence. "The last monarch whom it mentions by name is 'Darius the Persian' (*Ne* 12:12)—either Darius II (423-404) or Darius III (336-331) the last king of Persia".[5]

A great controversy dominated the life of the Jewish people in this period. It turned on speculation about the nature and the state of God's covenant with Israel at the time of the Persian wars with the Greeks, and in fact essentially fixes the parameters of debate on this theme where they stood when the "Common Era" opens five hundred years later.

In the beginning of this last Biblical period, what was immediately under debate was the nature of the role being played by Cyrus and his successors on the Persian throne. Behind that there was the issue of the relationship between the history of the covenant and global history. Cyrus was the latest representative of the type of man brought to dominate over the lives of men and nations by the secular workings of power politics. The original of his type was the Pharaoh of Egypt. From the Pharaoh to Belshazzar, the masters of the empires that surrounded the Israelites were unreservedly identified as enemies of the independence of Israel, with all that went with it: freedom of worship, cultic purity, civic morality, racial integrity—all the several facets of the one essential factor, political sovereignty. Now there appears Cyrus, a pagan like all his predecessors, but who offers himself as the instrument of the return of the people to Israel and the restoration of the Temple. Cyrus' decision disoriented everyone. First of all, Cyrus' decision suddenly opened up for the Jews a possibility of freedom of action that only fanatical seers (of whom Ezekiel is the type) had ever expected to see again. Secondly, the opportunity which Cyrus provided (return to Israel) seemed to fit what the major prophets had held out as the penultimate chapter of world history. Thirdly, the agent of all of this (Cyrus, himself) was a pagan man of power—not a Jew, certainly not of "the seed of Abraham".

It is not an easy matter to align all the elements in this controversy and identify consistent spokesmen for each viewpoint. But the theorizing, and preaching and prophesying on this theme ranged to such extremes that, with little imagination, we can make out all the permutations and combinations of all the arguments of the following twenty-five centuries of Jewish religion on the theme of the relationship between the history of the covenant and the history of the nations.

All participants in the controversy agreed that what was happening was in vindication of all those prophets who had spoken of the ultimate restoration of Israel. These (it must be recalled) are to be distinguished from the optimistic (or "comfortable") prophets who had consistently denied that Jehovah would allow Israel's defeat by pagan enemies, and who had of course been discredited by events. The prophecies of ultimate restoration were bound up in the prophecies of immediate doom made by Amos, Hosea, Micah, and of Isaiah, prior to the conquest of Israel by Assyria and the scattering of the ten tribes; and by Jeremiah, Zephaniah, Nahum and others prior to the conquest of Judah by Babylon and the exile of the people's leaders to Babylon.

Religious spokesmen of all types—prophets, priests and lawyers—as well as certain politicians in the coterie of the exiled Davidic princes in Babylon, were caught up in a frenzy, as it seemed now that the whole confused process of history, the rise and fall of empires from the beginning, had come into sharp focus. The defeat and "scattering" of Israel the proud majority had rejected in advance as an impossibility. After the fact, pessimists could see only defeat of all hopes.

The pre-exilic prophets had talked about the "sifting" of the people. Speaking before the period of the exile, Isaiah described Israel as the Lord's "Servant", whose sufferings would somehow accomplish the restoration of the kingdom (*Isaiah*, Chapters 42 and following). These words were now applied to the remnant who would return with the leaders of the restoration to Jerusalem, who would labour to restore the cities and the farms and above all, the Temple. The trials associated with the pre-messianic age were being lived out by the generation that was returning to Jerusalem. Clearly, God was master of History after all. He had raised up Egypt for one purpose, Assyria for another, Babylonia for another, and now Persia for yet another. In none of these cases, the prophets said, was there any independent or objective basis or origin for these empires. Apart from their function in the Messianic plan, there was no logic to their rise and fall.

As for Cyrus, the Jewish leaders had great difficulty in making sense of his personal responsibility in all of this. The "line" taken by the priests was that Cyrus should be understood as an essentially will-less instrument of a purpose he did not himself grasp. (This is the viewpoint of the prophecies of *Haggai* and *Zechariah*.) Though Cyrus does not understand his own motives, he is in fact moved by the God of Israel to allow the restoration and encourage the building of the

Temple. These specific deeds are required as the penultimate acts of the historical process. They will result (though Cyrus cannot guess this) in the advent of the messianic age, the exaltation of Israel, and the collapse of the Persian empire itself. It is unthinkable that Cyrus would desire or anticipate this outcome. He thinks he is the master of world-historical forces, like all the movers and shakers of the earth before him. He does not understand the mystery of the covenant as the inner meaning of history, and of Israel as the Suffering Servant of God's purpose to redeem humanity from the likes of himself and to restore men to a world without oppression. If history is organized as the scriptures say it is, as the story of the ultimate blessing of all mankind though the blessing of Abraham's seed, then this must be seen by the eye of faith. The eye that sees political power as the governing reality in historical life will fail utterly to see anything of significance in the present story of the Jews. It has to be assumed that it is the very innocuousness of the Jews that commends to Cyrus the idea of restoring them to their locale and their cult. He cannot, in the one policy, be consciously fulfilling the purposes that Jehovah has for Abraham's seed (and thus be a willing servant of its historical vision) and at the same time providing for the permanent security of his empire. He obviously believes he is doing the latter. He declares as much publicly.

The crux of the case of the Jewish leadership is that Persia and her Empire and the kind of unity established under it cannot have any independent meaning. The whole pattern of the rise and fall of empires is without intrinsic interest. Had Herodotus' *Histories* been put into their hands (about a century in advance of their publication) its premise would have seemed to them mad—a blasphemous misrepresentation of history as the evident workings of power.

We begin to realize what is at stake here when we reflect that our civilization's theory of history has for centuries followed Herodotus' example in insisting on the positive significance of what is *evidently* happening in history when told as the story of power. Christian theorists of history later accepted Herodotus' estimate of the significance of Persia's empire, and his estimate of the significance of the rise of Greece, and of the conflict of the two empires. And they followed Herodotus' successors in continuing the story of great power struggles as the organizing matrix theory of world history. Their ideological purpose was to make a case for God's preparation through the processes of secular history, of a unified world-civilization, the civilization of Rome, as the necessary matrix for the globalization of the promises of the covenant. Of this, much more later. For the moment, we have to make the point that here, where the story told by Herodotus crosses the path of the history of the ancient Jews, we find the Jews involved in a decisive review of their theory of the covenant which fixes for ever the limits of the distinctively Biblical theory of history.

∴

The first years of the restoration were depressingly disappointing for the remnant who had returned. They had to face the hostility of the local population. These latter included those Jews who had not gone to Babylon after 586, and who had in the eyes of the returnees, and probably in actual fact, sunk to a low level of cultic deviation and moral squalor. And there was the hostile population of the "Samaritans" (non-Jews transplanted by the Babylonians to the territories of the former Kingdom of Israel to displace the ten tribes, and who were determined to prevent the re-instatement of the Jewish cult based on Jerusalem. At the same time, the returnees felt betrayed by the Babylonian Jews who were refusing to "come up" (immigrate) to Jerusalem.

Far from being a glorious new beginning, it was turning out to be "the day of small things". (*Zechariah* 4:10) The project to rebuild the Temple had scarcely begun when a famine took hold. The depression was so keenly-felt, that the project was abandoned. (*Ezra* 1 to 6)

There seemed no way for the leaders of the returned remnant, themselves agents of the empire, to persuade the people that these paltry beginnings amounted to the dawn of the messianic age which (prophecy seemed uniformly to predict) would accompany the return to Zion. There seemed a real possibility that faith in the premises of the covenant would sooner or later collapse of their own splendid weight. The prophets' frantic exhortations on behalf of rebuilding the temple have to be seen in this light. Apparently there were some whose enthusiasm led them to publicly identify Zerubbabel with the Messianic Son of David. And it may be that Zerubbabel went along with this, and that the Persian authorities had to put him down, perhaps to remove him, even to execute him. (There is much recondite academic guesswork about this).[6] In any case, neither the Persians nor the masters of any of the subsequent empires to which Judaea belonged ever again allowed a descendent of the house of David to govern Judaea.

Whatever the exact nature of the events surrounding Zerubbabel's end, it seems likely that it figured among the many political upheavals that began in 521 when Cambyses (Cyrus' successor) died (see above, p. 50), and various sections of the empire gave their allegiance to various pretenders. Some scholars believe that these events may have inspired the urgent messianic message in the books of *Haggai* and *Zechariah*.[7] The political and religious leaders persuaded the people to return with vigour to the work of rebuilding the Temple which (as we have noted) they had abandoned in the depression that followed after the initial years of return. The disorder throughout the Persian empire was pronounced significant of the end of the rule of power in the world. The messianic fulfilment was imminent. All that remained was for the people of the covenant to build the Temple:

> Haggai in particular, scored the lassitude and indifference that allowed people to establish themselves in their own houses while letting Yahweh's house lie in ruins. He explained the hard

times the community had experienced as the divine punishment, for that indifference (Hag. 1:1-11; 2:15-19). Convinced that Yahweh had again chosen Zion as the seat of his rule, he viewed completion of the Temple as a matter of utmost urgency, the necessary precondition of Yahweh's coming to dwell among his people and bless them. Sternly separatist, Haggai urged the cutting of all contacts with religious syncretists in the land, which, he declared, were as contaminating as handling a corpse (ch. 2:10-14). Sensing the people's discouragement because the structure they were building was exceedingly modest, he fired them with the promise that Yahweh would soon shake the nations, fill the Temple with their treasures, and make it far more splendid than Solomon's (ch. 2:1-9). He even (ch. 2:20-23) addressed Zerubbabel in Messianic language, hailing him as the chosen Davidic king who would rule when imperial power, as it shortly would, had come crashing to the ground.... Like Haggai, Zechariah... spurred the people on [to the completion of the Temple] (chs. 1:16; 6:15), declaring that Zerubbabel, who had begun the work would by God's Spirit see it to a finish (ch. 4:6b-10a). He promised that Jerusalem would then be a great city overflowing its walls (Zech. 1:17; 2:1-5) as God's people—and Gentiles too (chs. 2:11; 8:22f.)—flocked thither from all over the world (ch. 8:1-8).[8]

Zerubbabel, as we have seen, was removed. But the work on the Temple went forward; and in 515 it was finished and dedicated. (*Ezra* 6:13-18)

> Yet, needless to say, the hopes voiced by Haggai and Zechariah did not materialize. David's throne was not re-established, and the age of promise did not dawn.[9]

Thus, the life of the Jews who had returned to Judaea was made extremely difficult by the alteration of mood between exhaltation and depression, which resulted from the determination of their religious leaders to bring on the messianic age through a great act of collective will.

Isaiah's message of universal hope

But there was a rival branch of prophets whose preaching at once took more realistic account of the facts of power politics in the world and provided a more elevated vision of God's ultimate purpose for history. This vein of prophecy outlasted the crises of the age of "restoration", and its accents are those which Augustine and later Christian theologians exploited.

Of this branch of prophets the founder is Isaiah. In the Book of *Isaiah* we are told that this pre-exilic prophet foresaw Cyrus' edict allowing the return and the restoration. Isaiah insists that it is the God of Israel who will being Cyrus to power, and who will cause him to act as he does. All the great historical movers are instruments of His purposes:

> Tell me, who raised up that one from the east, one greeted by victory wherever he goes? Who is it that puts nations into his power, and makes kings go down before him? ...Whose work is this, I ask, who has brought it to pass? Who has summoned the generations from the beginning? It is I, the LORD, I am the first, and to the last of them I am He. (*Isaiah* 41:2a,4.)

And he confirms that all of these historical forces are directed towards the restoration of Israel:

> But you, Israel my servant, you, Jacob whom I have chosen, race of Abraham my friend, I have taken you up, have fetched you

from the ends of the earth, and summoned you from its furthest corners, I have called you my servant, have chosen you and not cast you off. (41:8-9)

But all the frenzy involved in the Temple project and the reckless politics surrounding Zerubbabel, far from pleasing God, must be denounced as tactics to force the hand of God—to take the levers of history by force into the hands of men. The fatal fascination in the Temple project to that generation was that it seemed to bring the whole work of the covenant into focus as a project—like the Tower of Babel, again!—a magnificent, costly, even a heroic project; but still a definable and realizable human job. It had been forgotten that the ultimate goal was still as defined in *Genesis*: 12:3: the blessing of all the nations.

This is the note that is missing in the "priestly" line of prophecy:

It is too slight a task for you, as my servant, to restore the tribes of Jacob, to bring back the descendants of Israel; I will make you a light to the nations, to be my salvation to earth's farthest bound. (49:6)

Israel's work would not be finished until the whole purpose is accomplished for which Abram/Abraham entered into his covenant with God. It is not given to men to know the dimensions of the whole work. It is blasphemy to confine this work to the dimensions of a project that a single generation of men, however pious and otherwise self-denying, can reduce to a blue print for a building, or a political constitution, or a Book of Prayer, or a plan of social reconstruction (all of which figured in the work of that busy generation.)

Remember this, you rebels, consider it well and abandon hope, remember all that happened long ago; for I am God, there is no other, I am God, and there is no one like me; I reveal the end

The God of Israel and the History of World Empires

from the beginning, from ancient times I reveal what is to be; I say, "My purpose shall take effect, I will accomplish all that I please." I summon a bird of prey from the east, one from a distant land to fulfill my purpose. Mark this; I have spoken, and I will bring it about, I have a plan to carry out, and carry it out I will. (46:8-11.)

As for Cyrus, the "bird of prey from the east", Isaiah's verdict has implications that still can cause the reader some sense of shock. We recall that the "priestly" line on Cyrus was that he was essentially an unwitting (because pagan) instrument of a purpose which he did not grasp. Apparently there were some who found it hard to accept that the pagan Cyrus could be a divinely-chosen instrument, and tried to persuade themselves that he must have become converted, secretly or otherwise, to Judaism. Josephus says that Cyrus had in fact read the prophecies in *Isaiah* regarding himself, and was consciously fulfilling them. (*Antiquities*, XI, I:1f.) This seems unlikely at best, but has the advantage of keeping the decisive instruments of God's purpose within the line of conscious "men of faith" who follow from Abraham.

Isaiah's verdict is much more radical:

Thus says the LORD, your ransomer, who fashioned you from birth: I am the LORD who made all things, by myself I stretched out the skies, alone I hammered out the floor of the earth. I frustrate false prophets and their signs and make fools of diviners; I reverse what wise men say and make nonsense of their wisdom. I make my servants' prophecies come true and give effect to my messengers' designs. I say of Jerusalem, "She shall be inhabited once more", and of the cities of Judaea, "They shall be rebuilt; all their ruins I will restore". I say to the deep waters, "Be dried up; I will make your streams run dry". I say to Cyrus, "You shall be my shepherd to carry out all my purpose, so that Jerusalem may be rebuilt and the foundations of the temple may be laid."

Thus says the LORD to Cyrus his anointed, Cyrus whom he has taken by the hand to subdue nations before him and undo the might of kings.... For the sake of Jacob my servant and Israel my chosen I have called you by name and given you your title, though you have not known me. (*Isaiah* 44:24-45:1; 45:4)

It is the same God who is God of nature, who is God of Israel, who is God of history. If, in his sovereignty over nature he "says to deep waters be dried up", so in his sovereignty over history he commands and directs the deeds of Cyrus. But Cyrus is no automaton. He has been chosen by the God of Israel for his qualities, as was Abraham: He is identified (48:14) as "He whom I love". He is called by name, and taken by the hand, as was Abraham. He is, furthermore, "annointed" for his task, as David was. And all this it true "though you (Cyrus) have not known me!"

To Cyrus are applied, here and now (provisionally, as it were), all the titles that will be applied to Israel in the days yet to come, when the world will see openly what it now (because of Israel's humiliation) cannot see. He is the God of Israel's "shepherd" (*cf.* 40:11) He is the God of Israel's annointed (in Hebrew, מְשִׁיחוֹ "His annointed", his Mashack, "Messiah"; in the Septuagint, χριω, from which χριστος, Christ. These are the titles of Messiah.

The "outer" and "inner" visions of Hebrew prophecy

This conflict between the vision of history put forth by Isaiah on the one hand and the "official" or "priestly" school of prophets on the other, developing against the background of the history of the empire of Cyrus, exposes the fundamental tension between what might be called the "greater" and the "lesser", the "outer" and the "inner" aspects of the ancient Jewish theory of world history. The notion that has to be resisted is that this vision of the tensions involved in the covenant relationship is a breakthrough to a higher concept of the universal reign of Israel's God, coming as the end-product of a long evolutionary process of moral and intellectual struggle, starting from the Pentateuch's primitive vision of God as "the ego of Israel". The variety of historical adventures since Abraham's decision has inspired a kaleidescopic variety of expressions of the anomalies and paradoxes inseparable from the mystery of God's covenant with the Jews on behalf of all mankind. If we were now to work our way back through the Jewish scriptures earlier than Isaiah, with the main themes of Isaiah's complaint against the lesser visionaries still ringing in our ear, we should easily discover that this tension had always existed. The fact is that the extra-ordinary expectations of the age of return and the rebuilding of the Temple brought out this fundamental tension in an extreme form. The expectations attaching to the Temple project provoked a controversy which sheds a brilliant light on all the paradoxes bound up in the problem of how the covenant with Abraham's seed is accomplished in history. In that light, we can return to the many stories in *Genesis* (see above, pp. 86–88) having to do with the process by which the promise of the covenant devolved upon Isaac (but not upon Ishmael), and then upon Jacob (but not upon Esau). These are expressions in narrative, semi-legendary form, of Isaiah's thoughts on the question of the relation between the "sacred" history of the Jews and the "secular" history of the rise and fall of empires; between the Davidic kingship and Cyrus; between the "messiah" who is to come, and Cyrus who is, here and now, God's "annointed". In this same light, we should read again the story of the covenant with Noah (*Genesis* 8 and 9) and the frequent references in later scripture to God's commitments to all men and to nature itself under that covenant. In *Exodus* through *Deuteronomy* we find frequent instances of God's despair over the unworthiness of the Jews; sometimes only Moses' fidelity dissuades God from abandoning the covenant with Abraham's seed. (*E.g.*, *Exodus*, 32:11-14.)

This theme of the unworthiness of the Jews to be the bearers of God's purposes for all mankind is exposed in an especially harsh light during the "restoration crisis" of the late sixth-early fifth centuries B.C. But it had always been there in scripture, as an undertone, whenever the Bible speaks about the history of the Jews and the history of the world. God is preparing to accomplish, through the covenant with Abraham's seed, so great, so absolute a victory, for Himself and for man, over all that now separates both man and nature from Him, that all the Jews' most noble (let alone their lesser) efforts to get the measure of it all imaginatively *must fail*. Their failure of charity towards those not of Abraham's seed is, humanly speaking, inevitable. The risk of chauvinism is (given human weakness) built into the very fact of God's decision to *choose* at all. A failure of imagination with respect to the restoration of all things beyond history is similarly built in.

Historical realism

The fact of Israel's living within the covenant, and in active knowledge of the covenant, makes it impossible for her to turn her eyes away from history. The extra dimension (so to speak) of the "punishment" that Israel suffers within history is that which belongs to her realistic knowledge of history. Other nations are able (though only through perversity) to pretend not to notice the truly hopeless character of history, when viewed from outside the perspective of the covenant. For every other nation than Israel there seems to be at least a moment when it can let itself be deceived that it will live forever. Paradoxically, it is ignorance of history that sets up the innocent to want to be movers and shakers within it. If only they knew more about history, they would not fall into the trap of mistaking it as a place where they can find immortality. The ambitious skim through the record of the past, and find examples of glory. "Babylon" as always in scripture, is held up as the original of this bad example:

> Babylon has been a gold cup in the LORD's hand to make all the earth drunk; the nations have drunk of her wine, and that has made them mad. (*Jeremiah* 51:7.)

It will be seen that the Bible takes little stock of the idealistic and altruistic motives that men always offer for their interest in historical activity:

> They cry to me for help: "We know thee, God of Israel." But Israel is utterly loathsome; and therefore he shall run before the enemy. They made kings, but not by my will; they set up officers, but without my knowledge; they have made themselves idols of their silver and gold.... Do not rejoice, Israel, do not exult like other peoples; for like a wanton you have foresaken your God, you have loved an idol [margin: *or* a harlot's fee] on every threshing-floor heaped with corn. (*Hosea* 8:2–4 and 9:1.)

The prophets never allow us to forget the inevitably corrupting effects of power. Even the noblest historical characters end up harassing us all for their "harlot's fees" on our daily life.

Those Biblical scholars who are also familiar with the documentary sources for other ancient Near Eastern people note the striking absence in the Bible of anything resembling the glorification of kings and kingly power found consistently in other sources.[10] David, we recall, is the type of God's future "annointed"; but the sources make perfectly clear that he is no exception to the rule that power corrupts—most memorably (but not exclusively) in the matter of Bathsheba, the wife of Uriah. It is deeply significant that David, the figure the Biblical sources come closest to lionizing as a figure of historical success, is disqualified by God Himself, by very reason of his triumphs, from the privilege which (he claimed) he most coveted: to build a house of worship for God. (I *Chronicles* 28.)

The Jewish scriptures take a consistently realistic view of what happens in history, understood as a story of human agency. The habit of historical action, they say, leads to increased ambition; ambition leads to over-confidence; and over confidence to madness:

> [The king of Assyria says:] By my own might I have acted and in my own wisdom I have laid my schemes; I have removed the frontiers of nations and plundered their treasures, like a bull I have trampled on their inhabitants. My hand has found its way to the wealth of nations, and, as a man takes the eggs from a deserted nest, so have I taken every land; not a wing fluttered, not a beak gaped, no chirp was heard.... I will set my throne high above the stars of God, I will sit on the mountain where the gods meet in the far recesses of the north. I will rise high above the cloud-banks and make myself like the Most High.(*Isaiah* 10:13-14 and 14:13a, 14:13-14.)

This realism with respect to the motives and character of the princes of the earth did not, however, lead to withdrawal from history. On the contrary, it made the prophets intensely interested in history's detail. It is in the spirit of these prophets that Karl Barth was wont to say that the preacher should always carry the Bible in one hand and the day's newspaper in the other. The prophet's judgements do not invite our contempt for politicians. They do insist on realism, which entails the recognition that we are all just like them. We must pay close attention to the world of politics because, in fact, God is at work in that world, over-mastering these movers and shakers, putting them to accomplishing purposes which they do not intend. It is true of "the Assyrian" that "this man's purpose is lawless, lawless are the plans in his mind". (*Isaiah* 10:7.) But, "Shall the axe set itself up against the hewer, or the saw claim mastery over the sawyer, as if a stick were to brandish him who wields it, or a staff of wood to wield one who is not wood?" (*Isaiah* 10:15.) "The Assyrian! He is the rod that I wield in my anger, and the staff of my wrath is in his hand.... When the LORD has finished all that he means to do on Mount Zion and in Jerusalem, he will punish the king of Assyria for this fruit of his pride...." (10:5, 12a.) Thus punishment awaits all the brutality of the mighty in history. The "punishment" which specially belongs to Israel in this life, and of which Amos spoke, is the pain of the knowledge of history's real meaning, which their obtuseness spares the mighty in this life.

But on the obverse side of that peculiar "punishment" is a peculiar mercy. And this is the hope (of which the gentiles are in ignorance) that belongs to the end of all things:

> In days to come the mountain of the LORD's house shall be set over all other mountains, lifted high above the hills. All the nations shall come streaming to it, and many peoples shall come and say, "Come, let us climb up on to the mountain of the LORD, to the house of the God of Jacob, that he may teach us his ways, and we may walk in his paths." For instruction issues from Zion, and out of Jerusalem comes the word of the LORD; he will be judge between nations, arbiter among many peoples. They shall beat their swords into mattocks and their spears into pruning knives; nation shall not lift sword against nation nor ever again be trained for war. (*Isaiah* 2:2a-4)

Abraham Heschel writes:

> What is history? Wars, victories, and wars. So many dead. So many tears. So little regret. So many fears. And who could sit in judgement over the victims of cruelty when their horror turns to hatred...? Should not all hope be abandoned?
>
> What saved the prophets from despair was their messianic vision and the idea of man's capacity for repentance.... Over all the darkness of experience hovers the vision of a different day.

> "In that day there shall be a highway from Egypt into Assyria; the Assyrian will come to Egypt, and the Egyptians into Assyria, and the Egyptians will worship with the Assyrians. In that day Israel shall be a third with Egypt and Assyria, a blessing in the midst of the earth, which the Lord of hosts has blessed saying, Blessed be My people Egypt, and Assyria, the work of My hands, and Israel, My inheritance" (*Isaiah* 19:23-25)[11]

We know these proper names as belonging to historical nations of the time of Isaiah. We know that they have (incredibly!) their contemporary counterparts. What must we think of "man's capacity for repentance" in order to believe in the historical possibility of which this prophecy speaks? ("In that day there shall be a highway from Egypt to *Syria* and *Iraq*!") The prophets take us across the threshold of history into the realm of the redeemed human and natural reality that will replace this present one when all of the work of history is done:

> What to us seems inconceivable, to Isaiah was a certainty: War will be abolished. They shall not learn war anymore because they shall seek knowledge of the word of God.... Had the prophets relied on human resources for justice and righteousness, on man's power to achieve redemption, they would not have insisted upon the promise of messianic redemption, for messianism implies that any course of living, even the supreme efforts of man by himself, must fail in redeeming the world. In other words, human history is not sufficient unto itself.[12]

Thus, Biblical prophecy looks to the realization of man's expectations in the intervention of God's Messiah as the ultimate chapter in history—the chapter that will see the reconciliation of man-and-nature-together to God:

The God of Israel and the History of World Empires

Then a shoot shall grow from the stock of Jesse, and a branch shall spring from his roots. The spirit of the LORD shall rest upon him, a spirit of wisdom and understanding, a spirit of counsel and power, a spirit of knowledge and the fear of the LORD. He shall not judge by what he sees nor decide by what he hears; he shall judge the poor with justice and defend the humble in the land with equity; his mouth shall be a rod to strike down the ruthless, and with a word he shall slay the wicked. Round his waist he shall wear the belt of justice, and good faith shall be the girdle round his body. Then the wolf shall live with the sheep, and the leopard lie down with the kid; the calf and the young lion shall grow up together, and a little child shall lead; the cow and the bear shall be friends, and their young shall lie down together. The lion shall eat straw like cattle; the infant shall play over the hole of the cobra, and the young child dance over the viper's nest. They shall not hurt or destroy in all my holy mountain, for as the waters fill the sea, so shall the land be filled with the knowledge of the LORD. (*Isaiah* 11:1–9)

Summary

Turning from ancient Greek historians to the Jewish Bible we have found a broadening of our perspective on the meaning of history. Indeed, so broad is the perspective that it will no longer seem to us possible for any philosophy or science to contain it. The Jews are unique among the civilizations of the world in building their collective case for the largest meanings on the assertion that the *surest* and the *most important* things that we know about God we know from His activity in history.

There are many evidences of purpose in nature. The Bible is very interested in these, and speaks of such evidence as pointing towards God. And if we put our minds to it, we can uncover laws that undergird this purposive behaviour of nature. The Bible is always interested in these, and in fact regards the search for such laws as a pious activity. But the Bible consistently shows that the sum-total of all the laws that obtain in nature is not a true testimony to the will of God, because the will of God is engaged in transforming nature.

The ultimate law in the cosmos is God's covenant with man through Abraham, which is presently at work redeeming human nature, and indeed redeeming the whole matrix of nature. The laws that apparently describe the order of the cosmos in fact describe a tentative system of order. Philosophy and science more-or-less *describe* this tentative system of order. But there is a larger dynamic at work in the cosmos which is redeeming this otherwise doomed system of order. This dynamic is God's Plan.

• • •

These are the words of the LORD, who gave the sun for a light by day and the moon and stars for a light by night, who cleft the sea and its waves roared, the LORD of Hosts is his name:

If this fixed order could vanish out of my sight, says the LORD,
then the race of Israel too could cease for evermore to be a nation
in my sight.

These are the words of the LORD: If any man could measure the heaven above or fathom the depths of the earth beneath, then I could spurn the whole race of Israel because of all that they have done. This is the very word of the LORD.
Jeremiah 31:35–7

The ancient Jewish scriptures begin with descriptions of how an originally stable and permanent order of reality was established, but was subsequently set at jeopardy by man's defiance of the laws which governed that initial order. Therefore, systematic intellectual efforts can never get at ultimate truth about the human situation in the cosmos, since the human situation is being changed by God's action in and through time. If this is so, there is no possibility of finding the meaning-of-meanings through ontological speculation: that is, through exhaustive discovery of the patterns of coherence in this present reality.

The governing truth about reality is that it is being re-established according to a Plan—which is not inherent in its present, doomed "order", but which comes from outside of it, and includes a new and eternal order of reality. "For behold, I create new heavens and a new earth. Former things shall no more be remembered nor shall they be called to mind". (Isaiah 65:17) *The ultimate law in the cosmos is God's covenant with Abraham by which this new order of reality is being established.* Laws discovered by disciplined examination of present reality (that is, through science) are sub-laws of that ultimate law; they describe the present tentative order of the cosmos, and are in fact on the way to being set aside.

It must stand to reason that we could not work our way to this ultimate law through disciplined thought, since thought can only deal with the reality in which it finds itself. We could not find this Plan; we would have to be shown it. And it is precisely the Bible's case that in the history of God's covenant with Abraham we are told what we need to know about this Plan. "See how the first prophecies have come to pass, and now I declare new things; before they break from the bud I announce them to you". (Isaiah 42:9 and *cf.* 48:6-7)

The Greek philosophers (and ontological philosophers since) are unanimous in arguing that history is the intellectual discipline least likely to yield large meanings, because its subject-matter is the least "orderly". But what if this present order of reality is only tentative? What if there is some new reality in process of displacing it? On the face of it, history has the one qualification necessary for being the bearer of this meaning—that is, the very qualification which seems, in the eyes of philosophy and science to be its disqualification: its intractability to ontological philosophy.

Chapter 6

Convergence of the Graeco-Roman and the Ancient Jewish Theories of History

In this chapter, we have in view a block of time, approximately two centuries, or roughly speaking six generations of men, with the birth of Jesus of Nazareth roughly at its centre. It was during this period that there came about the convergence of the two previously discrete and distinct traditions for the recital of the whole story of the human past which we desribed in the four previous chapters.

Before convergence of these two traditions became feasible, there was a somewhat longer period of time (that is, roughly the fourth, third and second centuries B.C.) during which the two traditions remained distant—at first because of ignorance of each other, and then because of mutual contempt. Insuperable obstacles (both of a practical and of what we could call an ideological sort) separated them. Perhaps the greatest obstacle was the enormous disparity in their respective political auspices. The Greek tradition of historiography belonged to the culture of the masters of the Hellenic empire, and the Jewish belonged to one of the least significant and (in all senses) least accesible subject populations of the empire. This was the situation until the Maccabean revolt of the middle of the second century B.C. brought a sudden astounding transformation of the political fortunes of the Jews. (Of this, more below, pp. [157f.].) But we have some evidence that even before this time Greek intellectuals had at least heard of the Jewish world-view and had begun to reckon with it.

587/6   Babylonian destruction of Jerusalem and Temple, and beginning of Babylonian exile.

539	Cyrus of Persia's conqust of Babylon
538	Cyrus' edict allowing return of Jewish exiles to Judaea
520–515	The Temple rebuilt
525	Persian conquest of Egypt
493–479	Graeco-Persian war
431–404	Peloponnesian war
359–336	Philip of Macedon —his conquest of Greece, 338–337
336–323	Alexander of Macedon —his expedition against Persia, 334–330 —seige of Tyre, 332; in Palestine 332-1 —invasion of India, 327-326
306–203	Judaea ruled by the Ptolemies (Egyptian-based successor-state to portion of Alexander's empire)
264–146	Punic wars —Roman conquest of Macedonia, 168; of Greece 146
203–168	Judaea ruled by the Seleucids (Syrian-based successor-state to portion of Alexander's empire)
168	profanation of the Temple by Seleucid king, Antiochus IV ("Epiphanes")
168–165	Jewish revolt

Convergence

166–63	Hasmonean (Maccabean) Kingdom of Judah
129	Roman province of Asia established
88–84	Mithradates' war against Rome
66–64	Pompey's campaign—seige of Jerusalem by Pompey, 63
48–44	Julius Caesar, dictator
37–4 B.C.	Herod "the Great"
31 B.C	Battle of Actium
31–14 A.D.	reign of Octavius (later "Augustus") Caesar
14–37	Tiberius Caesar
26–36	Pontius Pilate *praefectus* of Judaea
30 (?)	crucifixion of Jesus of Nazareth
37–41	Gaius Caligula / 41–54 Claudius / 54–68 Nero/ 68–69 Galba, Otho, Vitelius / 70–79 Vespasian
66–73	Jewish revolt —destruction of Jerusalem, 70 —sanhedrin established at Jabneh by Johanan b. Zakkai, 70 —fall of Masada, 73
79–81	Titus/ 81–96 Domitian/ 96–98 Nerva/ 98–117 Trajan/ 117–138 Hadrian

132–135   Bar Kokhba war—Aelia Capitolina established on the ruins of Jerusalem, 135.

We must retreat somewhat in time to connect this story to the moment which we identified in the previous chapter as the original point of contact between the Greek and the Jewish historiography: the reign of the Emperor Cyrus of Persia. We spoke (pp. [127f]) of the return of some part of the exiled Jewish population from Babylon to Jerusalem, of the rebuilding of the Temple, and of the establishing of the province of Judaea—autonomous in all that really mattered except to certain political fanatics who may have hoped to re-install the Davidic dynasty. We spoke of the work of completing the canon of sacred scripture and the perfecting of the system of law and the religious cult. None of this made any impression elsewhere in the world. There were few Greeks who had ever travelled far enough outside the great cities of the east to have any reliable information about the remote community of Judaea. There may be a trace of some second-or thirdhand knowledge of the Jews in Herodotus' references to the practice of circumcision among "the Syrians of Palestine" (even though the practice itself he identifies as originating with the Egyptians [II:104, II:37.]) The earliest sure references to the Jews in Greek literature are roughly contemporary to Alexander the Great, i.e., late fourth century B.C.; and these are still from second hand. They offer some incorrect descriptions of their cultic practices, together with the judgement that they are "philosophers by race [who regularly meet to] discuss the nature of the Deity among themselves"[1] The earliest such references, for all their confusion about detail, all bear out one theme: that the Jews are a good source for speculation about the Divine—in which respect they are often compared to the Brahmans of India.[2]

These few earliest references by the Greeks to the Jews belong to the era of tranquility which followed the disappointment of the hopes of the immediate messianic endtimes in the days of Ezra and Nehemia (above, pp. 6 [132f]). The Jews left virtually nothing in the way of usable

[h]istorical documentation for this period, and so the Biblical historians [sp]eak of the "two lost centuries" between Nehemiah and the [M]accabees. It would be safe to say that everything belonging to the [tr]aditional life of the Jews lost prestige steadily with the Jewish elite [(n]ot altogether excluding the priests of Jerusalem themselves); while in [th]e cosmopolitan world of greater Persia virtually no attention was [pa]id to Judaism. Even in Jerusalem,³ but much more conspicuously in [th]e other centres of Jewish population, notably at Elephantine (in [E]gypt) and at Babylon, the Jewish elite tended more and more to [su]ccumb to the attractions of Hellenic culture. The innocuousness of [th]e Jewish intellectual traditions seemed (to the few outsiders who [w]ere aware of it) to have been conceded by the Jews themselves in their [de]cision to "close the canon" of sacred literature. Equally, the possibility [of] any future influence of Judaism in the religious destiny of other [m]en seemed to follow from the dogma that the prophetic age was now [ov]er. The official teaching was that prophecy would not resume until [th]e coming of Messiah. While Greek intellectuals produced a copious [lit]erature of philosophy, poetry, scientific speculation, and works of [his]tory and kindred fields of travel, biography, and so on, the intellec[tua]l energies of the Jews seemed entirely given over to fantastic [spe]culations about the end of times.

In 332, Alexander burst upon the scene, the Persian Empire was [sw]ept away, and all the subject-nations of that empire were now part of [a g]reat cosmopolitan empire in which the dominant language and [cul]ture was that of the Greeks. Intellectuals everywhere turned to the [Gre]ek language and Greek models and genres. This process was [esp]ecially conspicuous in historiography. The writing of history (and [suc]h related *genera* as military and political memoirs, biographies, [geo]graphical treatises) was often taken up with the motive of ingrati[atio]n to the new political leaders. This was true of the individuals who [did] the writing, and of the parties to which they belonged: a priestly [cast]e, a local aristocracy, a displaced but still ambitious royal family, or [an e]ntire nation. Accordingly, there was a tendency to tell one's own story while looking into the mirror of Greek civilization. This is notoriously true of the historiography of this period, and (so far as we can judge from what survives) is not least true of Jewish historians who wrote in Greek in this period.

A leading scholar in this field, Emil Schürer, wrote:

Pharisaic Judaism [whose influence was dominant in Judaea] as such had scarcely an interest in history. It saw in history merely an instruction, a warning, how God ought to be served. Hellenistic Judaism [i.e., among the Jews living elsewhere in the Hellenistic world] was certainly in a far higher degree interested in history as such. A knowledge of the history of the past formed part of the culture of the times. And no people could lay claim to be reckoned among the civilized nations, unless they could point to an imposing history. Even nations hitherto regarded as barbarian now compiled their histories and clad them in Greek garments for the purpose of making them accesible to the entire cultured world. The Hellenistic Jews also took their part in such efforts. They too worked up their sacred history for the instruction of both their own fellow-countrymen and the non-Jewish world. The most comprehensive work of the kind with which we are acquainted, is the great historical work of Josephus. He had however a series of predecessors, who laboured some upon longer, some upon shorter periods of Jewish history in various forms. Of these some set to work in modest annalistic manner (Demetrius), some with fantastic and legendary embellishments in *majorem Judaeorum gloriam* (Eupolemus, Artapanus), while some sought in a philosophical manner to represent the great Jewish lawgiver as the greatest of philosophers, nay as the father of all philosophy (Philo). But the Greek Jews occupied themselves not only with the older Jewish history, but also depicted—as Pharisaic Judaism had ceased to do—important occurrences, which they had as contemporaries

Convergence   155

experienced, for the purpose of transmitting them to posterity (Jason of Cryrene, Philo, Josephus, Justus of Tiberias). Many who carried on authorship as a vocation were active in both departments.[4]

It is interesting to note that our acquaintance with the surviving literature of this period[5] is almost entirely confined to what is incorporated into the histories written by early Christian scholars (notably, Eusebius.) (The same can be said of Hellenic historiography in general.) From these fragmentary materials we can make out something of the motive of Hellenic Jews in resorting to Greek models of historiography. While they were dignifying their own tradition by showing how well it lent itself to the retailing of the same glorious lessons as were to be found in the histories of the Greeks, they were simultaneously laying the groundwork of the case that Christian scholars of the fourth and fifth centuries would make for a special kind of *priority* belonging to the story of the Jews. Already Jewish scholars of the *diaspora* were demonstrating the gifts they have always shown for mastering the languages and literatures of their hosts, and for entering creatively into the philosophical debates extant in other cultures. Philo (mentioned here by Schürer for his historical essays) formulated the classic statement of the case that there must have been some early contact of the Greek philosophers with the "school" of Moses. There was already a theological preparation for this argument in speculations of the rabbis. When Josephus wrote his vindication of the antiquity of Jewish history—a book the size of the whole canon of the Old Testament, and which is the only item in this library of books of Jewish history written in Greek to survive intact—he summed up and elaborated the arguments of these writers.

Hengel writes: "The Jews were the only people of the East to enter into deliberate competition with the Greek view of the world and of history, whether they gave their 'historical' works the traditional form of a chronicle, the cryptic form of an apocalyptic outline of history or even the alien garb of Hellenistic historiography."[6] There is every evidence that the Greeks and the Romans were increasingly intrigued by this history, and its implications for their understanding of their own history and of world history.[7]

During the "two lost centuries", therefore, we can imagine that, in spite of their political innocuousness, the Jews were beginning to exercise some fascination for Greek intellectuals, particularly on account of their somewhat exotic reputation as "a race of philosophers", especially gifted in speculation about the place of the divine in history. As the rapid advance of the Roman Empire made the Greeks "historically-minded" again, the Jews became rather suddenly of interest to Greek intellectuals, in the light of the sudden resurgence of their national spirit under the leadership of the Maccabees. The Maccabean resurgence came exactly at the point when the Greeks themselves, and for that matter all the other nations of the Hellenic world were experiencing the crisis of nerve which preceded their conquest by the Romans.

We need to say something about the origins of the Maccabean revolt, as there is no understanding our interlocked themes of the prestige of Jewish historiography and political destinies of the Jews without some appreciation of the forces that were given expression in it. Judaea had been a province of at best secondary importance in Persia's empire, and her status was not changed when Alexander's empire replaced the Persian. It is a measure of the significance of Judaea that no reference to it occurs in the primary sources for Alexander's campaigns in Palestine and Syria. If, as Josephus (*Antiquities* II: 325-339) and certain Talmudic sources claim, Alexander actually visited Jerusalem at the time, the experience didn't register sufficiently with his entourage to survive in the records of his progress, through his new empire. When that empire was divided following Alexander's death, and Judaea ended up in the Kingdom of the Ptolemies, (by 306 B.C.) her status did not change. A century later (201–198) Judaea's leaders threw their support to the Ptolemies' rivals, the Seleucids, whose empire centred in Syria, expecting to gain some increase of autonomy and cultural prestige from a Seleucid succession. But these gains proved insignificant, and did not last long. In fact, things shortly got worse.

This was a period of stalemate in the great political world. The three successor-states to Alexander's empire had fought each other on and off for over a century, and had reached approximate equilibrium. Rome was involved in the first of her wars with Carthage, (264–241); in the later stages, (218–201 and 149–146), she would be drawn into Asia Minor, at first only to punish Carthage's allies, but finally to establish the foothold for her ultimate empire there. In the early third century B.C., the kings of the east were caught up in a frenzied competition for dignities to compensate for the frustration caused by this equilibrium of their relative powers, and (as it were) to improve their standing with the Divine in advance of the coming struggle with Rome.

An extreme instance of this was the decision of the Seleucid Emperor, Antiochus IV, to seize the Jewish Temple at Jerusalem and convert it to the worship of Olympian Zeus (167). At the same time he declared himself the living manifestation of Zeus ("Epiphanes") and demanded the worship of his subjects. The Temple's treasures were seized. He forbade the cult of Judaism, announcing the death-penalty for observance of the Sabbath and the rite of circumcision. He forced idolatrous rites on the population. To his astonishment, the population resisted wholeheartedly, in what some have claimed is the first instance of an entire nation risking martyrdom for the sake of religious conscience. Eschatological expectations ran high. Because the priestly families of Jerusalem had compromised themselves too often by concessions to Antiochus, unlikely leaders appeared in the persons of a family of priests from the small town of Modi'in, west of Jerusalem. Combining gifts of religious inspiration with brilliant techniques of guerrilla warfare, this family (the Hasmoneans), after many cruel setbacks, drove out the Seleucids and established a new dynasty of a new and independent Kingdom of Judah (166–63.) The Hasmoneans (also remembered as the "Maccabeans", after Judas nicknamed "Maccabeus", "the Hammer") were forced to defend their kingdom against the Syrians and their neighbours who sought to pick up some part of the Syrian possessions on Judaea's flanks. At some point, these wars of self-defense become wars of consolidation, and the consolidation shaded over into annexation; so that by the time that Rome had taken over as heir of the Seleucid Empire (renamed the Province of Asia), the Hasmonean Kingdom had almost recovered the dimensions of David's kingdom at the end of his reign.

Thus, just at the moment when all the other nations of the East—culturally so much more advanced, materially so much more prosperous, politically so much more sophisticated—were caught up in a crisis of nerve, as they awaited the onset of triumphant Rome, this apparently wretched and apathetic people had astounded the world by rising up in defense of their faith in an unseen God. This faith of the Jews, it appeared, was such an elemental force that, having now been aroused, it had not been satisfied by restoration of its Temple and cultic privileges, but had exploded into a movement of national assertiveness. The Hasmonean kings pushed toward new borders beyond those of the old province of Judaea, imposing its faith by mass-conversions of new subjects to north, east and south.

These accomplishments drew the world's attention to Judaea, with political consequences of the utmost importance. For our present purpose, the important fact is that the Jewish scriptures and their extra-scriptural literature now were widely read and eagerly searched for clues to explain this unexpected dynamism, and what it might portend for world history.

This sudden notoriety of the Jews and the enthusiasm we find among the Greeks for their history is all the more remarkable when we consider to what a low estate the study of history had fallen among the Jews themselves prior to the Maccabean revival. Several factors had worked together over the previous century and a half to inhibit the writing of history and speculation about history among the Jews. The historical sections of those books belonging to the canon which dealt with the period prior to the Exile had been written with the help of rich archives belonging to the First Temple; and these archives had been destroyed along with the Temple itself. The dramatic story of the Restoration and the rebuilding of the Temple and the city and its walls had now been fully told in the books of *Ezra* and *Nehemiah*, which would be canonized eventually (probably second century B.C.)—this having the effect of inhibiting further historical review of the period. Since the dissipation of the popular messianic expectations that had accompanied the completion of the Temple, the religious leaders had discouraged the people from seeking for signs of the times in world affairs. This went hand in hand, apparently, with a policy of discouraging further review of the historical past through the publication of new historiography. Some scholars speak of an eclipse of the spirit of historiography in this period;[8] but this is hard to believe in view of how intense that spirit had always been in the past, and how swiftly it came alive again in the Maccabean days. Suffice it to say that there is nothing, or practically nothing,[9] from the century and a half prior to the Maccabean revolt to remind us of the earnest and realistic historiography which is found in *Kings, Chronicles, Ezra,* and *Nehemiah*.

When Antiochus "Epiphanes" declared his intention to destroy the worship of the God of Israel, he awoke the Jewish people from this deepening habit of apathy with regard to the affairs of the great world of politics, and to a reconsideration of their own place in it. The Maccabean period is indeed distinguished for a great literary revival in all genres. We have many lively examples of Jewish wisdom literature, as well as poetry, and apocalyptic-visionary literature belonging to this period. But of greatest importance, from our point of view, is the revival of Jewish historiography.

Whereas the Jews who wrote history during the previous century and a half (see above, pp. 153–5) were Jews of the diaspora, to some degree alienated from the traditionalism current in Jerusalem, drawing their models from the Greeks, addressing themselves to the Greek *oikoumene*, and having no apparent influence on the people or leaders of Judaea—the historians of the Maccabean period were responding to an awakened sense of history in Palestine itself. Only a small portion of this literature survives intact [notably *I Maccabees* (c.100), *II Maccabees* (parts of which date from this period.)] But that such historiography was both abundant and varied is attested by the works of Josephus (?37 A.D.–95) who depended on these sources.

The appeal of Jewish apocalypse

Most people, when they think of the literature of this "period between the Testaments"[10] think of the books of speculation about the end of time, that is the "apocalyptic" books. *Daniel* is the one canonical model, but there is also an abundant "apocryphal" and "Pseudepigraphical" literature. It is of fundamental importance to recognize that speculations of the apocalyptic sort did not militate against the historical spirit, but in fact nourished it. There is no fundamental incompatibility between the instinct for historical research and the instinct for eschatalogical speculation. The fact is that the roots of the theory of history of our civilization are in this age when eschatalogical speculation was perhaps the principal source of the inspiration for scholarly-historical research.

Until early modern times, history was routinely told, in our civilization, within the framework of speculation about a master-pattern of the rise-and-fall-of-empires that can be drawn from the Jewish apocalyptic literature of the period we have here under review. The *Book of Daniel* had the greatest prestige in this connection. By the third century, the *Apocalypse of St. John* (the Book of *Revelation*) was regarded by Christians as having incorporated the insights of *Daniel* and of all the Jewish-apocalyptic literature inspired by that book, putting these all now into a form which Christians could proclaim in the light of the Christian gospel. Christian intellectuals of the third and

Convergence 161

fourth centuries further believed that they were now in a position (as Jewish intellectuals were not) to interpret the history of the Roman empire (further to the time of the Book of *Daniel*) in ways that to some extent vindicated those insights of the pagan (Greek and Roman) historians which had previously seemed incompatible with the theory of history of the Jews. The key to this reformed understanding of Roman history was, of course, the Church's dogmatic understanding of the life of Jesus of Nazareth and the promise of His return.

The Book of *Daniel* offers what purports to be an inspired understanding of the pattern of rise-and-fall-of-empires, culminating in what the Jews of our period took to be a preview of the present empire of Rome, the final world-empire. Certain messages are conveyed by the God of Israel, through the Prophet Daniel, about the circumstances that will precede the end of this present (Roman) empire. These take the form of "visions", rather than directly appropriable messages couched in objective, historical language. Different schools favoured different explanations for the cryptic character of these messages: (a) they are meant to be accesible only to an elite within Israel—that is, they are esoteric truths for the specially pious, or for the specially intelligent (this was the view of the Essenes, for example); (b) they are meant to be sufficient for present needs—further "revelations" before the end-time will make things clearer to all (this was essentially the view of the Pharisees); (c) they are an intellectual challenge, to be solved by diligent historical research. In this latter spirit, Jewish scholars, Greek converts to Judaism, and those whose standing was not quite that of formal converts ("God-fearers", in the eyes of the synagogue) poured over the apocalyptic literature, adding many new items to it. They diligently reviewed the canonical scriptures for further clues. They diligently studied current politics. Some assumed that behind the mere description of the succession of empires there must be a rhythm, or a discoverable articulation in the giving-way of one state of historical affairs to the next. To prove these theories, they devised elaborately-detailed charts and schemes. Behind these, there was much labour in archives: Greek, Latin, Egyptian, Syrian, Aramaic. The details of succession lists had to be confirmed. Synchronisms had to be established. Dates had to be exact. The vague conventional reckonings of the Greek historians (three generations to a century) no longer satisfied—not when what was at stake was the discovery of the exact articulation of the machinery of world-history.

The boldest of these spirits held out the hope of finding the master-rhythm: How long did the Assyrian Empire last before giving way to the Babylonian? How long did the Babylonian Empire last before giving way to the Persian? Then, how long did the Persian Empire last before giving way the the Hellenic Empires? Then, how long did the Hellenic Empires last before giving way to the Roman? A sub-problem: are the reigns of the Diadochi (the rivals who broke up Alexander's empire after his death) to be reckoned into the span of the Greek Empire? Or does a new cycle begin here?

The boldest spirits of all said that once all the detail had been confirmed an absolute arithmetic of rise-and-fall-of-empire would stand forth as the objective result of this research. This result would equip us to anticipate the date of the end of this *final*, Roman, Empire.

Most readers will recognize the main features of this speculation, and will know that it is still very much with us today. There have been periods of history when apocalyptic speculation was widespread and close to the surface. (The present age is clearly one of these: *the number-one best-selling non-fiction* book of the decade of the 1970's in the United States was just such a book: Hal Lindsey's *The Late, Great Planet Earth* (1971).[11] In other times, it is not so conspicuous nor popular. We need not enquire here into the logic that governs this pattern of rise and fall of interest in apocalyptic speculation. It is crucial to our present argument however to note that classical Christian philosophy of history was established when this sort of speculation had been running extremely high for at least five centuries (taking Augustine's *City of God* (413-426) as our benchmark); and that, while Christian interest in apocalyptic speculation derives immediately from the Jews, another source of it which must be taken account of is Roman historiography, which in turn had been profoundly affected by the musings of Greek, Hellenic, and Roman intellectuals upon the Jews, their history, and their historiography. Long before Augustine, the Hellenes and the Romans were testing these eschatological schema to see how the history of Alexander's empire and the rise and fall of political fortune since could be fitted into them.

In the course of establishing the discipline of academic history, roughly during the last two centuries, the recital of history has been radically separated from eschatological speculation. The integrity of the methods of academic history, painfully developed over this period of time, depend on this separation; *but* it does *not* follow, for the Christian historian, that speculation about the largest meanings that history bears gains by the exclusion of the eschatological dimension. We must distinguish between what is required for mature, critical, narrative—recital of history and what is required for mature speculation about meaning in history. And to most Christian theorists of history, prophetic speculation about the last things remains an indispensable part of the legacy.

In the two centuries which center on the Year One of the Common Era, Jewish historiography and Jewish eschatology together were stimulating the jaded minds of Greek-speaking intellectuals. The Greek mind was thus drawn back into the realm of speculation about history's largest meanings, after several generations when the tendency had been to denigrate history's noetic worth. The results are evident not merely in Graeco-Roman historiography, but in other branches of Graeco-Roman speculation, art, and poetry.

The fact seems to be that intellectuals in the Greek world had lost patience with the limitations placed upon speculation by the ontological bias of Greek philosophy, and had been tending for some time towards questions that were central in the Judaic tradition (and, for that matter, in the East in general.) This drift from ontological speculation towards speculation about the mysteries bound up in the

Jewish theory of history had been prefigured for some time in religious discussion. (We have already noted that long before Greek intellectuals knew anything substantial about the history of the Jews they had heard (and were fascinated by the intelligence) that the Jews were a race given to advanced speculation about the Divine.) Though scholars do not know much about the process, the result is clear enough: in the two centuries we have under review (c.100 B.C. to c. 100 A.D.) the key elements of the ancient Jewish speculation about the meaning of history would be carried, by overt and covert channels, into the heart of Graeco-Roman historical speculation and historiography.

By the beginning of the First century B.C., therefore, champions of each of these two previously distinct Greek and Jewish traditions of recital of the story of the whole human past had discovered each other and were beginning to brood about each other's claims. Both traditions were now increasingly tending towards speculation on the question of the unity of the human past (inspired by preoccupation with the emergence of the Roman Empire as the apparent residual legatee of all previous empires known to the Greeks and the Jews.) Both were now deeply interested in finding keys to understanding the pattern of the Divine action in history (in the pattern of rise and fall of empires), with the threefold purpose of (a) being reassured that history has always been under divine guidance; (b) understanding the present dynamics of history; (c) understanding the end (*telos*) toward which historical events are tending. And most remarkable of all: both traditions were now deeply infected with a sense of some pending intrusion of the Divine will and presence into human history of an unprecedented and maybe ultimate character.

Roman "messianic" expectations

Christian children have explained to them in their Sunday Schools the arguments (common to all the Books of the New Testament) about the manner in which Jesus fulfilled Jewish expectations regarding the

Messiah. It is not so well understood by most Christians that a parallel expectation dominated the historical speculations of the Romans. The references to this are less obvious to our present eyes, but they were fully appreciated by the early Christian preachers and scholars, and they figure importantly in the commentaries of the early "Fathers of the Church."[12]

There are two principal reasons for our tendency to overlook the references to Roman "messianic expectations. (Here we use the term "messianic", derived from the Hebrew, as a generic term for visions of a forthcoming national or popular deliverer.) One reason for this oversight is that the Enlightenment of the Eighteenth century was embarrassed by these evidences of Judaic superstition in the classical Latin sources, and therefore pretended not to notice them; secular scholarship has generally followed suit. And the second reason is that Roman messianic expectations were in large part derived from Jewish messianism, and co-opted into the Roman world-view.

To a considerable degree, the messianic expectations of the Jews had become an exoteric property. Much of Jewish messianic expectation had already been mulled over by the Romans, and the other nations within Rome's empire, and important elements had been incorporated into Roman and Hellenic theorizing about history. Thus, the case for Jesus of Nazareth as Messiah made in the gospels, in the Epistles, and in the Book of *Revelation* and which we perhaps think of as being addressed exclusively to the Jews is addressed as well to the great world of citizens of the Roman Empire, appealing to what they had already assimilated of Jewish messianism.

A practical demonstration of the convergence of both standards of practice of historiography and the content of historical speculation in these two pivotal centuries is achieved by reading the major surviving works of the contemporary Latin historians of the Roman empire (Livy [c.60B.C.–c.12A.D.] Sallust [86–34] Tacitus [c.56A.D.–120A.D.], and Suetonius [c.70A.D.–c.130A.D.]), the major works of the Jewish historian Flavius Josephus [37?A.D.–c.100]), and then reading the five historical books of the New Testament (*Matthew, Mark, Luke, John,* and the *Book of Acts.*)

To bring into focus the arguments of these pages, it would be useful to the reader to read at this point the first three chapters of the Gospel of Matthew. This Gospel stands where it does, as the first book in the Christian section of the canon not because of any misapprehension about its being the earliest Christian source,[13] but because it is the Gospel which begins by directly addressing the case for linking the story of the life, death, resurrection and ascension of Jesus of Nazareth with the story of the covenant of the God of all the nations with the people of Israel, (Matthew, Chapter One.) It then immediately links this story of the "New Covenant" to the story of the history of Rome, by fixing the story of the birth of Jesus in the reign of Herod, King of Judah, the client-king of Rome (Chapter Two.) The impact of this "gospel" of the Jewish disciple of the Jewish Messiah upon its audience of citizens of the Roman empire would depend entirely on their recognition of its opening proposition: that the expectations of the Jewish historians and the expectations of the Roman historians are both fulfilled in the story about to be told.

Everywhere in the Roman Empire, as the Gospels clearly assume, there was growing obsession with the possibility of some dramatic, imminent intrusion of the Divine into human affairs. Tendencies, once dimly understood from study of the pattern of rise-and-fall of empires, were becoming clearer as historians studied the legacy of historical speculation derived from the Greek masters and brooded over the fascinating themes of Jewish scripture.

Roman co-option of the messianic expectations of their eastern subjects

The place to begin this story of Roman co-option of eastern messianism is with the generation that fought the wars against Macedon, the Greek leagues, Syria and Pergamum (215–168.) This was the generation that, in a real sense, first admitted to itself the

Convergence 167

implications of Rome's becoming an empire—and furthermore, the presumptive heir to the whole process tending towards universal empire, which process (in the ancient world) gave world history its standing as a bearer of large meaning.

It is well known that in all genres the literature of this period shows the effects of a sudden mood of unease. From the beginning—in the days of Rome's conquest of her neighbours in Italy—there had always been voices warning against the risks of expansion. Outside populations would have to be absorbed or repressed: either way, traditional Roman virtues would be jeopardized and liberties would be lost. Now there was a whole new dimension to this theme. Now Romans were not merely the masters of an empire (that threshold was well past) but heirs of the ancient empires of the Greeks and the Asians. They were now about to step directly into the line of succession of world-empires.

Later historians (including Livy, whose history is the major history of Rome surviving from the Augustan period) record many stories of omens, auguries, and prophecies suddenly appearing in Rome in those days, bearing out that the Divine had chosen Rome for this role. (There were, among many other signs, a mysterious appearance of Romulus in the streets of Rome, and omens attending the founding of the Temple of Jupiter on Capitoline Hill.)[14] These were signs of confirmation to Roman citizens, to strengthen their self-confidence in the face of the contempt of the conquered. But, unfortunately for Roman peace of mind, there were omens of a disturbing kind as well. In "moments of expectant terror", when critical military campaigns were under way, or when politics were particularly disturbed, "prodigies multiplied. Statues sweated blood, monstrous animals and children were born, the earth shook, stones rained from the sky, fires broke out spontaneously.... An ox is supposed to have told a consul, 'Rome, beware'"[15]

The irony is that from the moment Rome embarked on the path of empire speculation immediately began on how it would all end! Such speculation seized all ranks of men from the most superstitious plebeian to the intellectuals.

> One could say that as early as Romulus plowed his furrow to mark the boundaries of his city, the idea of the end arose.... From the second century B.C. to A.D. 410, when the Visigoths sacked Rome, there were varied but recurring types of prophecise based on chronology and numerology. Seven was the prophetic number for the Biblical writers.... For the Romans, however, the magic number was twelve. The twelve vultures that Romulus saw supported the prophecy that the Empire would last twelve centuries or twelve millennia... Some of the theories that subdivided time into regular periods originated in Etruscan circles. Of particular interest was the theory of the Great Year, which would last either 365 or 440 years. When this period expired, eveything would begin anew, and only then would brotherhood reign and the lion lie down with the lamb. Given the difficulty in accurately establishing the advent of this new century, it was believed that the gods would provide a sign. Strange phenomena would certainly accompany or precede the revolving of the cycles, the end of a century, and the beginning of the next... The *Ludi Saeculares* were instituted as a festivity, repeated every hundred years in order to assure the safety of the community for the successive century. To mark the end of the year, it was the practice to hammer a nail into the Temple of Jupiter.
>
> Periodic renewal was reassuring and helped overcome the obsession with the end. Cicero writes, "It will happen at some future time that all this world will burn with fire...." "We are in the last age that the Cumaean Sibyl prophesied in her song," wrote Vergil, "and now the reign of Saturn will be renewed, and a new progeny will descend from above."

The Romans, athirst for stability, were ensnared in these contradictory versions of the future. Just as a new planet is immediately caught up in the rotating motion of the cosmos, so Rome, once she had entered the orbit of history, was forced to trace the entire parabola without ever being able to return to her point of departure.[16]

Compounding the doubts of patriots were the effects of "anti-Roman propaganda" (Mazzolani's term) emanating from the conquered lands:

[F]rom Carthage to Pergamum and from Alexandria to Epirus... [came rumors] about the imminent downfall of a nation that continued its relentless expansion. Mysterious connections were extablished between political events and natural cataclysms. The earthquake during which the island of Thera (modern Santorini) rose up from the Aegean Sea occurred in the same year that the Romans defeated the Greeks at Cynoscephalae (197 B.C.)... The anathemas of impotent wrath that the Jews had hurled against Alexander and the Kings of Syria, who first introduced the seeds of Western iniquity into their closed society, were again activated... When the Romans set foot as victors in the East, they felt themselves to be desecrators. Venerable deities dwelled in sanctuaries and grottoes, on the white summits of mountains that rose high above groves of olives and cypresses. And other divinities watched from the endless sparkling waves.[17]

There was of course no going back. And if the Romans were to go forward their intellectuals had to find ways to ward off the anxieties of their own people and the hostile propaganda of their subject-peoples. They must find answers to the question of the legitimacy—or better, the necessity, of their empire. All of the dogmas, theorems, visions, by which all the various peoples of this growing empire had understood their own great past had to be first learned, then confronted and appeased, and finally co-opted.

All aspects of the question of how nations come to have empires—how they were led onto the path of empire, what qualified then for empire, whether they "deserved" them, or "earned" them, or whether empire merely "befell" the nation (was it a matter of *law*, of *will*, or of *fate*?)—this had all been thoroughly worked over by Greek historians and theorists. The Romans immersed themselves in this literature, and soon became adept at turning its arguments to the purpose of justifying their own path to empire.

> [Rome] assimilated from the Greeks a cosmic vision and, at the same time, appropriated the civic virtues the Greeks had demonstrated when they stemmed the Persian threat from the East.... She took the story about the flight of the Trojan refugees to Italy and wove a legend around it to idealize her origins and to give her conquests the sanction of divine decrees. Aeneas, the Trojan hero, had escaped the flames of Troy and had fled to Latium to become the founder of a stern, vigorous race. By choosing Italy as the site for a new, exemplary race, he was obeying divine orders and transferring the spirit of his city to Latium. Trojan blood therefore ran in the veins of the Roman conquerors. The gods who presided over the founding of Rome had a premonition of her future grandeur. The desertion of Dido foreshadowed the Carthaginian Wars. From Cato, Naevius, Varro, and Dionysius of Halicarnassus, the legend was passed down to Vergil, and acquired the status of a national dogma that was to live on throughout the ages.[18]

The Greek tradition was inherently cosmopolitan. The dogmatic-theological premise of the universal regime in the Golden Age of the deities known to the Greeks made Greek historiography in principle

Convergence 171

adaptable everywhere. And in fact intellectuals all over Alexander's empire (including many Jews of the dispersion) had already pioneered for the Romans the path of adapting Greek models of historiography to the telling of their own story. But the Romans went a step further, claiming the history of the Greeks *as their own*. Morally it was a bold move, but intellectually it was an obvious one: Greece's mandate of Empire was transferred directly to Rome, through the hidden history of Aeneas; Rome comes of age in time to pick up the burden of empire from the heirs of Alexander's empire; the chapters from the point where Herodotus leaves off until Rome arrives to claim her rightful legacy are recapitulated under the heading of the apprenticeship of Rome. All the premises of Herodotus' theory of world history are directly appropriated and will continue intact under Roman auspices.

Far more difficult, morally and intellectually, were the challenges offered by the historical theories of the East. Every one of the nations of the East which were brought into Rome's empire retained in some form remembrances of former glory and dreams of vindication. The East was not any longer the source of the energies that organize empires. Their speculations about history were now understandably affected by resentment, but also by a weariness with history, told as the story of power. The *resentment* shows itself in fantastic speculations about the imminent appearance of a warrior-avenger against Rome, who will set the humiliated nation back in its rightful place at the head of the company of rulers of the world. The *weariness* with history shows itself in scattered rumours about the imminent appearance of a ruler unlike all the mighty men of power who have ruled before: a meek figure of transparent, irresistible moral authority—a shepherd-king (in some versions), sent by God, who would shame the kings of this world by his mere appearance in their midst into the voluntary surrender of their crowns, and usher in not merely a new human order of human love, but a new order of nature—the lion lying down with the lamb. This latter sort of speculation belongs to theory of history insofar as it looks to an imminent intrusion into human affairs of an ultimate kind, which puts an end to history.

It is well-known that speculations of this sort had found their way into Latin poetry—for example in the frequently-cited Fourth Eclogue of Vergil (70B.C.-19B.C.):

> Bless him, the infant with whom
> discontinues the era of iron;
> Bless him with whom will arise
> the new race that is gloriously golden....
> But that boy will partake of the life of
> the Gods;
> he will meet them.
> Meet all the heroes; and he
> will in turn by the gods be beholden.
> Over a pacified world will he rule,
> patriarchic in virtue.[19]

The immediate source of these notions is the so-called "Sybilline Oracles" (of which more shortly). The ultimate source is Jewish messianic literature.

We seriously mistake the force of these notions, however, if we think of them as mere poetic conceits. These notions deeply affected Roman self-understanding at the time, and are a powerful force in the historiography and in the history of these two crucial centuries. Whether it was poets or priests who inspired these speculations (and both did); whether the object of the speculation was an imminent natural cataclysm, a divine or semi-divine warrior-deliverer, or a shepherd-king, all of these fantasies were dangerous for Roman morale. They cast doubt on the theology that sustained the theory of history that sustained the legitimacy of Rome's Empire. And, worst of all, they seemed to have a subversive fascination for the Romans themselves.

Convergence

It is significant that at critical stages of the several civil wars within Rome, one or other of the rivals would invariably try to co-opt to his cause some or all of these Eastern prophetic-historical fantasies. It was not altogether clear to their contemporaries, nor is it to the historians, how far these Roman strongmen were in control of these fantasies. The pattern was established before the Romans arrived, by Alexander. He identified himself in several places with the legends of divine saviour-figures who were to come to redeem their people thus allowing his new subjects the option of seeing him as their vindicator when they could not tolerate accepting him as their conqueror.

This was the beginning of a dangerous game which saw Western military leaders co-opted by Eastern religious myths—the process which culminated in Emperor-worship, which so offended the Romans themselves, but came to be seen as the price of Empire. "Alexander" re-appeared again and again throughout the history of the Roman empire at the head of rebellions against Rome's empire. Mark Antony tried to co-opt the myth of Alexander *redivivus*, along with the messianic expectations of the Egyptians. After Nero was murdered, a cult was founded on the undoubted fact that he had claimed divinity and identified himself in particular with certain of these Eastern messianic fantasies: rumours spread that he was alive in Persia, and was preparing to lead the trumphant restoration of the Persian Empire.[20]

Practically every major Roman figure who went to the east was somehow or other caught up in this. It was a strange process: the western conqueror co-opted the local messianic role, then was himself post-humously co-opted to it. In Rome itself, the most rational politicians spoke of the cynicism of those who played these dangerous games, while the most superstitious were tempted to see signs pointing to divine forces that had to be appeased. In the middle, the pragmatists spoke of ways of accomodating these fantasies, to neutralize the historical theories that lay behind them.

Octavius Augustus probably belonged to the pragmatic camp. He came to see the absolute necessity (from the point of view of Roman statecraft) of Emperor worship after Antony had demonstrated the risks of leaving these mythologies and the theologies, the political theories, and the theories of history which they entailed, lying about for the use of adventurers:

> Augustus ...prohibited the Egyptian religion, expelled astrologers and seers alike, and ordered that all the Sibylline Oracles be confiscated from private houses and then burned. [Suetonius, *Augustus*, 31] Augustus's actions were prompted, as were those of his forerunners, by considerations of public order, since those oracles, reflecting Asian and Egyptian propaganda, spoke about the East's imminent retaliation against Rome. The end of Roman supremacy would be near when a woman reigned. [*Sibylline Oracles* 3:75-96; 8:190-212; 11:290 and 279.] Maybe this woman was Cleopatra, called the "Widow" because, *like* Isis, she has lost her husband Ptolemy *XIV*. At her sumptuous coronation in Alexandria in 34 B.C., she wore the attributes of Isis, while Antony appeared in the Eastern provinces as a new Dionysus, the divinity of the Asian proletariat, rather than as a Roman proconsul surrounded by lictors. In Alexandria, he had founded an Eastern empire antagonistic to the Roman Empire, open to alliances conflicting with Roman policy, with the Medes and the Parthians. His marriage to Cleopatra appeared as a wedding between divine beings, which would shower beneficent gifts upon mankind. He called his children Helios and Selene—that is, Sun and Moon, the two divine stars which cast their light over all human beings, not over one city or one elite class or one race of conquerors.
>
> All those regal trappings seemed to point to a cosmopolitan and egalitarian theocracy, which would have placed Alexandria

and Athens on the same level with Rome. In order to compete with that policy, Augustus wanted to turn the mystic expectations of the restless masses to his own advantage, and to give the Empire a unifying and providential character, while in Rome he adhered to the traditional images.[21]

Thereafter, it was a matter of public policy and official theology that all the historical expectations of all the nations of the world and all the supernatural expectations attaching to all national histories were fulfilled, completely and without remainder, in the life-in-time of the reigning Emperor and in his continuing life-beyond-time as a divine being.

The appeal of the Jewish vision of history

The first step towards understanding the impact of the Jewish vision of history upon Roman historiography is, therefore, to consider it in the context of the general Roman fascination for visions of redemption coming out of the East—of which we know enough to be able to say that this constituted a major political force, which time and again came near to splitting the empire. But we know as well that these visions of redemption were eventually co-opted by Rome—that is, brought into alignment with Roman-imperial ideology, the capstone of which ultimately came to be worship of the emperor. This policy failed only on one front: and that was in Judaea.

Hostility to Roman empire ran deeper in Judaea than anywhere else. We have already noted that the Jews had experienced an unanticipated resurgence of national self-assertion (in the Maccabean revolt against the Seleucids), precisely as the other nations of the eastern world were undergoing the crisis of nerve which laid them open to Roman conquest. For a long while, the Romans put off a direct effort at annexation of Judaea. But admiration for the Jews' example of fiery independence, and fascination for the theology that nourished it, had increasingly subversive effects, not only among Rome's conquered subjects but in Rome itself. Judaea was the source of a contagious ideology which jeopardized Rome's prestige everywhere.

Many Roman authors of Augustus' time speculated about the meaning for Rome of Daniel's visions. Mazzolani cites Dionysius of Halicarnassus (d. 7 B.C.?) and Velleius Paterculus (c. 19B.C.–31 A.D.); we can assume that these speculations were typical of a vaster literature that did not survive.[22] In Daniel's interpretation of Nebuchadnezzar's dream (*Daniel* 2), and in the angel Gabriel's interpretation of the vision given to Daniel (*Daniel* 7 and 8), there is foretold a succession of empires subsequent to Babylon's, each less noble than the one before. Of the five "kingdoms", four had run their course (Assyria, Babylonia, Persia and Greece.) The present "kingdom", Rome, must therefore be the last worldly kingdon. Roman intellectuals were persuaded by the apparent genius of the sixth-century prophet who had foretold the outlines of four subsequent centuries of world-history. They were enthralled by the many fantastic images which contained hints about what lay ahead for this last worldly Empire—their own Roman empire. Other apocalyptic books were constantly coming from the hands of Jewish writers, all bearing out the theses of Daniel's Five-Monarchy scheme, but adding new and yet more specific details to the catalogue of signs of the end-times.

Since Herodotus, Greek historians and their Hellenic successors had learned to think of the rise-and-fall of world-empire as the theme that gave shape to history—that made it possible to tell world-history as a single, unilinear human story. Jewish apocalypse accepted this objective estimate of the story of empire, and in fact made possible an even more earnest consideration of the theme, by insisting that it was under the absolute willful direction of the God of all reality. The God of History was also the sovereign God of the natural order. What was being accomplished in history, therefore, was not within the aegis of fate (as the Greek tradition had taught) but was the irresistible will of the sovereign God of All. But the great (and for the jaded Graeco-

Roman mind, the emancipating) *paradox* was that it was the ultimate will of the Jewish God of History to conclude the work for which He employed the nations and the Empires of this world by redeeming mankind from history itself.

The Jewish prophets spoke realistically of the world of power and the work of empire-building, regarding this as a necessary element in the story of God's provision of the practical conditions for the globalizing of human destiny. But they protested against the human habit of glorifying the human side of this work. On that side, it is a story of oppression. They looked toward a sudden intrusion of the Divine on behalf of the oppressed. The history of God's dealings with the Jews was a paradigm of the history of God's dealings with all nations. Properly understood, Israel's history revealed that God was the Nemesis of the evildoers who were the movers and shakers in the political realm, and the Saviour of the oppressed. Furthermore, God's final purpose for all humanity was being accomplished through that history of the Jews. The prophets looked to a sudden intrusion of the Divine into human history of behalf of the oppressed. This would necessarily take the form of an irresistible vindication of God's covenant with Israel. The hidden meaning of that relationship would be disclosed. That the tendency of historical events was from hiddenness to revelation, was reflected, some said, in the renewal of Jewish self-confidence represented by the Hasmonean Kingdom—a manifestation of great strength where previously there had been pitiable weakness. But the deepest spirits among the Jews said that even this Jewish national-state was not exempt from the rule that power corrupts. For deliverance from history, they said, we must continue to look to the coming of God's Annointed. Messiah's authority will be the perfect antithesis of the authority of men of power. It will be manifest in the purity of his love, depending not at all upon the fearful effects of the politician or the warrior.

For many Roman intellectuals these sorts of speculation were tantalizing alternatives to those they had inherited from the Greeks.

Many Romans felt that the religious insights behind these Jewish speculations were in some respects more congenial to their own religious legacy than were the more austere religious insights of the Greeks—at least as these latter were conveyed by Greek intellectuals. And for victims of Roman authority everywhere, Jewish messianic expectation had obvious appeal. Particularly fascinating to these two constituencies (and very unsettling to the leaders of Rome) were rumours that both Greek and Roman seers, belonging to the most ancient and authoritative circles of temple-priests and priestesses, had issued oracles that plainly endorsed the Jewish messianic message, giving these a priority over the religious legends and visions of the Greeks, the Romans, the Egyptians and all the others—in fact, subsuming all the promises contained in these latter under new prophecies founded four-square on Daniel's visions. These were the so-called "Sibylline Oracles".[23]

This is a controversial and somewhat murky theme. A few features are beyond doubt, however, and these are all we need for present purposes. The earliest of the oracles is the Third Book, parts of which are dated as early as 160 B.C. They were accepted in their time as true oracles originating as visions of the seers (sibyls) of several of the ancient pagan temples. One was supposed to have derived from the ancient Erythraean sibyl, and appears to predict to the ancient Greeks the fall of Troy and subsequent events. Another purports to derive from the ancient Cumean sibyl and is supposed to have been deposited in the Capitol by Tarquinius Superbus. (This is the oracle that figures in the Fourth Eclogue of Vergil, cited above p. 172.) It is now believed that they were in fact inventions of Jews of the dispersion, originating probably in Egypt. Their purpose was probably to establish the pre-eminent authority of the visions of Jewish prophecy by having it appear that pagan Greek and Roman seers had been inspired by visions parallel to those of the great Jewish prophets. This, if true, would bring indigenous Greek and Roman prophecy under the yoke of Jewish prophecy. In brief, the oracles rehearse the main themes of Jewish apocalyptic literature, especially stressing the visions of Daniel and those features that purport to tell of the rise and the coming decline of Rome. We know that the Sibylline Books were greatly feared by Roman leaders. The earliest of the oracles was supposed to have played a part in Cleopatra's ambitions.[24] For safety's sake, Augustus confiscated all known copies of all Sibylline Oracles, burned some, but apparently retained custody of others.[25] The predictable effect of this was to strengthen their reputation as underground, "occult" literature. Augustus perceived their subversive potential as propaganda speaking for the East's contempt for the West, providing fuel for the self-loathing that comes over intellectuals who are born into the conqueror's side of world-empire. Augustus shared the conservatives' fears of its appeal to the economically oppressed: it was becoming clear (as Mazzaloni puts it) "that social classes that in the era of classical literature were not writing [had] now joined the literary ranks."[26]

We must keep in mind in this connection the superstitious susceptibilities of Romans of all classes and all levels of learning. Politicians like Augustus knew the uses of superstition—which is not to say that they were above it, but rather that they were very much *of* it.

For example: the conspiracy of Catiline (63-62 B.C.) coincided with a year identified in the oracles of one Hystaspes as one fatal for Rome and her empire; he was supposed to have prophesied that it would be necessary in that year to identify, segregate and punish all evildoers if the people were to be saved. It was Cicero who brought this prophecy to the attention of the Senate and called for implementation of Hystaspes' remedy.[27] Similarly, at the time of Caesar's assasination several learned statesmen read into the record prophecies of the event. Some spoke of clear signs of the end of the world. Cicero and other contemporaries "speak of wonders that accompanied this event: 'Such a thick mist arose', said Vergil, 'that the people feared eternal night...' A comet was spotted—this, too, was confirmed by the oracle—and it was taken as the sign of war, famine, and death. The news of the appearance of the *sidus Julium* (Julius Caesar's star) spread as far as the Jews in Alexandria."[28]

Establishing the divine auspices of Roman authority

It is against this background that we have to see Augustus's decision to co-opt all of the messianic expectations with in his empire—domestic and foreign, overt and occult. He would align all these promises with the story of his own origins and establish a cult of himself and his office:

> ...Augustus wanted to turn the mystic expectations of the restless masses to his own advantage, and to give the Empire a unifying and providential character, while in Rome he adhered to the traditional images.
>
> These were years of tension and fervor, the years when an obscure prophet was born in Judaea. It is not important to identify the mysterious child that Vergil referred to in the *Fourth Eclogue*. The messianic contents of his poem and the oracular tones with which the poet announced the arrival of a new golden age certainly reflected the sentiments of his times: the earth would spontaneously produce fruit and grain, goats would bring milk to the houses, the herds would no longer fear the lions. These promises echoed Biblical texts and ancient prophecies.
>
> The hopes that followed the sufferings during the civil wars transcended national boundaries. They had a universal appeal, an expectation of cosmic renewal. Augustus was too shrewd not to understand this hope for the Millenium, and within limits he utilized it in specific ways. From the poets, he accepted hyperbolic eulogies that came close to deification; in the Eastern provinces he permitted his name, which was engraved on the coins, to be followed by the title "God the Saviour" [cf. *Matt* 22:19-20]; in Egypt, his name appeared among those of the gods.[29]

Convergence

The increasing disposition of Roman intellectuals towards a superstitious understanding of their own history made them susceptible to the Jewish vision of world history. This fact made it necessary for Roman leaders to co-opt Jewish messianism. By the time of the birth of Jesus of Nazareth, it was the established ideology of the empire that the messianic promises of Israel were fulfilled in the dynasty of Julius Caesar. The intellectuals seem to have fallen in line without much difficulty; certainly this is the case with the historians.

We have to stress here that over the previous two centuries tendencies in speculation on theory of history had prepared the Roman historians for this task. It needed no brutal imposition of the Emperor's will to bring the historians into line. Graeco-Roman and Jewish speculation about the general trends of history had been converging for at least two generations, as we have shown.

> Roman superiority over Israel was unequivocally asserted [by Tacitus and his contemporaries]... Tacitus [c. 56-c.120 A.D.] lived at a time when Rome was beginning to formulate her own messianic concept of history, according to which the universal kingdom would be established by a man sent from the heavens. The thought that this might not be a Roman was unacceptable to Romans, who were unable to transfer the expectation of the kingdom to the metaphysical sphere; national sentiment regarded it as ambition for worldly dominion.
>
> These were years when feelings ran high. The ancient rivalry between the East and the West was still alive. People were sensitive to portents and prophecies. Tacitus is aware of these currents, records them in his concise prose; imperturbably he relates irrational occurences and reports rumors that we also find in other sources: "Suddenly the doors of the shrine flew open and a superhuman voice cried: 'The gods are departing...'" [*Histories*, 5.13] The historian Josephus Flavius noted: "From above, they heard terrible voices that cried out: We are

departing!" [*The Judaean War* 6.300] These phenomena, recorded as occurring on the eve of the fall of Jerusalem, appear also in the Apocrypha, where they accompany the death of Christ. The ancient prophets thundered from the clouds amid lightning flashes: "Let us forsake this place!"....If the Empire was to be considered the bulwark of world order, universal solidarity must perforce be appealed to and ethnic and religious differences wiped out in order to achieve harmony. It seemed as if a premonitory shudder were running through the Roman world and inducing its inhabitants to huddle close together within the safe, protected *limes* (boundaries) of the garrisons. Only Israel, persisting in her prejudices, and her refusals, did not join in.[30]

In their histories of Rome, the Latin authors offered a justification for their Empire; and for this justification they depended upon three arguments: (1) that the Gods had provided for the emergence of that Empire by giving the Roman people the character of worthy conquerors; (2) that the Gods had provided for the leadership of this Empire, by providing a dynasty whose origins were legitimate because the gods themselves had participated in their foundation; and (3) that the promises entailed in all the theories of world history held by all the subject nations of Rome's empire were fulfilled in the story of Rome and in the adventures which brought the ruling dynasty to power. In all of this, the rival claims of Jewish ideology were always kept closely in view.

The founder of the dynasty of the Caesars was, of course, Julius (102 or 100–44 B.C.) At the beginning (67 B.C.) of the political maneuvering which would bring him into his dictatorship, we find Caesar laying the case for vindication of his regime by tracing his bloodline to that exclusive set of men who are the issue of gods and kings (on the divine side from Venus, and on the human-regal side from the Roman king Ancus Marcius).[31] Caesar inaugurated his regime with the decision to cross the Rubicon, defying his instructions to remain at his post in

Convergence   183

Transalpine Gaul, and marching against the Senate. The gods participated directly in his making of that decision:

> As he stood, in two minds, an apparition of superhuman size and beauty was seen sitting on the river bank playing a reed pipe. A party of shepherds gathered around to listen and, when some of Caesar's men broke ranks to do the same, the apparition snatched a trumpet from one of them, ran down to the river, blew a thunderous blast, and crossed over. Caesar exclaimed: 'Let us accept this as a sign from the Gods, and follow where they beckon, in vengeance on our double-dealing enemies. The die is cast.'[32]

As for Octavius (later called Augustus), who made the constitutional arrangements for perpetuation of the dynasty and effectively cut off the possibility of return to republicanism, divine legitimation of his regime is equally unambiguous:

> Augustus was born just before sunrise on 23 September, while Cicero and Gaius Antonius were Consuls, at Ox Heads, in the Palatine district; a shrine to him, built soon after his death, marks the spot. The case of a young patrician, Gaius Laetorius by name, figures in the published book of *Senatorial Proceedings*. Pleading his youth and position to escape the maximum punishment for adultery, he further described himself as 'the occupant and, one might even say, guardian of the place first touched at his birth by the God Augustus'. Laetorius begged for pardon in the name of his 'own especial god'. The Senate afterwards consecrated that part of the building by decree.
> In the country mansion, near Velitrae, which belonged to Augustus's grandfather, a small room, not unlike a butler's pantry, is still shown and described as Augustus's nursery; the local people firmly believe that he was also born there. Religious

scruples forbid anyone to enter except for some necessary reason, and after purification. It had long been believed that casual visitors would be overcome by a sudden awful terror; and recently this was proved true when, one night, a new owner of the mansion, either from ignorance or because he wanted to test the truth of the belief, went to sleep in the room. A few hours later he was hurled out of bed by a supernatural agency and found lying half-dead against the door, bedclothes and all....

At this point it might be well to list the omens, occurring before, on and after the day of Augustus's birth, from which his future greatness and lasting good fortune could clearly be prognosticated.

In ancient days part of the city wall of Velitrae had been struck by lightning and the soothsayers prophesied that a native Velitraean would one day rule the world. Confidence in this prediction led the citizens to declare immediate war against Rome, and to keep on fighting until they were nearly wiped out; only centuries later did the world-ruler appear in the person of Augustus.

According to Julius Marathus, a public portent warned the Roman people some months before Augustus's birth that Nature was making ready to provide them with a king; and this caused the Senate such consternation that they issued a decree which forbade the rearing of any male child for a whole year. However, a group of senators whose wives were expectant prevented the decree from being filed at the Treasury and thus becoming law—for each of them hoped that the prophesied King would be his own son.

Then there is a story which I found in a book called *Theologumena*, by Asclepias of Mendes. Augustus's mother, Atia, with certain married women friends, once attended a solemn midnight service at the Temple of Apollo, where she had her litter set down, and presently fell asleep as the others also did. Suddenly a serpent glided up, entered her, and then glided away again. On awakening, she purified herself, as if after intimacy with her husband. An irremovable coloured mark in the shape of a serpent, which then appeared on her body, made her ashamed to visit the public baths any more; and the birth of Augustus nine months later suggested a divine paternity. Atis dreamed that her intestines were carried up to Heaven and overhung all lands and seas; and Octavius, that the sun rose from between her thighs.

Augustus's birth coincided with the Senate's famous debate on the Catilinarian conspiracy, and when Octavius arrived late, because of Atia's confinement, Publius Nigidius Figulus, the astrologer, hearing at what hour the child had been delivered, cried out: "The ruler of the world is now born." Everyone believes this story.[33]

There follows a long list of portents accompanying Augustus's birth: certain dreams of his father and of others interpreted by soothsayers as prefiguring his world-wide regime. Further portents occur in his infancy and boyhood: his apparent powers even as an infant to command natural forces; natural portents; astrological portents, and the extraordinary signs in the entrails of sacrificial victims. Similar signs of providential intention prefigured his death and inspired the belief that he had become a god.[34]

Similar portents attended the births and deaths of the next three Caesars: Tiberius, Gaius Caligula, Claudius. In the case of the next Emperor, Nero, the gods provided supernatural evidences both of the legitimacy of his reign, and of their intention that his reign should end the Julio-Claudian dynasty.

Spectacular omens foretold the reign of Tiberius (reigned 14 A.D.–37 A.D.)[35] and of Claudius (reigned 41 A.D.–54 A.D.)[36] The mad excesses of Gaius Caligula (reigned 37 A.D.–41 A.D.) were inspired by his determination to actualize the messianic expectations inspired by the poets, the priests, and the historians:

> He adopted a variety of titles: such as 'Pious' 'Son of the Camp', 'Father of the Army', 'Caesar, Greatest and Best of Men'. But when once, at the dinner table, some foreign kings who had come to pay homage were arguing which of them was the most nobly descended, Caligula interrupted their discussion by declaiming Homer's line:
> Nay, let there be one master, and one king!
> And he nearly assumed a royal diadem then and there, doing away with the pretence that he was merely the chief executive of a republic. However, after his courtiers reminded him that he already outranked any king or tribal chieftan, he insisted on being treated as a god—sending for the most revered or artistically famous statues of the Greek deities (including that of Juppiter at Olympia), and having their heads replaced by his own.
>
> Next, Caligula extended the Palace as far as the Forum; converted the shrine of Castor and Pollux into a vestibule; and would often stand beside these Divine Brethren to be worshipped by all visitants, some of whom addressed him as 'Latian Juppiter'. He established a shrine to himself as God, with priests, the costliest possible victims, and a life-sized golden image, which was dressed every day in clothes identical to those that he happened to be wearing. All the richest citizens tried to gain priesthoods here, either by influence or bribery. Flamingoes, peacocks, black grouse, guinea-hens, and pheasants were offered as sacrifices, each on a particular day of the month. When the moon shone full and bright he always invited the Moon-goddess to his bed; and during the day would indulge in whispered conversations with Capitoline Juppiter, pressing his ear to the god's mouth, and sometimes raising his voice in anger. Once he

was overheard threatening the god: 'If you do not raise me up to Heaven I will cast you down to Hell.' Finally he announced that Juppiter had persuaded him to share his home; and therefore connected the Palace with the Capitol by throwing a bridge across the Temple of the God Augustus; after which he began building a new house inside the precincts of the Capitol itself, in order to live even nearer.[37]

The reign of Nero (reigned 54 A.D.–68 A.D.) was marked by auguries of the fall of his dynasty.[38] But especially fascinating in the case of Nero is that his reign brought a crisis of confidence regarding the messianic character of Rome's Emperor. Is it possible, people asked, that the universal kingdom might come to be centered else-where? How could it be that the gods could have invested so much authority in these Roman rulers—to the point where they are clearly to be seen as surrogates of some sort and yet have allowed so much shame to attach to these surrogates? A possible solution suggested itself to many minds: but it was highly paradoxical and a problematic one. Both Suetonius and Tacitus have something to say about the intriguing effect upon Roman rulers of *expectations of a world-ruler coming out of Jerusalem.* Suetonius notes that in Nero's last desperate days astrologers suggested to him that he could abandon Rome, and assume "another throne in the East; one or two even particularized that of Jerusalem."[39] When Nero was overthrown, no legitimate heir of the Julio-Claudian dynasty could be found. Power went to favorites of the army: first to Galba; then to Otho; then to Vitellius. In the year of Nero's displacement, the year that the Julio-Claudian line came to an end, many spectacular omens pointed to this intriguing conjunction of the universalist-messianic expectations coming out of Rome and those coming out of Judaea:

Nero, it seemed, had been warned in a dream shortly before his death to take the sacred chariot of Juppiter Greatest and Best from the Capitol to the Circus, calling at Vespasian's house as he went. Soon after this, while Galba was on his way to the elections which gave him a second consulship, a statue of Julius Caesar turned of its own accord to face east; and at Betriacum, when the battle was about to begin, two eagles fought in full view of both armies, but a third appeared from the rising sun and drove off the victor.[40]

Tacitus tells this same story (regarding the statue of Julius Caesar.)[41]

In the year following Nero's death, three military favorites (Galba, Otho, and Vitellius) ruled, and were overturned in succession. This is called the year of the three Emperors. The historians were able to find legends and omens securing the geneology of Galba[42] and Vitellius[43] to regal-divine liaisons on a par with those of the Julio-Claudian dynasty. The difficulties that these legends presented to men like Suetonius, who were typical in being both intelligent and pious, is spectacularly illustrated in the opening lines of Suetonius's life of Vitellius:

> Vitellius's family may have been an old and noble one; or it may have been of undistinguished and even mean extraction. Both views are held, and either might reasonably be discounted as due to the prejudice excited by his reign, were it not that these origins had been hotly argued about many years previously.
>
> Writing to Quintus Vitellius, one of Augustus's quaestors, Quintus Elogius described the family as follows:
>> You Vitellians are descended from Faunus, an aboriginal king of Italy, and Vitellia, who was widely worshipped as a goddess. At one time, you ruled over the whole of Latium, but later the surviving members of the family moved from Sabine territory to Rome, where they became patricians. For centuries after, Vitellians were to be found along the Vitellian Way, which runs from the Janiculum to the sea; and the people of one settlement in

Convergence   189

> that region asked the Senate's permission to defend themselves against the Aequicolians, under their own officers. Another group of Vitellians, serving in the Roman army during the Samnite War, were dispatched to Apulia and established themselves at Nuceria; but eventually their descendants went back to resume senatorial privileges at Rome.
>
> The popular story, on the other hand, was that the family had been founded by a freedman, one Cassius Servius, described as a shoemaker, whose son made a comfortable living first as an informer and then as a dealer in confiscated property, before marrying a common prostitute, the daughter of a baker named Antiochus, and fathering on her a Roman knight. The truth probably lies somewhere between these anecdotal extremes.[44]

But this no longer seemed to constitute the whole of a divine mandate. It was Vespasian who inaugurated the successor dynasty. Omens were reported authenticating Vespasian's endorsement by the Roman deities—although these seem more threadbare than those offered in vindication of the Julio-Claudian dynasty.[45]

The contemporary historians apparently agreed that the new factor in this mandate was provenance from the East.

> An ancient superstition was current in the East, that out of Judaea would come the rulers of the world. This prediction, as it later proved, referred to two Roman Emperors, Vespasian and his son Titus.[46]

The application of this "ancient superstition" to Vespasian and Titus seemed obvious because it was these two who crushed the uprising of the Jews against Roman authority (A.D. 67–73.) But it went deeper than that:

In Judaea, Vespasian consulted the God of Carmel and was given a promise that he would never be disappointed in what he planned or desired, however lofty his ambitions. Also, a distinguished Jewish prisoner of Vespasian's *Josephus* by name, insisted that he would soon be released by the very man who had now put him in fetters, and who would then be Emperor.[47]

This Josephus (c. 37 A.D.–c. 100 A.D.), a member of the highest priestly aristocracy of Judaea, was Governor of Galilee and commanded Jewish rebel forces there at the time of the insurrection. Persuaded of the hopelessness of the Jewish cause, he defected (under shameful circumstances) to the conquerors, was eventually given Roman citizenship and became a friend of both Vespasian and Titus. In his memoir of the insurrection he makes the case that the Roman Empire is manifestly God's instrument in the consolidation of a world-community, and he explicitly transfers the credentials of Israel's Messiah to the Emperors of Rome. Resistance to Rome's authority had been worse than folly: it was blasphemy.

> Anyone who ponders these things will find that God cares for mankind and in all possible ways foreshows to his people the means of salvation, and that it is through folly and evils of their own choosing that they come to destruction. Thus the Jews after pulling down Antonia made the Temple square, in spite of the warning of their prophetic books that when the Temple became a square the City and Sanctuary would fall. But their chief inducement to go to war was an equivocal oracle also found in their sacred writings, announcing that at that time a man from their country would become monarch of the whole world. This they took to mean the triumph of their own race, and many of their scholars were wildly out in their interpretation. In fact the oracle pointed to the accession of Vespasian; for it was in Judaea he was proclaimed emperor. But it is not possible for men to

escape from fate even it they see it coming. The Jews interpreted some of the prophecies to suit themselves and laughed the others off, till by the fall of their city and their own destruction their folly stood revealed.[48]

An alternative (disputed) text replaces the passage beginning "This they took to mean", with: "Some took this as a reference to Herod, others to the crucified miracle-worker Jesus, and others to Vespasian."[49]

Tacitus, writing from the perspective of cultured Rome, draws the same conclusions as does Josephus from the destruction of the Jewish community. In a graphic passage which describes the heroic but doomed defence of Jerusalem by the Jews he concludes:

Prodigies had occurred, but their expiation by the offering of victims or solemn vows is held to be unlawful by a nation which is the slave of superstition and the enemy of true beliefs. In the sky appeared a vision of armies in conflict, of glittering armour. A sudden lightening flash from the clouds lit up the Temple. The doors of the holy place abruptly opened, a super-human voice was heard to declare that the gods were leaving it, and in the same instant came the rushing tumult of their departure. Few people placed a sinister interpretation upon this. The majority were convinced that the ancient scriptures of their priests alluded to the present as the very time when the Orient would triumph and from Judaea would go forth men destined to rule the world. This mysterious prophecy really referred to Vespasian and Titus, but the common people, true to the selfish ambitions of mankind, thought that this exalted destiny was reserved for them, and not even their calamities opened their eyes to the truth.[50]

The convergence of two supernaturalist theories of world history

The conventional view of this chapter in the history of the idea of history derives from the Renaissance and continues its biases and preoccupations. It states that these two traditions of theory and practice of history, having started from altogether different premises, and having been inspired by utterly contrary instincts, now confronted each other as mutually-hostile alternatives. Neither could learn from the other, neither could borrow from the other, because their separate visions of meaning were totally incompatible: the Greeks groping towards what moderns will eventually know as the secular, scientific, and humanistic definition of reality; the Jews fixated upon the possibility of transcendent meaning, and thus contemptuous of the possibility of that kind of meaning which, though imperfectly perceived by the Greeks, was to become the measure of all meaning in our present civilization. In the chapter that follows, the conventional history of the idea of history describes the ancient Jewish tradition swallowing up the Graeco-Roman tradition, in consequence of the political victory of the Christians in the time of Constantine (the early fourth century). The scientific-critical spirit, which had allegedly been gaining ground in the Hellenic mind and had begun to guide the master-spirits of Graeco-Roman historiography, would then be shelved for many centuries, until its re-discovery in the classical renaissance which begins in the fifteenth century.

To give the reader some idea of the polemical implications, we should consider a vintage expression of this view:

> The Christian interpretation found the central idea of world-history in a religious and not in a political phenomenon, and it introduced into historiography a new and pernicious principle. Hitherto history had been perfectly free. Homer had indeed enjoyed an excessive authority among the Greeks, but belief in Homer was not a religious doctrine, and men like Thucydides

and Eratosthenes used the Homeric poems, just as we do, like any other ancient source. It was with imperfect methods and inadequate conceptions of the conditions of the problem that the Greeks had attempted to order the traditions of their own and other races into a consistent whole; but they had worked quite freely, guided by reason alone and unfettered by dogma. Christian historiography installed the superior guidance of an indefeasible authority, the divinely inspired tradition of the Jewish records, whereby they determined the general frame and perspective of the history of the world. This was the first appearance of the principle which Cardinal Manning expressed in his famous saying that dogma must overcome history, and which guides all the historiography of the Ultramontane school.[51]

Bury was in his time the most esteemed partisan of what might be called the classical-humanist, or secular-critical vision of history. This is the school that believes that Christian scholarship deliberately destroyed the prestige of the classical vision of history, and in so doing irreparably set back the progress of human thought and culture. Bury saw classical historiography making progressively accelerating strides toward a true science of historical inquiry—which, in one mood, he was inclined to date from the time of Hecataeus (fl. c. 500 B.C.),[52] but in another mood was inclined to date precisely from "the brilliant inspiration which occurred to the genius of Thucydides" (who died c.399 B.C.): namely, "the idea of studying critically and recording political events as they occurred."[53] Bury is not arguing that Graeco-Roman historiography had *achieved* the modern program of history-confined-to-political-events, but rather that certain master-spirits had grasped it; and that, had there not occurred the overwhelming distraction into supernaturalism under the inspiration of Christianity, the inertia of these several centuries of effort would inevitably have carried the classical mind into the pale of "scientific history." Bury admits that critical-scientific standards were only fitfully applied, even by the best historians, (at the head of which he places Polybius (who died c. 120 B.C.)[54]) But he is adamant about the *tendency* of Graeco-Roman history: away from amateur story-telling towards critical examinations of texts, away from supernaturalism towards rationalism in explanation, away from moralizing towards exact description of human behaviour.

Bury's case about the accomplishments of classical historians stands, of course, upon the secular-humanist's case about what we need to know and what we are able to know in general. Bury believed that purity of historical method and confidence about truth are possible only so long as speculation about the larger logic that governs history locates itself securely in "the political sphere." This is defined as the sphere of deliberate human action. It is delimited on the one side from the sphere of nature, and on the other from the sphere of the supernatural.

Bury shares with the other classical scholars (see above, pp. 52f) their disappointment that the prestige of historiography remained so low among the Greeks. And while his judgements on the general quality of the actual production of Hellenic historians is not as harsh as that of most scholars today (see the judgements of Finley and Hays, above pp. 53–5 and 74) he does admit that it does fall well below what the heirs of Thucydides ought to have delivered. And he admits that there must be a link between this fact of history's low standing in the company of the philosophers and the disappointing level of actual historiography production in the Hellenic world.

Particularly disappointing to Bury is the failure of the Graeco-Roman historians to find some convincing theorem for combining the arguments and discoveries of the historians into one synthetic history with something like the coherence and persuasiveness of Herodotus' now-irrelevant theorem (based, we recall, on the notion that all human history tended to come into focus in the conflict between Greece and Persia.) In the aftermath of Alexander's conquests, Greek

Convergence   195

culture, already firmly established in Asia Minor and influential in the great cities of Mesapotamia and Egypt, became the common culture of the intellectuals and the political masters everywhere in what was now the Hellenic empire. Greek standards of historiography spread to all corners of their Empire. (see above, pp. 153f) The result was an exponential increase in the volume of histories written, but no advance in the quality of this work. But, while the Greek language and Greek genres, methods and format travelled well, the unifying vision of Herodotus did not: it was no longer at the heart of Greek theory of history (see above, pp. 58f.) To the great embarrassment of partisans of the Greek tradition of historiography, there is no avoiding the fact that Greek theorists failed to find a way of bringing this various and far-flung Hellenic historical production into any sort of alignment, so that it could all be told as facets of a single story, having a single direction. The embarrassment becomes more acute as we move down the centuries into the Roman era.

There are thus two aspects to this story of the disappointing legacy of Greek historiography. One is the decline in the quality of historical scholarship; the other is the dissipation of the theoretical assumptions that made it possible to see world history steady and to see it whole. Is there a link between the decline of the habit of rigorous scholarship (which located, accredited, recorded and ordered the *detail*) and the decline of faith in the vision that it could all be told as a single, unilinear story?

In Bury's view the principal thing lacking throughout the Hellenic period and through the succeeding Roman Period until the triumph of Christian ideology, was a coherent theory of the unity of mankind.[55] It is not that there was any lack of philosophers or philosophizing. Bury reviews the main schools, and concludes that the philosophy best suited for the purpose was stoicism. The capstone of the history of the idea of history, Bury argues, should logically have been the incorporation of the method of scientific-critical inquiry into some appropriate statement of the stoic concept of universal human nature. That this did not happen is owing (says Bury) to the "vagueness" of the stoic doctrine of the unity of mankind. Had this doctrine been better elaborated and somehow yoked together with a theoretical defence of critical-scientific historiography, both partners would have benefited: the philosophers by being provided with a material vindication in the detailed story of history; the historians by having a philosophical justification to inspire and sustain the otherwise tedious work of recording, storing, and collating historical records.

This seems to me desperate and far-fetched. It was not the "vagueness" of the stoic or the other schools of philosophy that made them unfit to rescue historiography. There never was a time when philosophy was more precise and sophisticated than this—until the beginnings of modern philosophy, in the seventeenth century (the century of Descartes, Spinoza, Hobbes, Locke.) But neither in Graeco-Roman philosophy nor in early modern philosophy is there forthcoming a theorem fit to make a case which vindicates the practical work of historiography as work that yields the largest meanings. This is because of the necessary hostility between philosophy's notions of what constitutes authoritative meaning and history's claims to its own authority. And unless it is understood that history deals in the largest meanings, the loyalties and the energies of the best minds go elsewhere—into the ontological disciplines and into poetry.

The process we have described in this chapter is quite a different one from what we find described in the mainline tradition of history of historiography, exemplified by Bury. What we find in the mainline tradition is a story of two rival and incompatible traditions for discovering meaning in the past, each reaching a certain critical stage in its evolution, having proceeded by strikingly different methods (the one proto-scientific, the other still in the grip of myth and legend), having contrasting ideological foundations (the one groping towards what moderns will eventually know as the scientific-humanist definition of reality; the other fixated upon certain absolute meanings, allegedly revealed by direct action of the Divine in history.) On this view, quite different preoccupations have brought each to its separate dead end. Neither could learn from the other. Neither could even borrow from the other, because their separate visions of what was real were totally incompatible.

Bury himself concedes (as we have noted) that Greek and Roman historiography had not in fact gained any new ground (in the period we have under review) towards that scientific understanding of history which was (he tells us) the implicit goal of the intellectual adventure which begins, if not with Herodotus, then with Thucydides. And Bury's epigones in the field of Greek historiography generally follow him in this. But if one sets aside the expectations induced by reading these conventional studies of classical historiography and turns to sample directly the authors of the historical books of this period, one does not find that any such ambition guided these historians.

Modern scholars of Graeco-Roman historiography give us no reason to believe that in the historical literature that has *not* survived from this period there is anything to contradict the evidence of the substantial literature that has survived: namely, that the best historians had become more determined, not less determined, since the days of Herodotus to take into account the purposes of the gods when they talked about history. So it is that later on the choice for intellectuals of the Christian period was not to be between a historiography tending towards an essentially secular-humanist rationale and method and one fixated on supernaturalism, but between *two equally supernaturalistic traditions*.

Why should these historians be described as failing to reach a goal which they did not set for themselves? The goal of scientific-critical history on atheistic premises is one set by modern theorists of history. It is simply not true that the guiding star of the best minds of classical historiography was the same as that of the modern atheists. (I use the word "atheist" here in its correct sense: namely, to define someone who on principle does not explain things in terms of the purposes that God or the gods or the Divine in any form is assumed to have.) At most, it can be said that this notion occurred from time to time (notably, in Thucydides), but was abandoned. As secular-humanists tell the story, the objective of an atheistic philosophy of history, abandoned by the classical historians under the chilling influence of Christian supernaturalism, is then "recovered" in the Renaissance, worked up into a full-bodied programme in the wake of the discovery of scientific method in the generation of Francis Bacon, and subsequently implemented in practical historiography since the Enlightenment.

But, if there ever was among the Greeks a clearly perceived ambition to develop something like secular-scientific method, it was abandoned, because it failed to commend itself to the best minds. The notion that explanation becomes more profound as it becomes more atheistic did not persuade the best minds of the Graeco-Roman world. Scholars of the history of ideas can provide evidence of a development, in the Graeco-Roman world, towards atheistic explanation in the natural sciences, whose most complete embodiments are said to be Democritus and Protagoras. But these same scholars have to concede that the atheistic programme had been at best stalemated by the beginning of our period, even in the sciences. This stalemate secular-humanist scholarship sees as owing to the inordinate boldness of vision required for the transition from the supernaturalistic to naturalistic world-view. At that early stage of the progress toward rational thought, men were not ready (so the argument goes) to pay the price for the secular scientific method of explanation. That may be. But we owe it to the best minds of that time to hear them out on their own terms. When we do this, we discover that in fact they believed that the supernatural element had to stay in their recitals of the past. They believed that, whatever the sum of all the possible meanings of historical events, one element that was constantly present was Divine purpose.

Chapter 7:

The Gospels as Historical Testimony

It was there from the beginning; we have heard it; we have seen it with our own eyes; we have looked upon it, and felt it with our own hands; and it is of this we tell. Our theme is the word of life. (I *John* 1:1–2)

The paradoxical character of Jewish and Christian theories of history

The commitment of Christians to the study of history is secured by our dogmatic investments in a specific and limited sequence of events lived out in time. The events come first in our consideration. Then comes discussion about their meanings. Then comes speculation about how these meanings shed light on other meanings that we or other men think they know from the application of disciplined reason to the realities of life around us. We believe that these events, lived out in history—in absolutely (or "merely") particular places at absolutely (or "merely") particular moments in time—tell us the largest meanings that it is given us to know. The worth of everything else that men think they know, we establish by reference to the meanings that we have invested in these historical events. The events in question are the recorded events of the history of Israel, and the recorded events of the life, death, resurrection and ascension of Jesus of Nazareth.

When we think of these events, we strive to think of them in their perfect detail. It is to develop a mastery of this detail that we read the scriptures again and again. What we are after is not some distillation of meaning, achieved by combination of many similar stories or thoughts—not lessons, not propositions, nor a pattern that gets clearer as we distance ourselves from concrete detail. What we *want* is detail.

I think that most Christians see the meaning which belongs to this detail as having two faces, or two orientations, which I would here call the "greater" and the "lesser". The *greater* implication of these events is what we see when we stand (imaginatively) in place and time with them and look to the mystery of the whole destiny of men and their universe. We believe that these events have already accomplished in time what must be accomplished in this present life-in-time so that God may bring about the reconciliation to Himself of all reality outside Himself. The lesser implication of these events is what we see when we stand (imaginatively) in place and time with them and look to our own present singular life in time and to our eternal future as singular individuals. On this "lesser" side, we believe that these events have already accomplished in time what is necessary for the eternal reconciliation of ourselves to Him. Nothing will ever persuade us that the perspective from which we see what we claim to see is other than historical. As we believe that the end which God has in mind for us is already accomplished in eternity by His detailed, singular and irreversible actions in history, so we believe that our own detailed activities in this life have cumulative and irreversible consequences in eternity. This historical realism sets our religion in a class by itself.

Christian faith centers upon the story of the birth, the life, the death, the resurrection and the ascension of Jesus of Nazareth. It declares that these events accomplish the purpose for which God entered into His covenant with Abraham. Christianity lays claim to the theory of history which follows from Judaism's understanding of the meaning of Abram/Abraham's decision. It does not dissolve the paradoxes that adhere to this theory, but raises them to a new level of complexity.

Foremost among these (we recall) are the many paradoxes entailed in the notion of God's election of the people of Israel. How could the history of Israel be uniquely revelatory of God's purpose, while being so conspicuously a history of failure, even of humiliation? We recall that the scriptural canon was established (for the most part) during the time when Judaea was at her point of lowest esteem in the eyes of the nations. Ostensibly, the Jews were finished as a nation; and without a national foundation of its own, Judaism must be finished too. How could the God of Israel be sovereign, if He was not the God of History? How could He be the God of History if His alleged covenant-partner counted for nothing in objective historical reckoning?

The implications of this mystery are worked and reworked by the prophets of Israel. If the God of Israel is the Lord of History, then empires and kings and political forces in general must be His instruments. It must follow that the subjection of Israel to the empires of this world is not inconsistent with God's covenant with Abraham, in which is contained the Plan by which the world is to be redeemed: "...Those that bless you I will bless, those that curse you I will execrate. All the families on earth will pray to be blessed as you are blessed".

In the light of political realities since the day of Jerusalem's fall to Babylon, the prophets present the notion of Israel as the suffering servant of God's purposes for all mankind. This notion informs the paradoxical statements radiating from the axial proposition that Zion would someday be the centre of a new world-reality whose features would be totally in contrast to the features that the hitherto characterized history (See above, pp. 143-5). In this reality-to-come, man will not be in conflict with man, men will not be in conflict with nature, and mankind-and-nature-together will be reconciled to God.

Theology can deal with paradoxes, because theology accepts the existence of imperceptible reality side-by-side with perceptible reality. Philosophy cannot deal with paradoxes, because its entire concern is with perceptible connections between perceptible realities. If philosophy is presented with the proposition that a nation (in this case, the Jews, but in other cases the English, or some other generalized entity, such as the Church, the working-class or Democracy) is the bearer of the ultimate meanings of the historical process, then it must find ways of stating this proposition in terms of lesser and greater. If what the proposition claims is true, the meaning of the history of Israel must be *greater* than the meaning of the history of other nations. The meaning of the latter must be capable of being fitted inside the meaning of the former. But the ostensible significance of the history or Israel is defeat and humiliation. She presents her innocuousness as her qualification for consideration as the bearer of the highest meanings. Philosophy cannot deal with the propostions that Israel's faith offers in vindication of the sovereignty of her God. The theory of history that such a faith demands points nowhere that philosophy can follow. It points toward mystery.

Israel's faith says that the hidden secret of the whole structure of events which is ostensibly governed by the categories of power (the rise and fall of empires) is the life story of the people of Israel—the most conspicuous example of ineffectiveness known to those who studied history in the days when Judaea was a province of Rome's empire.

Christians believe that the purpose for which God entered into covenant with Abraham has been accomplished in the life, death, resurrection and ascension of Jesus of Nazareth. To believe this proposition commits one to all the paradoxes involved in the Jewish statements, and new ones as well.

Among these new paradoxes is this: that we make our claims with respect to the work of Jesus Christ in the past tense. We say that Christ *has accomplished* the Plan which God had for man before creation. To *begin* the accomplishment of this plan, God had entered into covenant with Abraham. He has now, in Jesus Christ, accomplished the plan. He *has accomplished* the purpose for which there is history. He *has accomplished* this—not merely set in motion its accomplishment, or disposed history toward its accomplishement—not *tentatively* accomplished it, or provisionally accomplished it, not (as Reinhold Niebuhr preferred) accomplished it "in principle".

If we are to believe with the Old Testament prophets that God is *about* to accomplish the purpose for which there is history, that He *is* accomplishing it now in the history of the Jews, despite the ostensible innocuousness of the Jews—then we are committed to believe a vision of things that defies appearances, and cannot be defended or explained-without-remainder by philosophy. Equally, if we are to believe with the Christians that God *has accomplished* in the life, death, resurrection and ascension of Jesus of Nazareth the purpose for which there is history—then again we are committed to believe in a vision of things that defies appearances, and cannot be defended or explained-without-remainder by philosophy. Christian theory of history is not reducible to philosophy. Its principal categories of explanation are theological. That is, our theory of history is invoked in order to deal with mysteries.

It is crucial to understand that Christian theology, like Jewish theology, is offered in explanation of the meaning of historical events. Christian theory of history embraces the meanings which the Jews attach to the covenant of God with Abraham, and insists that the fulfilment of the purpose behind that covenant is to be seen in the events of a singular human life lived in time. As the best evidence of its validity as theology, Christian faith offers a set of historical testimonies to the details of that life.

The gospels as historical testimonies

There can be no compromising or qualifying this matter of the historical character of the gospel accounts. It "matters" absolutely that the gospels are of the highest standard of historical reliability.[1] The argument has always existed that the message of Christianity can be appropriated from *lessons* that the New Testament contains, and without regard to the question whether these are "historical records". "But", says F.F. Bruce, "the argument can be applied to the New Testament only if we ignore the real essence of Christianity. For the Christian gospel is not primarily a code of ethics or a metaphysical system; it is first and foremost good news, and as such it was proclaimed by its ealiest preachers.... And this good news is intimately bound up with the historical order, for it tells how for the world's redemption God entered into history, the eternal came into time, the kingdom of heaven invaded the realm of earth, in the great events of the incarnation, crucifixion and resurrection of Jesus the Christ. The First recorded words of our Lord's public preaching in Galilee are: 'The time is fulfilled, and the kingdom of God has drawn near; repent and believe the good news' (Mark 1:15)".[2]

The writers of the gospels intended their accounts to meet and pass the best-established conventions for the presentation of historical materials. This is shown by their care in providing specific references to the best-known public events of the time. That these points of synchronism are not always as helpful to us as they were to the contemporaries is owing to the lack of surviving documentation for the public side of the record. Wherever such materials do exist, they bear out in every case the deliberateness of the gospel-writers in providing references to place and to time which could be tested by living contemporaries. This concern is common to all four gospel-writers, but it is most obvious to our eye when we read Luke, because of his concern to provide the fullest account for circulation among the gentiles—that is, for the audience furthest removed from the immediate scene of the events of Jesus's life, death, resurrection and ascension, and therefore in need of more pointers; more proper names of places and persons, more careful use of titles and geographical names.

> [Luke] sets his story in the context of imperial history. Of all the New Testament writers, he is the only one who so much as names a Roman emperor. Three emperors (Augustus, Tiberius, and Claudius [*Lk* 2:1, 3:1; *Acts* 11:28 and 18:2]) are mentioned by name; the Emperor Nero is also referred to but not by his personal name—he is the "Caesar" to whom Paul appealed [*Acts* 25:11, *etc.*]. The birth of Jesus is fixed in the reign of the Emperor Augustus, when Herod the Great was king of Judaea and Quirinius governor of Syria [*Lk* 1:5, 2:1f]. The commencement of the public ministry of John the Baptist, with which the "Kerygma" proper begins, is elaborately dated by a series of

synchronisms in the Greek historical manner [Lk 3:1f.], reminding the classical student of the synchronisms with which, for example, Thucydides dates the formal outbreak of the Peloponnesian War in the beginning of the second book of his *History*. Names of note in the Jewish and Gentile world of his day appear in Luke's pages; in addition to the emperors, we meet the Roman governors Quirinius, Pilate, Sergius Paullus, Gallio, Felix, and Festus; Herod the Great and some of his descendants—Herod Antipas the tetrarch of Galilee, the vassal kings Herod Agrippa I and II, Berenice and Drusilla; leading members of the Jewish priestly cast, such as Annas, Caiaphas, and Ananias; Gamaliel, the greatest contemporary Rabbi and Pharasaic leader. A writer who thus relates his story to the wider context of world history is courting trouble if he is not careful; he affords his critical readers so many opportunities for testing his accuracy.[3]

Luke's historical details are couched in more explicit language; the other gospel-writers are less explicit, more allusive. But there is no gradation in their concern for historical specificity.

Bruce offers[4] a succinct summary of the confirmations, from surviving contemporary literature (including Josephus, Tacitus, Dio Cassius, Cicero) and from subsequent archeological discovery, of the exactness of Luke's references (in his two Books, the *Gospel* and the *Acts*) to public events and the details of Roman administration. The value of these confirmations is not merely that they bear out for us the reliability of Luke; but—far more important—it is that they prove that Luke had gone to extreme lengths to provide specifics for the purpose of synchronism with the public life of Judaea and the Empire so as to establish his credentials for trustworthiness in all that he had to tell. The irony is that the record of Roman imperial affairs is now so meagre, relative to the abundant record of the life of Jesus which is in these documents.[5]

Incidentally, the same judgement has to be made regarding the standing of the texts of the New Testament relative to that of secular literature and the public record of the time. That is : considering the texts merely as texts, only the New Testament records, out of the whole literature of the time, can be proven with confidence to belong as they presently stand, to the time and place from which they purport to come. Because great numbers of manuscripts of the New Testament texts have survived there is little difficulty about establishing with confidence the texts of the originals. "The interval then between the dates of original composition and the earliest extant evidence becomes so small as to be in fact negligible, and the last foundation for any doubt that the Scriptures have come down to us substantially as they were written has now been removed. Both the *authenticity* and the *general* integrity of the books of the New Testament may be regarded as finally established".[6] "The variant readings about which any doubt remains among textual critics of the New Testament affect no material question of historical fact or of Christian faith and practice".[7]

Perhaps we can appreciate how wealthy the New Testament is in material attestation if we compare the textual material for other ancient historical works. For Caesar's *Gallic War* (composed between 58 and 50 BC) there are several extant MSS, but only nine or ten are good, and the oldest is some 900 years later than Caesar's day. Of the 142 books of the Roman History of Livy (59 BC–AD 17) only thirty-five survive; these are known to us from not more than twenty MSS of any consequence, only one of which, and that containing fragments of Books iii–vi, is as old as the fourth century. Of the fourteen books of the *Histories* of Tacitus (c. AD 100) only four and a half survive; of the sixteen books of his *Annals,* ten survive in full and two in part. The text of these extant portions of his two great historical works depends entirely on two MSS, one of the ninth century and one of the eleventh. The extant MSS of his minor works (*Dialogus de*

The Gospels as Historical Testimony

Oratoribus, Agricola, Germania) all descend from a codex of the tenth century. The History of Thucydides (c. 460–400 BC) is known to us from eight MSS, the earliest belonging to c. AD 900, and a few papyrus scraps, belonging to the beginning of the Christian era. The same is true of the History of Herodotus (c. 480–425 BC). Yet no classical scholar would listen to an argument that the authenticity of Herodotus or Thucydides is in doubt because the earliest MSS of their works which are of any use to us are over 1,300 years later than the originals.[8]

The New Testament documents present themselves to us as testimonies to historical facts, virtually untouched in any detail after nineteen hundred years. Their subject is the birth, the life, the death, the resurrection, and the ascension of Jesus of Nazareth. They were originally offered by persons fully acquainted with the conventions governing the presentation of historical testimonies as these were practised by the best contemporary historians, to an audience of contemporaries, who would assume these conventions as they read these testimonies.

All of the changes with respect to normal format, tone of recital, techniques of citation of source, and so on, which have resulted from the establishment of a distinct academic discipline of history in the last two centuries have not altered by one iota the standards governing the selection of statements for inclusion in historical testimonies, the criteria by which the historian judges the relative reliability of evidence, nor the rights and obligations of the reader with respect to the authority of statements presenting themselves as "historical facts".

The gospel-writers have gone to great pains to make clear that the events they are dealing with were historical events; and that they (the gospel-writers) stand in exactly the same relationship to these facts as historians always do to the facts they narrate; and that we stand in relation to their stories precisely as readers of historical accounts are always understood to stand. It is impossible to miss the dogged way in which they provide for the reader's need to see these as events like other events, for which there were thousands of living eye-witnesses, who knew the exact locations where the events took place, and who knew all the controversies attaching to the events and the Man. They have provided everything they can think of to assist the living readers of these texts in locating the sites of these events and the living witnesses to them. So striking is these authors' determination to elicit the real-life setting of the story they have to tell—so unexpected and so unprecedented is this sort of realistic preoccupation, in the context of the whole tradition of classical literature, that one eminent classical scholar has bluntly declared that these gospels amount to not less than the first truly "realistic literature" to come into the world.[9]

Quite apart from the abundant specific references to time and locale which we can see in these texts, there must be countless specific allusions that of necessity are lost on us. It happens that we are living in an age of accelerating improvements in techniques of archeology and unprecedented opportunities for archeological research. This work brings to light constantly new evidences of specific allusions to time, locale, and other details of realistic setting.[10] Indeed no events of that time, and none for the span of several centuries either side of that time (with the one arguable exception of the last days of the life of Socrates) are in the same class with these events of the birth, life, death, resurrection of Jesus of Nazareth—*as historically documented events.*

How do we account for the monstrous misrepresentation of this situation which passes as the "state-of-the-art" in academic New Testament hermeneutics? Here we are routinely informed that the authors of the gospels could not be dealing historical evidences, as we understand "history" or "evidence", for the sufficient reason that the mind of that time had not yet discovered what these things were! There are variations in the way the "problem" is expressed. According to some, the problem is that the mind of the time "lacked our modern grasp of historical fact" (otherwise called "the canons of historical criticism", or a "scientific appreciation of historical understanding").

The Gospels as Historical Testimony 209

According to others, the problem is that people of that time, while vaguely aware of standards of historical factuality (otherwise called "facticity"), were "indifferent" to them, or "uninterested in them", or even determined not to yield to them, because they had some higher purpose in view than mere historical recital.

There is no possibility of a middle-ground in this matter. When we encounter such double-talk as "historicized theologoumena" (Raymond Brown), we can be quite sure we are dealing with a bad conscience.

What does it mean that Rudolf Bultmann and Eric Auerbach have before them the same texts, and are impelled by the same passion for truth—and that one can announce with scholarly sobriety that the authors under review (the gospel-writers) are utterly without interest in historical detail; and the other, in the same sober tone, that the detail of place, setting, characterization and so on is so massive and so obtrusive that we must concede that we are at the source of all the realistic literature of our civilization? What it means, I believe, is that the implications for *us* of our accepting or rejecting the authority of *the message that is conveyed* in this realistic material is so overwhelming that we are tempted to seize upon any formula that allows us to distance ourselves from it—no matter how perverse.

Current academic philosophy of history and the challenge of the New Testament record

It amounts to dogma within the company of academic philosophy of history today that one cannot responsibly speak in the same breath of historical testimonies on this side and that side of the establishment of the modern academic discipline of history. It is simply posited that the changes in the manner and spirit of historiography that began in the age of Ranke (1795-1886) have revolutionized the way in which men judge the truth and falsity of statments made about the events of the past. This dogma is linked to that other dogma: that "modern science" brought into the world a whole new set of qualifications for judging between true and false statements. It is this "scientific understanding" that releases us from the control of the witnesses of past events. Marc Bloch wrote: "We [the heirs of nineteenth-century historical science] have acquired the right of disbelief, because we understand, better than in the past, when and why we ought to disbelieve".[11]

It is this intimidating pair of dogmas that has frightened so many New Testament scholars out of the posture of respect towards the New Testament documents which is due to their extraordinary soundness as historical testimonies (let alone what is due to them as dogmas of their church).

The assumptions which currently rule in academic-theological discussion of this theme were set at the end of the decade of the 1960's,[12] when the pre-eminent names in this field of New Testament hermeneutics were E. Käsemann, Gerhard Ebeling, G. Bornkamm and James M. Robinson.[13] The principal authors in this field were all epigones of the German theologian, Rudolf Bultmann. They start where Bultmann starts: disqualifying the gospels as historical testimonies in anything like the normal sense, insisting indeed that their authors could never have had anything like the motives of historians, since their purpose was to "proclaim" certain meanings derived from certain absolutely unique events.

The logic runs something like this. The story the gospel-writers had to tell centred on the resurrection—an absolutely unique event. But precisely because it was absolutely unique it could not be spoken of in historical terms, since to speak of events historically means *explaining* them in terms of the class of events to which they belong. Being in the grip of the effects of their experience of the Resurrection, the witnesses who told the stories which appear in the gospels recalled everything that had happened previously as belonging already to that world beyond this world where the limitations of our natural life will be (or, in the light of the resurrection, already *are*) overcome. They could not, in these circumstances, be expected to care about "historical" exactitude.

The Gospels as Historical Testimony

What they wanted to convey to us was the marvelous and extraordinary transhistorical (eternal) dimension in which all of what happened really happened. Thus, what mattered was not what the eye saw (unassisted by faith) but what things really meant ("in the light of the Easter-faith").

A non-historian and a non-believer, the literary critic Frank Kermode, provides a plain man's paraphrase of these theologians' case, stripped of the jargon of the guild: the New Testament accounts are "free narrative inventions", "fictions inserted into a history-like record on a later consideration of what ought properly to have occurred".[14]

Thus (these theologians say) the models that must be consulted before considering the stories which the gospels tell are not any of these known to historians past or present, but rather the models of mythology. Hence, the primary task of hermeneutics is "demythologizing".

C.S. Lewis, in an address to theological students,[15] presents a devastating critique of what passed in the 1950's for critical-scientific hermeneutics. His principal target is the shoddy logic that underlies their methods of textual criticism; and to this criticism he brings the insights of a literary critic and author of fiction.

> ...whatever these men may be as Biblical critics, I distrust them as critics. They seem to me to lack literary judgement, to be imperceptive about the very quality of the texts they are reading. It sounds a strange charge to bring against men who have been steeped in those books all their lives. But that might be just the trouble. A man who has spent his youth and manhood in the minute study of New Testament texts and of other people's studies of them, whose literary experience of those texts lacks any standard of comparison such as can only grow from a wide and deep and genial experience of literature in general, is, I should think, very likely to miss the obvious things about them. If he tells me that something in a Gospel is legend or romance, I want to know how many legends and romances he has read,

how well his palate is trained in detecting them by the flavour; not how many years he has spent on that Gospel.... [For example, a commentary on the *Gospel of John* regards that gospel as] a "spiritual romance", "a poem not a history", to be judged by the same canons as Nathan's parable, the Book of Jonah, Paradise Lost, "or, more exactly, *Pilgrim's Progress*." After a man has said that, why need anyone attend to anything else he says about any book in the world?... Then turn to John. Read the dialogues: that with the Samaritan woman at the well, or that which follows the healing of the man born blind. Look at its pictures: Jesus (if I may use the word) doodling with this finger in the dust; the unforgettable ην δε νυξ (xiii, 30). I have been reading poems, romances, vision-literature, legends, myths all my life. I know that not one of them is like this. Of this text there are only two possible views. Either this is reportage—though it may no doubt contain errors—pretty close up to the facts; nearly as close as Boswell. Or else, some unknown writer in the second century, without known predecessors or successors, suddenly anticipated the whole technique of modern, novelistic, realistic narrative. If it is untrue, it must be narrative of that kind. The reader who doesn't see this has simply not learned how to read. I would recommend him to read Auerbach [i.e., Eric Auerbach's *Mimesis*, mentioned herein, pp.208–209][16]

Few scholars could match the qualifications of C.S. Lewis for judging the worth of the literary-critical conclusions of these scholars. Certainly, I find his judgements compelling. For just as Lewis doubts their "wide and deep and genial experience of literature in general" on the basis of their characteristic one-liners about the features of myth, so I think should the student of history doubt their wide and deep and genial experience of history on the basis of their characteristic one-liners on historiography.

The Gospels as Historical Testimony

The first step in coming to grips with the logic of the dominant school of New Testament hermeneutics is to recognize that it begins by assuming that a verdict has already been handed down from academic philosophy about the limits of historical knowledge. Whether or not our theologian directly alludes to the literature of academic philosophy of history, the fact is that the Bultmann school accepts absolutely the definitions of history's authority conventionally provided in that literature. In this company, the overriding preoccupation for at least a half-century has been with the problem of the content and nature of "historical excplanation".[17] Following David Hume, academic philosophers in the British tradition have borne down doggedly on the proposition that the historian's purpose is to *explain* a series of events to which he is testifying. To do this, he must depend on generally-accredited patterns of recurrence *in nature*. His goal, as an historian, is to be believed. To be believed, one must be seen to be explaining things in terms of what we all accept to be the laws governing all occurrences of the kind in question. Historical explanation is thus (in the philosopher's vocabulary) "nomological", that is, it proceeds by appeal to well-accredited *laws* of human and/or natural behaviour. Historical understanding is (in this view) dependent entirely on scientific understanding. The various branches of science determine the limits of possibility in life. The historian decides which combination of specific sciences is required for an adequate description of the event in question; but the authority of the science which is called into the examination of a question is absolute. It is axiomatic, in this camp, that nothing that the source says about a particular event can have the authority to contradict what science *knows* to be possible with respect to events of the kind in question. Knowledge of what is and is not possible is the province of the science which deals with events of the kind in question; and it is this knowledge that frees us from the control of the witnesses of past events, giving us the key we need to isolate that portion (if any) of their testimonies which is historically possible.

This logic has dominated academic-philosophical discussion of "historical explanation" since at least the eighteenth-century. Its classic expression (as already noted) is generally regarded to be by David Hume (1711–1776).[18] The possibility of recommending this procedure as Christian theology occurred later to David Friedrich Strauss (1808–1874),[19] and gained ground steadily until it became a pillar of liberal-Protestant theology prior to the First World War.

Conscious of these reigning dogmas of academic philosophy of history (that all explanation is nomological, that the measure of all factual truth comes from the empirical sciences, and that history, which deals with particular and non-repeatable events is least fit to yield true statements of the quality required by science); tantalized by the modernist's doctrine that the march of science gives to moderns an altogether unprecedented "right of disbelief"; but *finally, alarmed* at the outcome for faith if the facts of the gospel are left to stand in the company of other "merely historical" truths—the liberal theologians have retreated to the position that the gospels do not belong in the category of historical documents at all. They are a proclamation (*kerygma*) of truths too large for history to retail. The historical foundations of the events of the gospels are, at most, of marginal concern—some say irrelevant. The more pious of these scholars speak of the *kerygma* as bursting out of the bounds of historical methodology as Christ burst the bounds of death.

A particularly sedulous application of the Bultmannian hermeneutics is R.R. Niebuhr's *Resurrection and Historical Reason* (1957). Here we are told that the gospel writers were not the least interested in "mere facticity"—or "happenedness"[20] (a level of reality apparently akin, but not identical to "throwness into existence".)[21] Another spokesman of this school tells us that we should not "wish to fall back into the biographical approach, with its interest in chronology, topography, and psychology... [recognizing that we are] not in a position to lay bare the facts of history, to give a clean description of 'what actually happened.' Anyway that would be beside the point."[22] And

The Gospels as Historical Testimony

another: "...the *kerygma* calls for a total encounter with the person of Jesus, in which the self is put in radical decision. Therefore it can only regard as illegitimate a scholarly career which becomes in the long run no more than a distracting fascination with historical details about Jesus, details which may occupy the memory, move the emotions, prod the conscience, or stimulate the intellect, but fail to put the self in radical decision."[23]

It is surely not difficult for anyone not yet carried beyond the point of no-return by over-exposure to this sort of theological baffle-gab to see why such scholars might put little stock in anything which promises "*merely*" to "occupy the memory, move the emotions, prod the conscience [and] stimulate the intellect".

Were it not for the fact that this style of hermeneutics has been for so long the dominant one in the departments of theology, one would feel bound to apologize for getting down on all fours with it, as we have done over the last several pages. But this is a book about theory of history. And to speak of the premises of our Christian theory of history (as we are doing here in this chapter) without taking into account the present state of discussion on this point among the theologians might seem irresponsible. It is possible (though in any case irrelevant to the authority of our argument) that in academic departments of theology the pendulum has begun to swing away from the "de-mythologizers".

Still, the fact remains that the authority of the gospel testimonies is necessarily vulnerable in controversy—and this *not* because there is anything lacking in their credentials as historical testimonies, but precisely because the authentic historical testimony is by nature the most *vulnerable* of all kinds of authority. The present point is that we cannot deal fairly with the question of the *relative* credibility of these testimonies if the theologians will not allow that they are even *meant to be* historical testimonies. We do not claim that the testimonies of the gospel-writers are absolutely irresistible. No historical testimonies are. But there is no hope of making any case for the gospels at all if we deny that the authors even meant them to be taken seriously as historical statements.

The project of denigrating the "historical" seriousness of the gospel-writers had its beginnings in D.F. Strauss, at a time when European scholarship was generally dazzled by the accomplishments of the new schools of academic history deriving from Leopold von Ranke (1795–1886), and when no end of fantastic judgement was permitted regarding the literature and faith of the "pre-scientific past", provided there was a generous amount of solemn talk about *myth* to fill in the great spaces of ignorance which then existed regarding the history of the ancient world. The Bultmannian phase of this exercise came long after these great spaces had begun to be filled by the discoveries of modern archaeology and philology;[24] by which time, however, the habit of patronizing the gospels (and the Biblical texts generally) as documents of little historical value had become so deeply ingrained among the academic theologians as to seem irreversible. Not coincidentally, Rudolph Bultmann was a declared admirer of Martin Heidegger's philosophy.[25] Bultmann's dogmas took hold in the hour of greatest prestige of European existentialist philosophy, the school of philosophy most hostile to the case for meaning in history. At the same time, philosophy of history in the English-language universities was a province of the analytical school, which was totally preoccupied with the red-herring of "explanation" and ruminations on the "nomological model". Academic historians, meanwhile, had nothing to offer to the question of the historical credentials of the gospels, having farmed-out these responsibilities to the guild of academic philosophy. By outspending the more orthodox scholars in sheer manic energy, and depending on the low prestige of historical knowledge in academic philosophy and theology, and while the academic historians were out to lunch, the Bultmannites were able to achieve the standing of conventional truth for the notion that the New Testament documents were the very opposite of what their authors claim in every line: namely, historical documents. It was also crucial to

The rights of historical testimony

Here we are at the still point of the story of the prestige of history in our civilization. Our answer to the question of the historical foundation of the Christian creed must control our answer to the question of the character of historical authority in general.

What are the rights of historical testimony *vis-à-vis* other kinds of knowledge? What is historical knowledge? How do we recognize it when we meet it? What must a testimony have to qualify as historical evidence? What do its witnesses owe to us? What do we owe to their testimonies?

It is an inescapable fact that the modern sciences have given us a fuller description of what routinely happens in the world—that is, a clearer understanding of the regular processes that underlie routine happenings in the world. But it is an evasion of the challenge which history always presents to say that these accomplishments have given us a new "right of disbelief". The contemporaries of the writers of the gospels fully understood, for example, that virgins did not conceive and bear sons. They were not an iota more nor less free than we are to disbelieve this claim with respect to the child Jesus, (as it is made in *Matthew* and *Luke*.) (Is it really necessary to point out that this presumption is the basis of Joseph's behaviour in *Matthew* 1:18–25?) If they believed it nonetheless it was because they were persuaded of the authority of the witnesses to the life of Jesus to accept what they otherwise "knew" to be impossible. Such a fact as this contradicted the "facts of life", for them no less than for us. All the undoubted advance that the sciences have made in describing the processes involved in the conception of new human lives neither adds to nor subtracts from the simplicity of the issue involved. There are today devout gynecologists who confess without reservation the dogma of the virgin birth, and there are masses of scientific illiterates who reject it.

The question is this: on what basis do we generally believe what a historical testimony tells us?

The answer is: we believe when and insofar as we have confidence in the author of the testimony.

The issue of the reliability of an historical witness is *absolutely* unrelated to whether or not the witness can *explain* what he has witnessed. The witness may or may not have an explanation for the event. We may have to supply our own explanation. Frequently we do find ourselves supplying better explanations, after the fact. But for the actual occurrence of the event we depend absolutely on testimony of people who were there—and who may be lying to us. The "facticity" of the event owes nothing to the plausibility (to us) of any *explanation* that the alleged witness may offer. His credentials as a witness come down to these two: (a) was he there? and (b) would he lie to us (or could he have been deceived?)

There is a mountain of the dullest academic literature ever conceived (see footnote 17) reared on the fallacious proposition that it is the daily work of historians to process received explanations of past events into newer works which embody better explanations of the same events. The work of historians is to *tell* the past. They depend for this work upon prior *tellers* of the past, and ultimately upon original witnesses—who may or may not have had explanations, but who certainly had something to *tell*. Whether or not we accept what we are told along this chain of recitations turns not on the cogency of the explanations, but on the credentials of the witnesses.

A man might lay claim to having seen a thoroughly routine event, so that nothing in his story presents any difficulties for our powers of explanation. Yet he might be lying about having seen the event. Perhaps the event never happened. The fact that the "witness" never claims any knowledge of any possibility that violates the patterns of regularity we are accustomed to is of no help to us in judging his

The Gospels as Historical Testimony

qualifications as a witness. These we decide on other grounds. If we are persuaded that our witness would not lie to us, we have no "right of disbelief", deriving from our knowledge of what routinely happens in life, to interpose between his testimony and ours. If we absolutely cannot believe that there is a kind of reality in the world which could contain the alleged event that he claims to witness to, then we must reject his witness. He is deceived, or he is lying to us. If we absolutely will not accept what he says, we are interposing another kind of authority between ourselves and his alleged authority as an historical witness. But, we cannot in this case claim to be rejecting him on *historical* grounds. The statement that "things like that don't occur in this world" is not an historical judgement.

Voltaire, for example, condemned Herodotus as the "father of lies" because of the "absurd" stories that Herodotus told about the behaviour of people in the ancient past. In particular, Herodotus' story that in ancient Babylon fathers required their daughters to serve as temple prostitutes for one night as part of an initiation rite, Voltaire rejected as "a calumny on the human race".[26]

The first principle of Voltaire's philosophy of history was that human nature is always and everywhere the same. His "knowledge" of human behaviour ruled out acceptance of Herodotus' story. Voltaire regarded this as the judgement of an historian. But it was certainly not. It was a scientific or philosophical judgement—specifically, an anthropological one.

But if we reject at one place the testimony of our alleged witness because it is "impossible", then we have no right to regard as historical the parts of his story that do fit what we already think we know; or, if we do exercise such a "right", we should admit that it is not historical judgement that we are using but scientific or philosophical judgement.

Here lies the difference between historical testimony and all other kinds of knowledge. *Its right to contradict science and philosophy is absolutely unqualified.* But if it is sovereign on this side, on the reverse side it is extremely frail. It depends entirely on the moral authority of a singular human individual who may be lying to us or who may be deceived (see above, pp. [84-86]).

The fact is that *all historical testimony is first and last proclamation* (*"Kerygma"*). It may be associated with an explanation; but that is incidental to its authority. Historical testimony amounts to statements made by persons who claim to have been witnesses, or to be faithfully retailing the testimony of witnesses. The facts they testify to cannot be tested by us: that is the only reason for our needing their testimony. If we had direct access to the facts, we could handle them with philosophic or scientific method.

All of this is contrary to the spirit of most academic-philosophical agonizing on this subject, which begins and ends with the red-herring of "explanation". "Explanation" assumes dependence on what Gerhard Maier calls "analogous classification". But the whole point about historical recital is that it deals with unique events. There is always a limit to the possibility of "explaining" a singular event in terms of other events of a like kind. And when it comes to judging a statement that a particular event *happened* in the now-unreachable past, it is entirely irrelevant what class of events it might seem to belong to. "To be sure" says Maier, "as long as one makes analogous classification a precondition for acceptance, much in the world of the Bible remains without foundation". We go further: as long as one makes analogous classification a precondition for acepting *any* alleged historical testimony, one is avoiding the question of its qualification as historical fact. "But how", says Maier, "can the *pure* historian without further ado reject something just because it happens only once? What can be experienced and what has analogies can certainly not be declared synonymous".[27] That is the issue in a nutshell. Every historical event is an event that happened only once. What we need to know is: what happened. The question is not: Do military men tend to cross rivers? but, Did Caesar cross the Rubicon?

Furthermore: contrary to popular assumption, the authority of historical testimony does not tend to vary with the distance in time between ourselves and the witnesses; nor does it necessarily increase as the number of witnesses increases. The audience is always radically at liberty to reject historical testimony—no matter how recent and no matter how numerous and consistent the witnesses may be. (Was there ever an event that had more witnesses than the Holocaust of the Jews of Europe? Yet books have appeared under scholarly auspices, and in the lifetimes of hundreds of thousands of such witnesses, denying the fact of the Holocaust; and they are (at this writing) selling well. Again: there never was a political administration that provided so much documentation about itself, nor had so many qualified academic historians in its employ as the Kennedy administration. Yet every month a new book appears to challenge one or more of even the most apparently secure truths about it. Will we ever be closer to understanding all the facts and the real motives behind Kennedy's actions in Cuba? Is there any *fact* with respect to the Kennedy assassination that is more secure than the *facts* respecting the miracle of the feeding of the five thousand? Isn't it irrelevant to our confidence with respect to these two events that all the witnesses of the latter have been dead for nineteen-hundred years, while thousands of the witnesses of the former are still alive? and that there are stacks upon stacks of photographic records of the former and none at all for the latter? Those who declare themselves satisfied with regard to the facts of the Kennedy assassination do so because they consent to believe the testimonies upon which a certain story depends. Those who are not satisfied say that the story is at vital points faulty because someone is lying to us or is himself deceived. It all comes down to the matter of confidence in our *own* ability to judge character and motive. We think we know when we are being lied to. We think we know the signs that indicate when a person is self-deceived.

A textbook case of historical fact: Caesar-crossing-the-Rubicon

I once attended a public debate held in a University on the theme "The Resurrection of Jesus: Myth or reality". The New Testament scholar on the panel (the one confessional Christian in the group of five) prefaced his theological statement with the assertion that he assumed the historical integrity of the evidences for the Resurrection, but that he did not feel professionally competent (being a theologian, and not an historian, nor a philosopher of history) to explain what an historian might say about the normal tests for "proving" historical reliability. This was, perhaps, a correct position for him to take, in the context of an academic debate. However, the philosophers on the panel took immediate advantage of the theologian's modesty, re-interpreting what he had said as a repudiation of the "historicity" of the New Testament texts in question. "None of the writers of the Gospels, of Acts, of the Epistles, claimed to be writing 'history'", said one. "The canons of historical science, as we know them today, were developed in the nineteenth century", said another, "and from this it follows that these first-century sources are not historical sources". "These materials are essentially 'mythical', 'legendary', 'poetical', 'proto-historical', 'primitive', 'naive'; but infinitely 'human', 'moving', 'sincere', said they all, falling over one another in their condescension. But, "Notice the many contradictions in the stories. Notice how they fail to explain this detail, that detail...." "These events" (said one) "do not belong in history books, in the company of say,....."

I knew instantly what the example was going to be. I have been through debates like this one before. I have read the current philosophers of history on this theme, and I have heard the current theologians as they wrestle with this theme; and the example is always the same:

"...Caesar crossing the Rubicon"!

Why does *Caesar-crosing-the-Rubicon* have this status as the outstanding example from ancient history of solid historical fact? What

The Gospels as Historical Testimony

is the origin of this conventional coupling of *Caesar-crossing-the-Rubicon* with the *Resurrection-of-Jesus* as examples of (on the one hand) the securely-founded historical fact and (on the other hand) the supremely undocumented and undocumentable "event"?

It may be that this convention is of much longer standing than I know. But I think I know where to find the source of its present prestige among the New Testament scholars: namely, in R.G. Collingwood's, *The Idea of History*.[28] During the 1950's and the 1960's discussion of historical epistemology (i.e., how we know what we know about the past) revolved around the formulations of R.G. Collingwood. This was true, at least, in courses on theory of history given by academic historians. These latter believed that Collingwood was the philosopher who best understood the special features of historical testimony.

Collingwood, it should be stressed, was perfectly at one with the world of academic philosophy in believing that the central issue was the problem of "explanation". But he offered conclusions to the effect that the method of explaining things historically resulted in knowledge of a kind that gave a deeper satisfaction than did scientific knowledge, because it was knowledge of human thought rather than of abstract processes. And this (so far as I can see) is the basis of the misplaced love that historians had for him.

Collingwood's theory about the special nature of historical explanation turns on his famous distinction between what he called the "inside" and the "outside" of events. The natural sciences (according to Collingwood) deal strictly with "the outside of events", and their ways with events are, of necessity, unemotional, dispassionate, objective. The human sciences, however, deal with human agents; and when this material is in question, merely external observation is inadequate. Human will, the capacity of individuals to intrude their own decisions into the whole cluster of forces that act upon them, removes human activity from the scope of the method of the natural sciences. And history is the model for all the human sciences:

> The historian, investigating any event in the past, makes a distinction between what may be called the outside and the inside of an event. By the outside of the event I mean everything belonging to it which can be described in terms of bodies and their movements: the passage of Caesar, accompanied by certain men, across a river called the Rubicon at one date, or the spilling of his blood on the floor of the senate-house at another. By the inside of the event I mean that in it which can only be described in terms of thought: Caesar's defiance of Republican law, or the clash of constitutional policy between himself and his assassins. The historian is never concerned with either of these to the exclusion of the other. He is investigating not mere events (where by an event I mean one which has only an outside and no inside) but actions, and an action is the unity of the outside and inside of an event... His work may begin by discovering the outside of an event, but it can never end there; he must always remember that the event was an action, and that his main task is to think himself into this action, to discern the thought of its agent.[29]

Collingwood's methodology is basically easy to retail; but, like all such programmes that have come out of systematic philosophy, it depends for its force upon a carefully developed critique of alternative programmes, which in this case runs over some two hundred pages of Collingwood's *Idea of History*, and does not admit of condensation.

English-language theologians of the Bultmann school rushed to embrace Collingwood's concepts and soon were putting them to a purpose that runs absolutely contrary to Collingwood's whole philosophy. Bultmann himself was (so far as I can discover) the first major theologian to discover the uses of Collingwood.[30] The one-line

The Gospels as Historical Testimony

references of Bultmann's English-speaking *epigoni* to Collingwood have a certain uniformity about them and (to be blunt) a derivative flavour. Unlike these followers, Bultmann appreciated the limited usefulness of Collingwood's theories for a "Christian-existentialist" theory of history. The followers seem only to have noted the congenial parts, and have gone beyond Bultmann in lumping Collingwood with Dilthey, Croce and other quite disparate theorists of history into one monolithic "school".

The starting-point of the de-mythologizers was the collapse of their confidence (under Bultmann's influence) in the recoverability of the facts of Jesus' historical life. But, they say, Jesus Christ is more to us than a life recorded in such meagre and doubtful detail. If the objective or external facts of Jesus' historical existence are unrecoverable—or too few to be of service for more than "a historical novel"[31] then it is essential to find our way back to Jesus Christ by some *inside* route. "The new historiography has, as it were, opened up a 'second avenue of access' to the historical Jesus in addition to the first avenue provided by the *kerygma*. This 'second avenue' has not existed since the time of the original disciples who had both their Easter-faith and the faith and the factual memory of Jesus".[32] And here is Collingwood, the most esteemed of modern philosophers of history, the key to whose argument is the magic phrase, "the inside of events".[33] To turn the *kerygmatic* key in the lock of the Gospels is obviously the same operation (say these theologians) as what Collingwood called getting on the "inside" (or thought-side) of what is happening in the life of the historical person called Jesus. This makes possible a "total encounter with the person of Jesus, in which the self is put in radical decision".[34]

It must be noted that it is Collingwood's alleged emphasis upon the recovering of the historical "self" which makes him useful to these scholars. "The point of departure for Robinson is the inability of the older objective historical methodology to grasp the inward existential reality of Jesus' life. He therefore takes up the new weapon [not an inappropriate word!] of modern historiography, handed on by W.

Dilthey and more recently by R.G. Collingwood, as a means of access to the innermost being or selfhood of the historical Jesus".[35] It is also worth noting that it is standard procedure to offer Collingwood's name as merely the most recent and prestigious of a school of philosophers offering a common 'existentialist' approach to the problem of history: Dilthey and Collingwood are apparently regarded as the hard core, but the company is often expanded to embrace Heidegger and Bultmann. (Macquarrie writes: "The three thinkers who seem to have the greatest influence on Bultmann's view of history [Collingwood, Dilthey, Heidegger] ...show a certain affinity in their several approaches to the problems of history, and since this affinity centres on the relating of history to the historical existence of the historian himself, we find it convenient to speak of an 'existentialist' approach to history").[36]

But Collingwood, an idealist, and totally out of sympathy with anything the least redolent of existentialism, had no confidence whatever in the recoverability of historical 'selfhood'! In fact, he explicitly forbade his readers even to think about biography as a legitimate possibility for the historian:

> Of everything other than thought, there can be no history. Thus a biography, for example, however much history it contains, is constructed on principles that are not only non-historical but anti-historical. Its limits are biological events, the birth and death of a human organism: its framework is thus a framework not of thought but of natural process. Through this framework —the bodily life of the man, with his childhood, maturity and senescence, his diseases and all the accidents of animal existence—the tides of thought, his own and others', flow crosswise regardless of its structure, like sea-water through a stranded wreck. Many human emotions are bound up with the spectacle of such bodily life in its vicissitudes, and biography, as a form of literature, feeds these emotions and may give them wholesome food; but this is not history. Again, the record of immediate

experience with its flow of sensations and feelings, faithfully preserved in a diary or recalled in a memoir, is not history. At its best, it is poetry; at its worst, an obstructive egotism; but history it can never be.[37]

How could anyone have read that passage, and then have concluded that Collingwood stood for a programme of historiography based upon the recovery of the 'selfhood' of historical persons? About all that can be said in extenuation of the Bultmannites is that the passage I have cited is Collingwood's only explicit reference to the problem of biography; so that they may have overlooked it. But there is no reason to think that Collingwood, had he lived to flesh out his incomplete manuscript, would have felt it necessary to expand this reference to biography and to develop his objections. From the point of view that he had so carefully developed over three-hundred-odd pages there is nothing whatever to be said in favour of biography. It is, as he clearly states, the one traditional approach to history which is impossible under his method, and that because of a rigidly idealistic conception of psychology which should make his name anathema to existentialists.

Either the Bultmannites have not read Collingwood, or they have deliberately suppressed the key to his argument, which is as far removed from an endorsement of an existentialist approach to history as Bishop Berkeley's philosophy was from being an affirmation of materialism. The truth seems to be that they are so impatient to be done with anything which up to now has gone under the name of genuine historical work that they have clutched at every stray bit of wisdom bearing the name of a good contemporary historian or philosopher, in order to construct a new definition of historical method which, in effect, explodes the function of history altogether. The Bultmannites admit—in fact they glory in the admission—that all the evidence is in, and that further research into the life of Jesus is out of the question.

These theologians have seized upon, and misrepresented totally, Collingwood's epistemology in order to proclaim that true knowledge of Jesus is of a sort absolutely and by definition closed to historical examination. To confirm the distinction they want to make between the knowledge we have of the "events" of Jesus' life ("existentially" acquired) and "merely historical" knowledge (the knowledge we have of other events from other lives) they thoughtlessly seize on the example which Collingwood happened to be using when illustrating how historians "explain" things: the classic example of *Caesar-crossing-the-Rubicon*. The standing of this event in the literature on New Testament hermeneutics as a veritable fetish for the historically-reliable fact is I suspect to be traced to its place in Collingwood's text. It figures there as the centre-piece of an argument about the peculiarities of the historian's methods of explanation.

Whatever the theme—"causation-in-history"; objectivity in history"; "the nature of documentary evidence"—there we always find *Caesar-crossing-the-Rubicon*, never itself examined, but always thrown into the positive side of the scale as the measure against which we weigh the case for something more problematical.

How and why did *Caesar-crossing-the-Rubicon* acquire this virtually fetishistic status? Why did Collingwood choose it? Perhaps it is because everyone has some sense of the vast historical consequences that have followed from the event, and therefore everyone senses that the "facticity" of the event must be on the same level of greatness as the consequences. But, there could hardly be a worse choice as standard of relaibility of historical evidence. And the fact that it has beome conventional to place this event in tandem with the matter of the Resurrection presents a perfect occasion for reflecting on the extent to which the matter of historical reliability has become a business of rumour rather than actual experience. (Here I am speaking of scholarly discussion, but the fact is that popular under-standing tends to follow behind the scholarly convention).

The Gospels as Historical Testimony

The fact is that no one even knows where the Rubicon river is! (In contrast, the site of the crucifixion and the gravesite of Jesus have been identified within a matter of a few square feet at most, having been pointed out continuously to visitors since the day of the events in question.) Any one of several widely-separated streams might have been the actual frontier of Caesar's province and Italy. There are no first-hand testimonies to Caesar's having crossed the Rubicon (wherever it was.) Caesar himself makes no mention in his memoirs of crossing any river. Four historians belonging to the next two or three generations do mention a Rubicon River, and claim that Caesar crossed it. They are: Velleius Paterculus (c. 19 B.C.–30 A.D.); Plutarch (c. 46–120 A.D.); Suetonius (75–160); and Appian (second century.) All of these evidently depended on the one published eye-witness account, that of Asinius Pollio (76 B.C.–5 A.D.)—which account has disappeared without a trace. This contrasts dramatically with the situation with respect to the New Testament documents. Reliable and nearly complete manuscripts of the New Testament are extant from the mid-Fourth century, while there are fragments of such quantity, quality and variety from as far back as the mid-Second century as to make it possible for us to say (following Sir Frederick Kenyon, see above p. 206) that "both the authenticity and the general integrity" of the material in question "may be regarded as finally established."

The identification of the crossing of the Rubicon with the momentous and irreversible decision to seize authority over the empire is explicit in Plutarch—from whom, evidently, we get the notion of this as the type of all momentous decisions in history:

> When he came to the river Rubicon, which parts Gaul within the Alps from the rest of Italy, his thoughts began to work. Now he was just entering upon the danger, and he wavered much in his mind, when he considered the greatness of the enterprise into which he was throwing himself. He checked his course and ordered a halt, while he revolved within himself, and often

changed his opinion, one way and the other, without speaking a word. This was when his purposes fluctuated most.[39]

Plutarch says that Caesar uttered a certain set of words in Greek before stepping towards the Rubicon; Suetonius has him speaking a rather different set of words—in Latin. Suetonius says (see above, p. 183) that "an apparition of superhuman size and beauty was sitting on the river bank, playing a reed pipe," and that it was this "sign" that persuaded Caesar to cross the Rubicon.[40] Plutarch doesn't mention this or any other apparition. Caesar, as already noted, has nothing to say about any of this; and his is the only surviving eye-witness account. What Asinius Pollio wrote, we have no way of knowing.

(Incidentally: neither Collingwood nor any other philosopher of history I have ever read who drags in the case of *Caesar-crossing-the-Rubicon* ever takes any account of the apparitions mentioned by Suetonius when "explaining" what Caesar was doing—even though this is the only place in the documents where anybody offers a *specific* explanation for this *specific* decision! This means that they have entirely by-passed Suetonius in their attribution of motive for these events. They are entitled of course to feel that this as an implausible motive for such a great deed. But when they do dismiss it from consideration they are appealing to their own philosophy and not to *historical* evidence.)

Now, we should be willing to accept that Caesar crossed a frontier on the way back to Rome from his province in Gaul. A good date (though conjectural) is January 10, 49 B.C. And there is nothing much wrong with calling this event, "*Caesar-crossing-the-Rubicon*." With that deed Caesar committed himself to civil war, and many profound consequences have followed, with which we still live. But details of the sort that would make crossing the Rubicon a part of our understanding of Caesar and of these consequences do not exist. It is fantasy to suggest, as Collingwood does, that we can re-think Caesar's thoughts on this occasion. We have no evidence for his thoughts, unless it is in the report of Suetonius, which Collingwood never acknowledges. Nor have we any other circumstances of the occasion. But then, many colorful episodes which are confidently reported in the history-books are of this sort; and the damage that would follow from discrediting their "historicity" would not, after all, be very serious.

But it is an altogether different sort of case with the history of the Risen Christ. Unless we have eye-witness testimonies to the event, and unless we trust them, we have no right to cling to the story of the Risen Christ and to the ineffable consequences that follow for our singular lives, and for all men, and for the cosmos too!

Two frontiers: a River and a Tomb

"Look, the hour is coming, has indeed already come, when you are all to be scattered, each to his home, leaving me alone.... In the world [the Greek reads, "the cosmos"] you will have trouble. But courage! The victory is mine; I have conquered the *cosmos*!" (*John* 16:32–33.) Anticipating—as He could, having the perspective of Eternal God on events that, from His earthly-human perspective were yet to come!—His conquest of death, and of all the demonic realities that prevent the reconciliation of man to man, and of man to nature, and of man-and-nature-together to God, He announced His victory over the cosmos. His disciples did not understand. But they lived to see the day that He went unresisting to death. Others (Joseph of Arimathea, and Nicodemus—not of the Twelve) saw His body into the tomb, and overlaid it, to cover the shame of its inevitable decay with sixty pounds of myrrh and aloes. And then, a huge rock, and a guard of Roman soldiers posted, on pain of death, to prevent any and all possibility of mischief.[41]

Now, to return to the Rubicon. No one today that I know of has invested anything in Suetonius' story about the apparition. Most of us have our minds made up about that sort of possibility. Our views about the plausibility of such an occurrence have been formed out of reading in books whose subject matter is general religious possibility, comparative religion, psychology of religion, religious anthropology, *etc*. And in any case, I am not forced (as an historian) to declare an interest in this particular possibility, given that this story alleged to derive from Pollio, is not seconded by the story in Plutarch. So I am off the hook there.

But there is no authority and no guidance (in terms of general religious possibility) to assist me in the matter of the empty tomb. Nobody claims—least of all do Christians claim!—that the event was an instance of a general religious possibility. There is no possibility of "analogous classification".

The irreducibly essential notion in the case of Caesar crossing the Rubicon is a frontier of some kind; which Caesar crossed, thus initiating a civil war. Since the evidence which purports to give some character to the frontier itself (the Rubicon) is useless, we say: "Assume it. It does not matter. Make a leap of faith! As for the apparition, that is optional: the evidence is not good." The Rubicon is thus left standing as a *notion*—a valuable *notion*. That is all it is. But that is all, for this purpose, that we need.

But the thing at issue in the matter of the empty tomb *is* the empty tomb. A "notion" like the Rubicon will not serve. The "historicity" of the frontier itself is the thing at issue. The eye-witnesses claim that the Unique Son of the Unique God rose as the first (so far, the Unique) member of our human race to enter into Eternal Life. There is no way that we could have views on the general possibilities governing the matters said to be at issue there. Hence, we are absolutely dependent on the eye-witness accounts. These witnesses have our entire faith in their hands. If they are deceived, or if they are lying to us, then (as Martin Luther put it) we are doomed.

If we see some reason not to believe these alleged eyewitnesses, we can call them liars or judge that they were deceived. But we cannot avoid the issue by saying that the "historicity" of the matter is an optional notion.

The Gospels as Historical Testimony

But thank God, we have eyewitness testimonies to the empty tomb. But then, when we say just that, we immediately see how circular the situation is: We *do* believe these unique things done by the unique God because we have unique human eyewitness accounts to give warrant to our belief. If we knew *a priori* that the event was probably true, we could indulge in an act of faith—like the one which keeps *Caesar-crossing-the-Rubicon* in place in the history books.

We must put out of our heads entirely the modern-scholarly-chauvinism that says that the rules of historical evidence were invented in the Nineteenth Century. They were well established in Graeco-Roman practice centuries before the Christian era. They are clearly presumed in the statement of purpose which forms the prologue to the Gospel of Luke (i.e., *Luke* 1:1-4).

There is no event, public or private, in the history of the world for which there is eyewitness testimony more compelling than that for the discovery of the empty tomb on Easter morning. Here are a few essentials of the case:

1) the locale, the day, the time,—everything about the setting is identified precisely. And this is done in writing and addressed to an audience composed largely of persons alive at the time of the alleged event, and many of them within walking distance of the alleged situation;

2) all the stories about the empty tomb and the subsequent appearances of the Risen Lord are told by the alleged eyewitnesses (Peter from Mary; Mark from Peter; Luke from Peter and others; Paul from Peter and others);[42]

3) the eyewitness accounts are not uniform—as follows logically from the circumstance that the different eyewitnesses arrive at different times (some go away and then return); and there is a variety of combinations of witnesses.

There is thus a variety of detail; there are parts of some testimonies that are difficult to reconcile with parts of others, but nothing in any testimony that flatly contradicts anything in any other testimony. The

234   The Greek and Hebrew Origins of our Idea of History

variety in content, taken together with the wide range of responses of the several characters to the same alleged events absolutely undercuts the stupid theory that the disciples got together and made the whole thing up. If they had done that, we would have an official story as tidy and as consistent in detail as the official story on the other side.

From those who don't like the official story from the Jewish and Roman authorities, but who cannot bring themselves to call the eyewitnesses liars or deceived, we get no end of preposterous theories. (It was dark; they went to the wrong tomb. Jesus "swooned," recovered, wandered away. The execution itself was a charade. The authorities took the body.) People who need opportunities to exercise creative imagination in lieu of historical criticism, would be better off turning these gifts to *Caesar-crossing-the-Rubicon*, where there is no embarrassing firsthand testimony, none at all, to cramp their style.

But no one has ever done this—to my knowledge.

Why?

I think it is because we all want to believe that Caesar crossed that Frontier. It seems to be required by everything that follows. The few students of history who are aware of the frailty of the testimony (the silly apparition; the confusion about Caesar's alleged words; the absence of reference in Caesar's own memoirs) are content to press on and pretend not to notice. Let's just assume that the usual laws of reality require that he and his army crossed a more or less standard size stream in a more of less routine way, and that it was a frontier, and that Caesar's crossing it set in motion irreversible effects of the greatest historical importance.

But in precisely the same sense it is required that Jesus passed that frontier of which the Easter story speaks. The difference is, of course, that here (at the Tomb) we cannot simply guess at or assume the means and the circumstances (as we can at the River). We are forced to face the eye-witnesses down. But many people will do anything rather than look those eye-witness in the eye. It is not the paucity of evidence that forces people to these hare-brained fantasies in explanation of the empty tomb. It is rather the embarrassing fullness, and the healthy variety of it.

The dogma of the Incarnation: the first premise of our theory of history:

The Jews said, "Now we are certain that you are possessed. Abraham is dead; the prophets are dead, and yet you say, 'If anyone obeys my teaching he shall not know what it is to die.' Are you greater than our father Abraham, who is dead? The prophets are dead too. What do you claim to be?"

Jesus replied, "If I glorify myself, that glory of mine is worthless. It is the Father who glorifies me, he of whom you say, 'He is our God', though you do not know him. But I know him; if I said that I did not know him I should be a liar like you. But in truth I know him and obey his word."

"Your father Abraham was overjoyed to see my day; he saw it and was glad." The Jews protested, "You are not yet fifty years old. How can you have seen Abraham?" Jesus said, "In very truth I tell you, before Abraham was born, I am." (*John* 8:52–58.)

The central "mystery" or "secret" of which Christians are "stewards" (I *Corinthians* 4:1) is that of the Incarnation of God in Jesus Christ. One of the many facets of that mystery shows us a man like ourselves (the Son of Man) living a life-in-time like our own, who was (is) also identical in authority with God, the Creator of all reality apart from Himself, Whose own being is eternal, knowing no beginning, no subdivision of moments, and no end.

As a son of man, Jesus of Nazareth lived a singular, human, life-in-time, and shared our perspective on time. As a singular individual, born in a moment of time into the stream of time, he had to be taught about the past of his family and his community, about his race, and about the history that stood behind the political realities in which he would live. We have to think of him as radically ignorant of all of these matters of fact until his elders informed him about them.

To see this side of the mystery of the Incarnation with the seriousness it demands we must try to uncover from our own memory, and then to rehearse as deliberately as we can, in our own minds, the process by which we learned as children to locate ourselves in time. We had to be taught certain mental strategies for grasping that our parents were in time before we were in it (a forbidding thought, that tantalizes as it frightens children, as thoughts of monsters do.)

It is difficult for us to reconstruct this mentally. But we all recognize that there was a process of learning that went into acquiring our sense of the radical separateness of past from present, and of past and present together from future. Hardest of all is acquiring the sense of time as extension, and how the various features of the landscape of the past stand in relation to one another. Every parent knows how children persist in questioning on this theme: how old is everything, relative to everything else? How old are you? How old is grandad? When grandad was a boy, how old were you? Where was I?

Out of all the grown-up talk about the past, we eventually learn that there are landmarks by which the grown-ups order the event-filled past. Things are located a certain distance on this side of that side of when George died, or (ditto) "the War." By stages (this depends on the level of seriousness of the discussion that takes place around us) we become aware that there is a hierarchy of these landmarks, and that at the head of this hierarchy is *history*.

There are certain principles that have to be mastered if we are to come to terms with our real place in time. We have to learn the trick of thinking of blocks of time to which our own presence does not belong. And we have to grasp that there are meanings attaching to the events of that time in which we are not present. Instruction in these principles begins very early, and continues through our lifetime—for the fact is that we never really come to terms with this. Something in us resists the exercise, and this tendency to resist is a clue to the most important spiritual principles. There is, in other words, a tension between the two processes of instruction: in the truths about our human situation in time and in the truths about our eternal situation.

Jesus lived an authentic, singular-human life-in-time, subject to the limitation of all such life. In his life, as in ours, there was the experience of learning. Before he learned something, he did not know it. There was a time before he knew his own name, or the names of those around him; before he knew that he had been born in Bethlehem. That he had been taken as an infant to Egypt. That there had been a house in Egypt before there was this house in Nazareth. That he was Joshua ben Joseph, descended from the line described in *Matt* 1:1–17 and *Luke* 3:23–38. That he was as Jew. We have to grasp the fact that as a man he shared the anxieties that belong to our being "creatures of allotted time" (as Karl Barth expresses it.) Yet we know that he declared himself to be identical in authority with the Lord, the Creator God of the book of Genesis, the God of Abraham, Isaac and Jacob. While he lived in our human time, he lived and reigned simultaneously in eternity.

As the Son of Man, he must have lived really in the course of human time. He must have chosen and rejected. Before he chose, opposite alternatives were radically open, as they are to us. (The temptation narratives make this point [Matt 4:1–11 and parallels].) Before things happened to him, he was ignorant of them. He learned (as something new) of John the Baptist's death at Herod's hands (*Mt* 14:12–13). His mood and his immediate plans were changed by this news—which surely makes the point that the death of John was not a fact for him before he learned of it: it was "news" to him, no less than to the others.

Elsewhere, he is portrayed as speaking with sovereign confidence and knowledge of what lies ahead. He expressed fear of what he *must* face (*Mk* 14:33:—..."horror and dismay came over him!") In Gethsemene, he spoke as though his end (which he had already predicted) was still undecided: ("'Abba, Father,' he said, all things are possible to thee; take this cup away from me...." [*Mk.* 14:36 and parallels]). He spoke of all that would befall Jerusalem after his death and Resurrection. He spoke of the destruction of the Temple and the massacre of the population. He spoke of them as certain judgements. (*Lk* 19:39–44, 21:5–38, and parallels.)

It is an intrinsic part of our confidence in his authority over our lives that he fully shared our humanity—therefore, like us, he had to learn, to fear the unknown, to doubt the unseen. New things happened to him as they do to us. He was not play-acting. He suffered anxiety in respect to the future and he could be dismayed by "news" in the present. But we are no less committed to the belief that he spoke with the authority of He who is sovereign over all the events of past, present, and future time.

There is no possibility of our grasping this. Our dogma requires us to believe it, and we should not apologize for it. But to try to visualize it or to conceptualize this reality is, in my view, perhaps worse than apologizing for it. We have no right to speak as though we can see anything from the perspective of eternity. If we attempt to do so, we alienate our hearers, who know that we do not stand where God stands, and we thus discredit the Gospel. The challenge of thinking from the perspective of eternity is on a par with the famous challenge not to think of an elephant. Simply to have the proposition stated gives away the fact that we are helpless to deal with it. Nowhere in the Gospels does Jesus offer an insight into what eternity "is like." Nowhere does he speak to us as though we could share the perspective he had from eternity.

But we *do* find Jesus speaking to us from that perspective. But in all such instances we find that what is said from the perspective of eternity is coupled with a statement from the perspective of the singular human life-in-time. In other words, we do find him speaking *simultaneously* from the perspectives of a singular life-in-time and the life-in-eternity.

The Gospels as Historical Testimony

Let us consider some passages where Jesus addresses himself directly to the issue of his authority. For example, there is the series of confrontations between Jesus and his adversaries which are grouped together in chapters 7–10 of the Gospel of *John*. The *New English Bible* groups these chapters into one section with the useful title: "The Great Controversy". The "controversy" is over the matter of Jesus' authority. Jesus' miracles have aroused expectations that he might soon declare himself as Messiah. (7:25–31.) He accuses the religious leaders of wishing to kill him (7:19–20.) Their animosity, he says, will result in his having "to go away to him who sent me" (32–33.)

Is this "going away" to be understood as a future event? Obviously. It refers to the pending outcome of his controversy: he will be arrested, tried, crucified, he will die and then "go away to him who sent me". After that (further into the future), "'You will look for me, but you will not find me. Where I am, you cannot come'.(34.) So the Jews said to one another, 'Where does he intend to go, that we should not be able to find him?'"(35.)

Jesus had shifted tenses on his listeners. He spoke of "where I am going." In the next instant, he was speaking of "where I am." Where he will be is where he is. Where he will be is likewise where he came from.

The effect of this is disconcerting to all his listeners—infuriating to his adversaries. He spoke from a perspective which we cannot share, not even imaginatively. He spoke from the perspective of the One who lives eternally, Who is therefore before all things and likewise will be after all things. He could therefore say: "I know where I came from, and where I am going." (*John* 8:14.) "My home" is in eternity (*John* 8:23.) He *is* there now as he tells them that he has come from there (that is, that he *was* there.) If we have not been prepared for this, the effect of these passages will be like being at the wheel of a vehicle whose transmission is suddenly *possessed*, and is shifting its gears eccentrically, of its own will.

The events of his life in time are *also* events in eternity. *These events are the eternal referents of all the events that belong to the sacred history of the Jews.* Thus, Abraham, who stood at the head of this chain of events *now* (in eternity) knows the meaning of these events. Or (it is equally true to say): Abraham (now, in eternity) looks *back* on the completion of the events of Jesus' life-in-time—even now as Jesus, speaking (at this moment-in-time, before these events have been completed) looks *forward* to them. Thus: "Your father Abraham *was* overjoyed to see my day; he *saw* it and was glad" (*John* 8:56-7.)

But how does this man, born like all humans in a moment of time, living a singular life-in-time, moving from past, through present to future, know what Abraham *saw*? How does he come by the perspective that allows him to speak of Abraham's present vision of things? And what does he intend by speaking of Abraham's present vision of things in the past tense ("Abraham was overjoyed to see my day")?

Abraham "saw this day". Abraham's life-in-time moved toward these events, the events of Jesus' life-in-time, which are the previously hidden (soon to be revealed) fulfilment of the covenant-history which Abraham's life set in motion. Jesus' hearers know that Abraham in his own lifetime did not see "this day." Jesus is portraying himself (who *is*, before Abraham was born) looking *now* upon Abraham, who in turn is looking *back* upon the completion of the covenant—which (as Jesus of Nazareth speaks, at this moment of his life-in-time) lies ahead.

This unnerving liberty that Jesus takes regarding the *tenses* that properly apply to events of his life-in-time and to their meanings, is the broadest of all the clues he gave to the character of his messiahship. The implications of these words were much more unnerving to his adversaries, (as the Gospels clearly state) than the hints that are in his miracles, even those miracles involving the raising of the dead! It baffled all the witnesses, friendly and hostile.

Jesus conveyed to his friends the mystery of his identity by speaking to them simultaneously from the perspective of eternity and of the life-in-time. The texts obviously convey this faithfully: the reactions of the listeners are described as ranging from exasperation to disorientation. His disciples were unnerved by these confrontations with religious leaders and were in no position to justify what his adversaries considered a perverse game with words. But while they could not vindicate him, neither could they leave him: "So Jesus asked the Twelve, 'Do you also want to leave me?' Simon Peter answered him, 'Lord to whom shall we go? Your words are words of eternal life.'" (*John* 6:67–68.)

But unlike the first hearers of these words, we can see everything that he did and hear everything that he said in the light of the historical knowledge of his death, resurrection and ascension. The meaning of what he was claiming is plain. Towards the end, when he was preparing them for the knowledge of his death and resurrection, they did begin to see it. He said: "'I came from the Father and have come into the world. Now I am leaving the world again and going to the Father.' His disciples said, 'Why, this is plain speaking; this is no figure of speech.'" (*John* 16:28–29.)

How He who came from the Father, and therefore belonged to eternity, could be unreservedly in the world and fully human, belonging without deceit to our limited life-in-time, Jesus nowhere offers to explain. *How* he was simultaneously in time and in eternity cannot be visualized by us. It cannot be grasped or thought through. But it can be stated plainly. It is no figure of speech.

There is a striking difference in the way in which John (on the one hand) and the synoptists (on the other) convey this fact of his speaking simultaneously from the perspectives of time and eternity. The gospel of John is notable for conveying Jesus' addresses at length; and in the course of these addresses we find the abrupt and deliberate shifting of tenses within a single sentence which we have noted already. In the other gospels, the effect is of Jesus stepping episodically out of the perspective of his life-in-time and announcing something unexpectedly, and seemingly out of context, from the perspective of eternity.

When his seventy emissaries returned from their preaching mission, He said in greeting to them: "I watched how Satan fell, like lightning out of the sky." (*Luke* 10:18.) But Satan had not fallen. Satan has still not fallen. This is a statement from the perspective of eternity, after the work is accomplished for which Abraham entered into covenant with God; Satan's fall *will* (from our perspective in time) be true as past event when the lion shall lie down with the lamb. Jesus sees here and now the "moment" of His *future* triumph over Satan.

Elsewhere, he sees other moments in the history yet-to-come between His crucifixion in time and the end of all things. When He entered Jerusalem at the beginning of the week that ended with His crucifixion, He was greeted by the crowds: "Blessings on him who comes as king in the name of the LORD!" (*Lk* 19:38.) The pharisees told Him to rebuke the crowds. But He replied:

> "I tell you, if my disciples keep silence the stones will shout aloud." When he came in sight of the city, he wept over it and said, "If only you had known, on this great day, the way that leads to peace! But no; it is hidden from your sight. For a time will come upon you, when your enemies will set up siege-works against you; they will encircle you and hem you in at every point; they will bring you to the ground, you and your children within your walls, and not leave you one stone standing on another, because you did not recognize God's moment when it came." (*Lk* 19:39–44.)

In that moment he saw what Josephus describes in the *Jewish War* (6:2 and 12:2) and (says Edersheim):

> He wept...not with a still weeping (εδακρυσεγ) as at the grave of Lazarus, but with loud and deep lamentation (εκλαυσεν). The contrast was, in deed, terrible between the Jerusalem that rose before him [as he entered, *Luke* 19:37] in all its beauty, glory, and

The Gospels as Historical Testimony 243

security, and the Jerusalem which He saw in vision dimly rising on the sky, with the camp of the enemy around about it on every side, hugging it closer and closer in deadly embrace, and the very 'stockade' [N.E.B. = "siege-works"] which the Roman Legions raised around it; then, another scene in the shifting panorama, and the city laid with the ground, and the gory bodies of her children among the ruins; and yet another scene; the silence and desolateness of death by the Hand of God—not one stone left upon another! We know only too well how literally this vision has become reality, and yet, though uttered as prophecy by Christ, and its reason so clearly stated, Israel to this day knows not the things which belong unto its peace, and the upturned scattered stones of its dispersion are crying out in testimony against it [written in 1883.] But to this day, also do the tears of Christ plead with the Church on Israel's behalf, and His words bear within them precious seed of promise."[43]

The synoptists present these "visions" as episodic. But we must not imagine that Jesus' grasp of the eternal perspective was episodic. We cannot expect the gospel writers to succeed in recreating the consciousness of Jesus. We assume they were not trying to. No more than we, could they see time from the perspective of eternity. John's characteristic way of conveying the simultaneity of Christ's eternal and human perspective on time is in his citing of Jesus' sovereign ways with the tenses of verbs. These passages offer a insurmountable challenge for philosophy. The synoptists describe episodes in which Jesus speaks from the perspective of his knowledge of eternity. These present equally insurmountable challenges to "psychology".

But we are really falling into a trap if we try to systematize the dogma in this way. There is no way of grasping this matter. But it can be stated plainly—it is not a figure of speech. His actions and his words were controlled by the Plan of which he was the Master. He knew how the story ended. He is the author of the timetable which controls the events of his life, which are in turn the measure of the meaning of all the events of history. He stood (stands) at the end of time—of that time and all previous time, and all subsequent time (including our time) and he knows how it ends. "This is not a figure of speech."

In the light of this, we can see that his behaviour would not be controlled by calculations of political forces or social forces or probabilities of success and failure. The disciples thought (as we do) in these terms. And having thought everything through they argued with him about what he should do. In *John* 7 they announce to him that, having thought all things through, *they* believe this to be the *right time* for him to go up to Jerusalem. They had tested public opinion, and they knew enough about the history of their own people to know what were the objective pre-conditions for success. But he knew how the story ended, and what must be done and how and when. "The right time for me has not yet come, but any time is right for you" (*John* 7:6.) All times are more or less "right" for us who have to calculate probabilities and risk and hope in everything we do. There is always something to be said for acting and there is always something to be said for not acting yet; and always reason to think that we should have acted sooner. "They [the disciples] can go up to Jerusalem at any time; Christ cannot, for he stands in the midst of the divine plan of salvation, whose *kairoi* are definitely fixed by God."[44]

Chapter 8:

Christ the Lord of Time

The Christian theory of history is the only theory of history whose authority derives from history itself. It is the only theory of history which concedes to history the authority to contradict other knowledge.

On the Jewish view, history has the authority to contradict philosophy because it delineates the Plan of God, which tends to the overcoming of the present order of Being. Such a proposition could not be built on the premises of Greek thought—and indeed there is nothing in Greek thought that even hints at it. It could never occur to any Greek thinker that Being itself was the product of the will of God. As that thought could not occur, *a fortiori* the thought could not occur that the whole order of Being could be changed, *re-ordered*, by the will of God. Being was *being*: the sum-total of all that is and all that can be thought. Our reason works for us because Being (or at least that part of it that we need to be familiar with in order to live according to the will of the gods) is orderly: i.e., governed by laws. Everything that is, is to be understood as an instance of some class of things, governed by law. The possibility of a meaning intrinsic to history is as unthinkable as the possibility of Being which is subject to a will which is extrinsic to itself. In fact the one possibility implies the other. And thus to speak of history's *own authority* (the Greeks believed) was to deny the foundations to reason itself.

The Greeks, however, clearly regretted the impossibility of making a case for history's own authority. They were drawn to history, in certain moods, but could not find any way of defending its authority without endangering the footings of philosophy. The post-Christian man has sought to keep a place in his heart for history, but is embarrassed by the fact that the footings of our theory of history were established in dogmatic theology. Nineteenth-century philosophy of history was in essence an effort to discover some rationale for history after philosophy itself had been separated from those dogmatic-theological footings. It sought to express in consistent terms *and without reference to Christian dogma* possibilities of meaning into which disciplined reason gives us no passage at all. Inevitably, the post-Christian mind has given up on philosophy of history altogether. It has no time for any theory which concedes to history the authority to contradict its philosophy or science.

Teleology and eschatology

I have found it useful at several places in this book to bring my argument into relief by the device of extensive critique of an opposite or at least antagonistic argument. Now, before drawing together the threads of my argument in summary, I want to consider carefully the argument of a little book which in recent years has become the favourite choice of college teachers of history who wish to give their students a taste of theory of history and need a single book for the purpose. The book is E.H. Carr's, *What is History*?[1] The main appeal of this book to the historians is that it seems to offer the most positive case for continued confidence in the value of the study of history, while taking into account the low prestige of history among the philosophers. At the same time it unwittingly exposes (on my reading) the fact of the historians' continued practical dependence on propositions which are indefensible except on dogmatic-Christian grounds. The poignancy in this is made all the clearer by the fact of the author's explicit hostility to Christian theology, and his consequent effort to banish theology from theory of history.

Carr's description of the present state of the idea of history is roughly as follows:

For two hundred years, he argues, all the history that was worth reading had been written on the assumption that the historical process is working out some purpose, working towards some goal. But nowadays, there is a widespread feeling that the political setbacks of the twentieth century have discredited the progressive view of history. But this, he argues further, is only a partial truth. The larger truth is that the majority of nineteenth-century historians had a simplistic vision of progress which circumstance has not vindicated, and which a more realistic philosophy would never have entertained: "The notion of a finite and clearly definable goal of progress in history, so often postulated by nineteenth-century thinkers, has proved inapplicable and barren."[2] Believing that they were promised an absolute, uniform, cumulative and ubiquitious process; and discovering that in many ways the mid-twentieth century was less to their liking than what they thought they knew about the eighteenth century, the public and guild of historians have both turned against progressive interpretations of history's meaning. This is especially true of those classes of people and those nations who have lost certain privileges as a result of the advances in the liberties and privileges of the previously unprivileged. ("All this talk about the decline of civilization...[as A.J.P. Taylor observed] 'means only that university professors used to have domestic servants and now do their own washing up.'"[3] It was a mistake to believe (as the Enlightenment did) that history was the story of "progress towards the goal of the perfection of man's estate on earth".[4]

Nonetheless, Carr feels that something of abiding worth has come from our experience of this misguided faith in linear and cumulative progress. The spell of medieval historiography had to be undone; and in the gap left following the exorcising of that spell, there grew the superstition of linear and cumulative progress towards the goal of perfection. While that faith reigned, an entirely new and entirely adequate science of history was quietly developed. It contained a "standard of significance, which is also a standard of objectivity...[by which historians] distinguish between the significant and the accidental."⁵ This standard corresponds, within the secular theory of history, to the notion of divine purpose in the medieval (eschatological) theory. If the objectivity of this modern standard is doubted today, it is because of the unfortunate assumption that it derives its validity from faith in "progress toward the goal of the perfection of man's estate on earth." People wrongly assume that since the latter confidence is discredited, they must give upon the hope of finding meaning in history. This explains the current force of either "mysticism" (defined as "the view that the meaning of history lies somewhere outside history") or "cynicism" (defined as the view "that history has no meaning, or a multiplicity of equally valid or invalid meanings, or the meaning which we arbitrarily choose to give it.")⁶

In fact, Carr argues, the standard of objectivity and of significance established by the Enlightenment was the right one. All it needs for its justification is continued faith that history has direction. And this faith does not entail—morally, logically, or in any other way—the expectation that perfection will be achieved in history. It merely requires a notion of "the absolute"—

> ...something still incomplete and in process of becoming—something in the future towards which we move, which begins to take shape only as we move towards it, and in the light of which, as we move forward, we gradually shape our interpretation of the past.⁷

This sense of the absolute still needs to be based upon faith in progress. But faith in progress does not require an "eschatological" foundation—only a "teleological" one: it is sufficient that we have "the sense of direction in history"—"the future in our bones." The authority of progress justifies our acceptance of "success" as the criterion for inclusion in that selective record of the past which we call history.⁸ We are assured of "objectivity" in our judgments, so long as

Christ the Lord of Time

we allow the future to judge the past. This orientation towards the future is what gives history its distinctiveness as a field of inquiry. It is the heart of its method. It is what qualifies it as a distinct "science".

> Our criterion is not an absolute in the static sense of something that is the same yesterday, today, and forever: such an absolute is incompatible with the nature of history. But it is an absolute in respect of our interpretation of the past. It rejects the relativist view that one interpretation is true in its own time and place, and it provides the touchstone by which our interpretation on the past will ultimately be judged. It is this sense of direction which alone enables us to order and interpret the events of the past.[9]

> The historian's interpretation of the past, his selection of the significant and the relevant, evolves with the progressive emergence of new goals... The old interpretation is not rejected, but is both included and superseded in the new. Historiography is a progressive science, in the sense that it seeks to provide constantly expanding and deepening insights into a course of events which is itself progressive.[10]

> Thus, the historian of the 1920's was nearer to objective judgement than the historian of the 1880's and... the historian of today is nearer than the historian of the 1920's; the historian of the year 2000 may be nearer still. This illustrates my thesis that objectivity in history does not and cannot rest on some fixed and immovable standard of judgment existing here and now, but only a standard which is laid up in the future and is evolved as the course of history advances.[11]

> ...history is meaningless in a static world. History in its essence is change, movement, or—if you do not cavil at the old-fashioned

word—progress... History properly so-called can be written only by those who find and accept a sense of direction in history itself.[12]

It is to meet this need for recovery of the sense of history as purposive (because forward-directed), that Carr has offered the response of a working professional to the question: "What is history?" Carr's case seems to have a distinctly logical side and a distinctly moral side (though Carr himself does not offer this distinction.) Curiously: what I see as the logical side of the case is reminiscent of the logical side of Augustine's case. That is: Carr discovers the possibility of history's speaking to us with authority arising directly out of our speculation about the elusiveness of our "present". We try to grasp the notion of the present directly; but we find that we cannot grasp the thought of the present except as we include the notion of its process into some future. This reveals to us that "The present has no more than a notional existence as an imaginary dividing line between the past and the future... It would, I think, be easy to show that, since past and future are part of the same time-span, interest in the past and interest in the future are interconnected."[13]

The "moral side" (as I call it) amounts to a call to recognize that we are being less than mature (or perhaps less than civilized, or perhaps less than modern) if we do not keep the future before us as we read about the past. "The line of demarcation between prehistoric and historical times is crossed when people cease to live only in the present," Carr says—evidently forgetting that he has earlier declared that it was logically impossible to live in the present—"the present [having] no more than a notional existence as an imaginary line...!" That line of demarcation is crossed when people "become consciously interested both in their past and in their future."[14] He quotes Huizinga with approval: "historical thinking is always teleological."[15] And to clinch the case, there is a third sort of argument—the argument from instinct: "Good historians, I suspect, whether they think about it or not, have the future in their bones. Besides the question 'Why?' the historian also asks the question 'Whither?'[16]

I have no interest in denying Carr's case so far in any of its aspects. I would agree that, if they are to be logical, if they are to be responsible, if they are to keep sane, historians cannot talk about the events of history unless they accept as the minimum meaning of those events that they are being moved forward by some at-least-intrinsic dynamic that derives from the future—and this notwithstanding the fact that the future is not yet. But Carr fails, as atheistic logic at this test must fail, to provide a reason for believing in this future which is not yet. Carr cannot avail himself of precisely the class of argument that is needed to show that the future is able to work an effect on the past, because he will not, as he puts it, "resort to mysticism". "Mysticism", in Carr's usage, stands for any form of "the view that the meaning of history lies somewhere outside history, in the realms of theology or eschatology."[17] Carr distinguishes between a "teleological" and an "eschatological" reading of history, and urges that we embrace the former and reject the latter.

The matter at issue is whether we can have a "teleological" view that is not, both practically and theoretically, also an eschatological one. Carr's case for separation inadvertently exposes (as I believe) the logical and the practical impossibility of the operation.

In aid of his case, Carr offers a brief history of the "linear view of history."[18] This, Carr suggests, is "an invention of the Jews", embodied in what Christians call the books of the Old Testament. Despite fits of insight into this "linear" reality (notably in Herodotus,[19] on Mondays, Wednesdays and Fridays), classical historians had been overwhelmed by the cyclical quality of man's historical experience, and had accordingly "assimilated the processes of history to the processes of nature."[20] But the Judaeo-Christian view is not merely linear, says Carr; it is also teleological.

During the Renaissance, Carr explains, the Judaeo-Christian method of reading history was stripped of its burden of "theodicy". The resultant method is secular, but still "teleological" in that secularists, no less than Christians and Jews, can only talk about history by positing some future referant toward which events move. To talk about history is to describe events in motion forward. If "past history" is a tautology, so it would seem is "teleological history".

> It was the Jews, and after them the Christians, who introduced an entirely new element [into the classical tradition of historiography—which, as we have seen, was hobbled by the "cyclical" persuasion] by postulating a goal towards which the historical process is moving—the teleological view of history. History has thus acquired a meaning and purpose, but at the expense of losing its secular quality.[21]

Carr has already said that we must reject the view that finds the meaning of history "outside history", "in the realm of eschatology". What then, is the difference between an "eschatological" view of things and a "teleological" view of things? In ordinary usage, we speak of an "eschatological framework" when the energy, or the dynamic, or the source of the purpose that drives events forward is thought to be in God's keeping. But where it is argued (as for instance by Marx) that the end toward which history is working is not in God's keeping (there being no God), then the energy or the dynamic or the source of the purpose that drives events forward is seen as contained exclusively and without remainder within the historical occasions themselves; and on this premise, history is read "teleologically" but not "eschatologically".

It is crucial to Carr's indictment against the Judaeo-Christian view of history that because the Jews and the Christians read history "eschatologically" they read history as "theodicy". Immediately following the passage just cited (i.e., "It was the Jews, etc. ...") comes this sentence: "The attainment of the goal of history would automatically mean the end of history: history itself became a theodicy."[22] This particular slander against the Christian view of history's meaning was

Christ the Lord of Time

first established in the Enlightenment. So effective was the propaganda on this matter by the Voltairean theorists of history, that it is even today as stoutly declaimed and as blithely undocumented as by Voltaire himself. Nevertheless: contra Voltaire—and contra Carr, and contra Karl Popper[23] and contra Peter Gay[24]—it does not follow that an eschatological view of history is a view of history-as-total-theodicy. It does not follow from the belief that God does everything for a purpose that we are privy to His mind. Secular theorists of history have been determined since Voltaire first suggested the theme to hang the charge of theodicizing upon Christian historians holus-bolus. Carr tells the story of the liberation of history from "the medieval view":

> The Renaissance restored the classical view of an anthropocentric world and of the primacy of reason, but for the pessimistic classical view of the future substituted an optimistic view derived from the Jewish-Christian tradition. Time, which had once been hostile and corroding, now became friendly and creative: contrast Horace's 'Damnosa quid non imminuit dies?' with Bacon's 'Veritas temporis filia.' The rationalists of the Enlightenment, who were the founders of modern historiography, retained the Jewish-Christian teleological view, but secularized the goal; they were thus enabled to restore the rational character of the historical process itself. History became progress towards the goal of the perfection of man's estate on earth.[25]

There is a good deal that is shifty in this brief passage. I want to seize on a few of the discrepancies of thought that we find here, precisely because they are so blatant, and afford us a relatively easy opportunity to point up certain fallacies which inform the modern theory of history—which, in the much more subtle handling of Peter Gay[26] for example, are harder to detect, though they are the same fallacies.

Gay and Carr would agree on the main features about how the modern theory of history came about. First, there were the Greeks and the Romans, "basically unhistorical" people, who, when they thought of history at all, took "a cyclical view which assimilates the process of history to the processes of nature." The Christians "introduced an entirely new element" into this pre-historical stuff, making it at last historical; this they did by "postulating a goal towards which the historical process is moving—the teleological view of history."

In the next breath, Carr unwittingly contradicts his entire case. "History has thus [in the transition from the classical zeitgeist to the Judaeo-Christian] acquired a meaning and purpose, but at the expense of losing its secular quality." We can't have this both ways: either the Greeks wrote history or they did not. He has just told us that the addition to the Judaeo-Christian element turned what the Greeks and Romans used to write into history. Now he speaks of the Christians taking the "secular quality" out of "history". What history?

He has already told us of a "line of demarcation" that is crossed when people "become consciously interested both in the past and in their future." Only those on the far side of that line of demarcation know history. "Historical thinking" (he quotes Hunzinga) "is always teleological". The Greeks obviously belong on the "pre-historical" side of his line. By this logic, the addition of the teleological element can turn pre-historical thinking into historical thinking. But then, if you take the teleological element out, you obviously cannot describe what you revert to as history. And (reading the process forward again) you cannot say that the Christians took the "secular quality" out of the classical tradition of "history".

And even if we overlook this inconsistency and agree to call this pre-Christian literature "history", is it true in fact to say that it was "secular" in quality? If the word "secular" here means what it usually means, it certainly does not apply to the literature of the Greeks and Romans generally, nor by exception to the work of its "historians", including the two great names, Thucydides and Herodotus. There is no lack of tributes to God and the gods in these latter. In fact, if we want to read history as "theodicy" (in the correct, dictionary sense of the word), we will find more of that sort of history in Herodotus than in Augustine.

My point is that history did not become "theodicy" incidentally to its becoming "full of purpose" (eschatological). If Carr had kept to his original presentation—that the possibility of writing history enters the classical world with the Christians—then he would have a coherent, consistent, and I would say totally correct case. We would then have an argument for reserving the word "history" for narratives of the past which are deliberately teleological. We would then have also a prima facie case for saying that the Christian view of the human situation in time made "history" (in this correct definition of the word) possible.

"Time, which had once been hostile and corroding now became friendly and creative," writes Carr. When had time been "hostile and corrosive?" When did it become "friendly and creative?" He wants to present the secularizing of the medieval view as having provided a *return* to a positive, forward-looking view of history—which, by his own original thesis, was not there in the first place.

If Christians saw history as "friendly and creative" it was because they believed that time had been redeemed—because the Redeemer was active within history. We cannot abandon this crucial heart of the Christian view of history without also abandoning our view of history as "linear".

In the Christian view of things there is, Carr says, "a goal" for history. Correctly, we should rather speak of "an end" rather than "a goal". Christians believe that what lies ahead of all past and present event is in principle decided and achieved now. From the perspective of eternity, history is over now. In the Incarnation, Crucifixion and Resurrection of Jesus Christ the end of history, as prefigured in the Covenant of God with Israel, is accomplished, and what remains is the manifestation of this accomplishment. All Christian theorizing about history's meaning depends upon this religious vision—which may be absolutely real or absolutely unreal, absolutely true or absolutely untrue, but certainly cannot be "secularized"! It is because time (in the light of this faith) is known to be contained in eternity—"redeemed", or "completed", or "healed"—that events-in-time are susceptible to being accepted as "friendly" (in Carr's trivialization of that vision) or "creative" (ditto).

Our Christian faith has provided the world with a dynamic confidence in history which depends on our understanding that history is tending towards a completion of all meaning. We see that completion of all meaning approaching us down the path of history itself. We know what we know about this meaning because we are told it from the only perspective from which it could be known—that is, from eternity. This is plain speaking. It is not a figure of speech.

The dogma of the Incarnation tells us that insofar as there is meaning in our singular lives it is because we live in history. This is another way of saying that insofar as there is meaning in our singular lives it is because we live in Christ. The way in which man participates in eternity is revealed in history—in the history of the life on earth of Jesus of Nazareth, which is the fulfilment (in history and in eternity) of the History of Israel, which is at once the paradigm of the history of all other nations and the centering theme of world history.

• • •

> When all things began, the Word already was. The Word dwelt with God, and what God was, the Word was. The Word, then, was with God at the beginning, and through him all things came to be; no single thing was created without him... So the Word became flesh; he came to dwell among us, and we saw his glory, such glory as befits the Father's only Son, full of grace and truth. (*John* 1:1–3,14.)

Christian theorists of history have not always been as forthright about this as they ought to be: *a faithful Christian theory of history stands on dogma, not on philosophy*. Dogmatic faith has consequences for thought. And these can be legitimately (i.e., faithfully) and productively expressed in the vocabulary of philosophy (as in the words of John, just quoted). (In truth: the only philosophy worth having is that which does express the consequences for thought of what we know dogmatically.) But there is no possibility for Christians of a free-floating philosophy of history.

Modern philosophy of history began as a program for stating in consistent, objectively irresistible terms the possibilities for thought that during the entire medieval period were believed to follow from the dogma of the Incarnation. Inertia is the full and sufficient explanation for the fact that philosophy of history, divorced from Christian dogma, did not vanish without trace into the province of ontological philosophy.

The process I refer to here began outside the academies in the Age of the Enlightenment (notably under the influence of empiricists, following the example of David Hume) and then moved inside the academies (where the most significant influence was the idealistic philosophy of Hegel and his *epigoni*) in the mid-nineteenth century. The collapse of the prestige of philosophy of history is now nearly complete.

Arthur Link succintly summarizes the outcome:

> Now, the historian, along with most other intellectuals in the modern world, long ago concluded that Biblical faith was irrelevant, that it did not validate his methodology. No sooner had he repudiated the Biblical foundations, however, than scientists themselves began to undermine reasons for believing in scientific certainty. These two great erosions have by our own day gone a long way toward destroying the intellectual and faithful foundations of historical methodology.[27]

The truth is that disciplined reason gives us no passage at all into any meanings of which history might speak with its own authority. The post-Christian mind gladly concedes this. Its investments are entirely in the sciences. It has no time for authentic philosophy of history—that is, for any theory which concedes to history the authority to contradict philosophy or science.

A faithful Christian theory of history begins with the dogma of the Incarnation. It begins, that is, with the proposition that the most important things we know about the whole course of the human progress through time we know because we are *told* them with the authority of the only One who could tell us. We are told these things from the perspective of eternity (which we cannot share, even imaginatively.) We are told them in words, and we see them enacted in deeds in this life-in-time.

Karl Barth writes of the life-in-time of Jesus:

> At the heart of all other times, both before and after [is] the time in which God Himself was this man, and therefore had time, a life-time. It is the Creator of all reality distinct from Himself who, taking flesh of our flesh, also took time, at the heart of what we think we know as time.... All other times are now controlled by this time, i.e., dominated, limited and determined by their proximity to it.[28]

It is *not* the case that Jesus' life-in-time (being the life of the Eternal lived in time) somehow collapses the normal distinctions between past, present and future (as the "existentialists" would have it). On the contrary, the life of the Eternal in time fixes the distinction between past, present, and future: "In and with this present [the life-in-time of Jesus], eternity creates in time real past and real future, distinguishes between them, and is itself the bridge and the way from one to the other."[29]

The dogma of the Incarnation is the ground of our confidence that singular-human meaning is permanent, and that it is secured for eternity in the same way and by the same power as historical meaning. We are told that the singular life of Jesus of Nazareth accomplished finally in time the purpose for which there is all human history. This singular life accomplished the purpose for which Abraham and all who belong in the sequence of men who act deliberatly in obedience to God are committed: the reconciliation of all men to all other men, of men to nature, and of man-and-nature-together to God. The outcome of this work is to be a new order of being.

The dogma of the Incarnation tells us that a singular life-in-time has (in the past tense) won irreversible victory over the limitations which belong to the finitude of this present order of being. The eternal is already in our midst. The entire process of history is working out the victory of eternity over being. If all this is true, history had the authority to tell us truths that contradict the truths that describe being. But we can say this of history only if we can say what we have just said of Jesus of Nazareth:

—that his authority is the same as the authority of He who is in the Jewish Bible called the God of Israel;

—that his life, death and resurrection have accomplished in time and in eternity the purpose for which Abraham entered into covenant with God. Of this latter (the covenant) we have already said:

—that it preceded creation;

—that it is the purpose for which there is creation;

—that it is the decisive content of all human history.

In John's Gospel we find on the lips of Jesus this recurring formula: "...the time approaches, indeed it is already here" (*inter alia* 4:23, 5:25.) The prophets spoke in a similar vein. (For example: *Ezekiel* 7:2–3: "An end *is coming*... The end is *now* upon you.") Like the prophets he spoke of what must follow because of what is and what has been. That is, he assumed a moral economy at work in history. What will happen must happen because human actions lead to appropriate and inevitable consequences. This moral economy is the warp of human history. But, again like the prophets, he assumes that there is a divine economy of grace, which is the woof of human history. Unlike the prophets, he speaks confidently of the end-result of the work of the economy of grace. This is because he speaks from the perspective of eternity.

Jesus spoke of the actions of his life as somehow governed by the whole of the historical past. What he will do, he *must* do because the entire history of the covenant is fulfilled in him.

In the process which *begins* with Abram/Abraham's decision all mankind are reconciled to God. This applies to all the generations prior to Abraham and generations subsequent. This process *ends in* the events of the life, death, resurrection and ascension of Jesus of Nazareth. Thus all that the prophets said with respect to this process is fulfilled in him. It has to be stressed again that the prophets spoke of this process of reconciliation as the ultimate law of the cosmos. There is a created order because there must be this work of reconciliation. In a moral sense, therefore, history, or the purpose for which there is history, must be thought of as preceding creation. There is no point in making promises about man's reconciliation to God if we leave out the natural order. Man suffers because he is not at one with nature. Nature punishes him with pain, and finally kills him. Therefore, the reconciliation of man to God necessarily requires a new order of nature: nature reconciled to God—the lion lying down with the lamb, the child playing at the hole of the adder. It follows from this that the whole order of nature is undergoing redemption as a by-effect of the redemption of man, which is the work of history, and which is *being done* by the work of Christ. Paul wrote: "For the created universe waits with eager expectation for God's sons to be revealed. It was made the victim of frustration, not by its own choice, but because of him who made it so; yet always there was hope, because the universe itself is to be freed from the shackles of immortality and enter upon the liberty and splendour of the children of God." (*Romans* 8:19–22.)

Jesus makes this explicit when he speaks of nature's processes as sub-processes of the history which he is fulfilling. He directs his hearers to the fields and he says that the time is ready for God's purposes for man to be accomplished. (*John* 4:35) He "curses" the fig-tree (*Lk* 21:29–31) for not bearing figs. But is it not "out of season" for figs? Not from the perspective which he has already assumed as accomplished by his death, resurrection and ascension.

Again, *later*, several hours nearer to his death by crucifixion, he resumes the human perspective in time. Walking to the place of crucifixion, he tells the crowds "...if these things are done when the wood is green, what will happen when it is dry?" (*Lk* 23:30–31.) He is not yet dead, and his resurrection has not followed from his death, or his ascension from his resurrecton. Where he had "cursed" the fig-tree a few days before for not knowing the news that nature is redeemed by his *accomplished* deed in history (accomplished, that is, from the perspective of eternity), now (days later) he contemplates disconsolately the long passages of history yet to come: generations yet unborn, but for whose sins he is about to die. There is more *history* yet to come before the relation between *man* and *nature* is what it will be when man-and-nature-together are reconciled to God. The relation between man and nature is still what it always was and always will be until the whole work for which he is about to die is accomplished. Meantime, it is right to draw "metaphors" from nature for what is happening in history. So long as there is still *time*, there will be new birth, and growth, and green wood turning over long periods of time into dry. All that is in nature still tends towards death. There is much history still to come. And in that realm too, the tendency towards death will continue, so that in later ages this age of Pilate and Tiberius Caesar will seem relatively "green". This moment in time (minutes before his death in time) is like green wood before dry wood. Yet, in the light of the end of times, the new creation is already accomplished.

In the Greek language, there are two words which we translate into the English language by the one word "end". They are τελος (telos; *pl.*

teloi) and εσχατογ (eschaton; *pl.* eschata). Christian theory of history starts with the premise that the end (telos) for which there is creation is accomplished now in eternity, as the result of the work of the life, death, resurrection and ascension of Jesus Christ. We have yet to see the final things (*eschata*); but we know that everything that happens in history tends towards these final things. And we know the centre from which comes the singular impulse which sets all historical happening in motion towards these *eschata* and this *telos*. This centre is a singular life-in-time (that of Jesus of Nazareth), lived in a particular place, composed of unrepeatable and ostensibly long-gone events—a life crossed (like all lives) by countless details of the lives of countless other singular individuals; issuing (like all lives) in the death of that singular life; and continuing (like all lives—*but this* is something we did not know before, and had to be shown *historically*) in resurrection and ascension into invisible realms.

God's reconciliation of all reality outside Himself *to* Himself is in force now, in all the realms of reality, following upon the vindication of Jesus' life and death in His resurrection. Though the events of Jesus' life and death occurred in a limited section of time, their effects were accomplished in eternity: that is, in that dimension in which there is even now no distinction between then and now.

Many religions—perhaps all, in one way or another, but with the one clear exception of Judaism—can entertain the thought that God might somehow have been incarnated specially in a singular life (for example: Vishnu in Hinduism.) But nowhere else than in the Christian dogma does this notion expand to the vision that a singular life, entering into the plane of history and leaving it again, accomplished *finally*, (i.e., in time and beyond time) the purpose for which all of history takes place.

Our statement that God has a plan for history, which is indeed already accomplished, does not mean that the plan is the only reality that we see in human life in time. We see real human deeds, having real, cumulative, and enduring effects. All this (says Karl Barth) "does

Christ the Lord of Time

not mean that [the particularity of individuals], their activity and their efforts, and the endless variety of happenings which go to make up world history as a whole, will later be ironed out and destroyed in favour of an all-comprehensive and unified plan".[30] This is the link between our confidence in the endurance of history's meanings and our confidence in the endurance of our own singular meanings:

> It cannot be said of Jesus Christ that He merely has lived. It must also be said that as the One who has lived once He lives and will live. To avoid misunderstanding, we add that He does not merely do so spiritually but physically, in the very spatio-temporal form of his then history. As the One who has lived, He has no need of later recollection to live continually. Risen from the dead, He has appeared and been manifested to His own. His history has been, but it has not passed. It is the promise given also to our histories, that one day they will have been, but will not have passed."[31]

The dogma of the Incarnation tells us that we are not wrong in expressing singular human life-in-time as an eternally significant story. In the light of the Incarnation, every man, anywhere, who has ever seen his own life and the life of those he loves in this way (and we suspect that most men have always done so) is vindicated. Christian dogma states that all human decision is of irreversible and eternal significance. The material of history, being the sum-total of all these meanings, is of the same quality: it is of irreversible and eternal significance.

The Gospel unmistakably turns our attention to the realm of history. The very form and substance of the scriptures is historical. we are directed to the plane of historical happening, not in order that our "interest" (to use Kierkegaard's term) in the matter of our singular existence should be extinguished, nor diminished, nor set in context.

The Gospel shows that the end (*telos*) of our singular existence is realized by God's activity within the historical realm.

The relation of the realm of singular meaning to that of historical meaning is not that of a lesser to a greater. It is not the case that either fits inside the other. It is rather that the meaning of each is revealed in and upheld by the same activity: the life of Jesus of Nazareth. The Christian gospel makes the same equally extreme case for the enduring meaning of the singular life-story and the cumulative human story; and it provides, in the dogma of the Incarnation, the bridge between the two.

Endnotes

Chapter 1: Prolegomena: Our Civilization's Dynamic View History

1. George Woodcock, *Gandhi* (London: Fontana, 1972), 22

Chapter 2: Herodotus: His Enquiries into History

1. Herodotus, *The Histories*. Translated by Aubrey de Selincourt, 1954. (Harmondsworth: Penquin Books, 1954), 13. These are the opening words of the book.
2. See, *inter alia*, Michael Grant, *The Ancient Historians* (New York: Scribner's, 1970), 15; and J.B. Bury, *The Ancient Greek Historians*, 1908 (New York: Dover, 1958), 15–16.
3. R.G. Collingwood, *The Idea of History* (Oxford: Oxford U.P., 1946), 266f.
4. Grant, 62–3
5. Grant, 36 and 59; A.D. Momigliano, *Studies in Historiography* (London: Wiedenfeld and Nicolson, 1966), Chapter 8: "The Place of Herodotus in the History of Historiography," 127–142.
6. Grant, 62.
7. Grant, 59.
8. Grant, 65. This judgement is seconded by Momigliano, *loc. cit.* He concludes: "The stupendous development of the study of Greek and Oriental history in the last three centuries would never have happened without Herodotus. Trust in Herodotus has been the first condition for the fruitful exploration of our remote past." (141.)
9. Grant, esp. 52–56.

10. Another common approach dismisses all of Herodotus' remarks of ostensibly pious or superstitious character as cynical gestures to a superstitious audience. An extreme example of this tactic is K.H. Waters, *Herodotus the Historian* (London: Croom Helm, 1985), esp. Chapter 8: "Religious and Moral Attitudes," 96–118.
11. William F. Albright, "Judaism, the Ancient Near East, and the Origins of Christianity," in Norman F. Cantor (ed.), *Perspectives on the European Past: Conversations with Historians* (New York: Macmillan, 1971), Volume I, 38–62. *Esp.*, 50.
12. Bury, "Lecture One: the Rise of Greek History in Ionia," *op. cit.*, 1f.
13. Bury, 7–8.
14. David Diringer, "The Biblical Scripts," in P.R. Ackryod and C.F. Evans, *The Cambridge History of the Bible.* Vol. I (Cambridge University Press, 1970), 18–19; and Waters, 15.
15. Grant, 16.
16. *Histories*, II:145. There survive only fragments of Hecataeus' two prose works, *Journey Round the World* and *Genealogies*. See Grant, 18f; and Bury 8f. It is believed that Alexander the Great used Hecataeus' books as his guide on his campaign into India. (Grant, 417.)
17. Bury, 27–8; M.Grant, 18f.; and Denys Hay, *Annalists and Historians: Western Historiography from the Eighth to the Eighteenth Centuries* (London: Methuen, 1977), 4–6.
18. See M. I. Finley, *Aspects of Antiquity: Discoveries and Controversies* (Harmondsworth: Penguin, Second edition, 1977), Chapter 15: "The Year One", 185–199.
19. Grant, 19.
20. B.A. Van Groningen, *In The Grip of the Past: Essay on an Aspect of Greek Thought* (Leiden: E. J. Brill, 1953), 104–6.
21. Grant, 33–4, 43; Oswyn Murray, "Greek Historians," in John Boardman, J. Griffin, and O. Murray (eds.), *The Oxford History of the Classical World* (Oxford: Oxford U.P., 1986), 188–190.

22. Immanuel Kant, "Idea for a Universal History with Cosmopolitan Intent" (1784), in Carl J. Friedrich (ed.), *The Philosophy of Kant: Immanuel Kant's Moral and Political Writings* (New York: Modern Library, 1949), 116–131.

Chapter 3: Elements of the Ancient Greek Theory of History

1. Grant, 45.
2. Grant, 45–6.
3. O. Murray, "Greek Historians," *loc. cit.*, 186–203; and Moses Finley, *Ancient History: Evidences and Models* (New York: Viking 1986), esp. chaps. 2 and 3.
4. Bury, 30–31.
5. M. I. Finley, *The Use and Abuse of History* (New York: Viking, 1975), 22–23.
6. Josephus, *The Ancient History of the Jews: A Reply to Apion*. (Teubner text, ed. by S.A. Naber, as printed in A.J. Toynbee, *Greek Historical Thought* (New York: Mentor books, 1952) 63–9.
7. Finley, *Use*, 24.
8. Finley, *Use*, 32.
9. R. W. Southern, "Aspects of the European Tradition of Historical Writing. 1: The Classical Tradition from Einhard to Geoffrey of Monmouth," *Royal Historical Society Transactions*, 1970 (Volume XX), 173–196.)
10. Southern, 175–6.
11. Southern, 177.
12. Stanley Jaki tells the related story of "the pessimistic logic of eternal recurrence" and its baneful effects on the development of scientific thought. The idea of creation out of nothing was universally rejected among Greek thinkers, "...by all who were known as dogmatists in antiquity, namely the Aristotelians, the Atomists, and the Stoics. As to the academic skeptics, they were, as they are now, the very last

ones to favour a creation out of nothing.... The claim that the world itself was intelligent could be and was mercilessly held up to ridicule.... With no transcendent intellect emerging on the horizon, with the world proved to be without intellect, all that remained was to fall back on the human mind, for which nothing was more normal than to settle with the customary.... [T]he rise of science needs the broad and persistent shaping by the whole population, that is, an entire culture of an intelligibility embodied in the tenet about a personal God, the creator of all." This set of conditions, necessary for the rise of science, came about, says Jaki, in what we now call "the Middle Ages". Stanley Jaki, *The Road of Science and the Ways to God* (Chicago: U. of Chicago Press, 1978), Chapter Two: "Lessons in Greek" (pp. 19–33.) The quoted portion is from 31–33.

13. From the *Collected Works of Plato*, Oxford text, ed. by J. Burnet. Vol. 1: *Politicus*. As reproduced in Arnold Toybee (ed.), *Greek Historical Thought*, 129–130.
14. Plato, in Toynbee (ed.), 130.
15. Frank E. Manuel, *Shapes of Philosophical History* (Stanford: Stanford U. P., 1965), 7. Further insight into the Greek concept of time and its bearing on historical understanding can be found in academic literature on comparative religion, as e.g.: Joseph Campbell (ed.) [Eranos–Jahrbuch], *Man and Time*: [Papers from the Eranos Yearbooks, volume three] (New York: Bollingen Foundation/Princeton University Press, 1957), especially the essays: Henri-Charles Puech, "Gnosis and Time," 38–84; Mircea Eliade, "Time and Eternity in Indian Thought," 173–200.
16. Abraham Heschel, *The Prophets: An Introduction*, 1962 (Harper Torchbooks edition, New York, 1969), II, 44.
17. C.A. Patrides, *The Grand Design of God: the Literary Form of the Christian View of History* (Toronto: University of Toronto Press, 1972), 1–2.
18. Diodorus of Agyrium (ca. 90–20 B.C.), "Library of Universal History" (from Book I, chapters 1–5). Reproduced in Toynbee (ed.), 48–49.

19. Diodorus, in Toynbee (ed.), 49.

Chapter 4: Elements of the Ancient Jewish Theory of History

1. See P.R. Ackroyd and C.P. Evans (eds.), *The Cambridge History of the Bible* (Cambridge: Cambridge U.P., 1970), Volume I, Chapters 5: "The Old Testament in the Making", and 6: "Canonical and Non-Canonical"; B.S. Childs, *Introduction to the Old Testament as Scripture* (Philadelphia: Fortress Press, 1979), Chapter 2: "The Problem of the Canon," 46–67; F.F. Bruce, *The Books and the Parchments: How We Got Our English Bible*, revised 1984 (Old Tappan: Revell, 1984), Chapter 8: "The Canon of Scripture", 86–104; and R.K. Harrison, *Introduction to the Old Testament* (Grand Rapids: Eerdmans, 1969), Part Four, Chap. IV: "The Old Testament Canon," 260–288. Shorter accounts can be found in basic Biblical reference works, *inter alia*: M.S. Miller and J.L. Miller (eds.), *Harper's Bible Dictionary* (New York: Harper and Row, 1973), articles: "Canon", "Bible", and "Sources"; J.D. Douglas, *et. al.*, (eds.), *New Bible Dictionary* (Wheaton: Tyndale. Second edition, 1982), article: "Canon of the Old Testament."
2. John Bright, *A History of Israel*. Second edition (Philadelphia: Westminster Press, 1972), 23–4.
3. See, in addition to Bright:
   J.H. Hayes and J.M. Miller, *Israelite and Judaean History* (Philadelphia: Westminster Press, 1977); Millar Burrows, *What Mean these Stones?* (New York: Meridian Books, 1957); Siegfried H. Horn, "Recent Illumination of the Old Testament," *Christianity Today*, June 21, 1968, 13–17; Paul W. Lapp, *Biblical Archeology and History* (New York: World, 1969); W.F. Albright, *From the Stone Age to Christianity*. Second edition (New York: Doubleday "Anchor" edition, 1957); W.F. Albright, *Archeology, Historical Analogy, and Early Biblical Tradition* (Baton Rouge:

Louisiana State U.P., 1966); R.K. Harrison, *Introduction to the Old Testament*, Part Two: "Old Testament Archeology," 83–143. Gary A Herion, "The Role of Historical Narrative in Biblical Thought: The Tendencies Underlying Old Testament Historiography," in *Journal for the Study of the Old Testament* 21 (1981), 25–53. James B. Pritchard, *Ancient Near Eastern Texts Relating to the Old Testament*, 3rd edition with supplement, (Princeton: Princeton University Press, 1969); Robt. M. Polzin and Eugene Rothman (eds.), *The Biblical Mosaic: Changing Perspectives* (Philadelphia and Chico: Fortress Press and Scholars Press, 1982); B.S. Childs, *Memory and Tradition in Israel* (London: S.C.M. Press, 1962); Millar Burrows, "Ancient Israel," in R.C. Dentan (ed.), *The Idea of History in the Ancient Near East* (New Haven: Yale University Press, 1955), 101–130; Rudolf Smend, "Tradition and History: A Complex Relation," in D.A. Knight (ed.), *Tradition and Theology in The Old Testament* (Philadelphia: Fortress Press, 1977), 49–68; C.R. North, *The Old Testament Interpretation of History* (London: Epworth Press, 1946); R.C. Culley, "Oral Tradition and Historicity," in J.W. Wevers and D.B. Redford (ed), *Studies on the Ancient Palestinian World* (Toronto: University of Toronto Press, 1972), 102–116.
4. W.F. Albright, *The Archeology of Palestine*. Revised edition (Harmondsworth: Penguin, 1960), 127–8.
5. Nelson Glueck, *Rivers in the Desert*, 1949), cited by Herman Wouk, *This is My God* (New York: Doubleday, 1959), 292.
6. Hay, 1.
7. Harrison, *Introduction to the Old Testament*, Part Five, Chapter I, B: "Semitic Historiography", 295–302.
8. These examples are from Bright, 182–3 and 187.
9. While appreciating the difficulty of the question, and acknowledging my lack of the expert knowledge to follow the details of the debate, I am drawn to the arguments of Umberto Cassuto, *The Documentary Hypothesis and the Composition of the Pentateuch* . Trans. from the

Hebrew by I. Abrahams (Jerusalem: Magnes Press, 1961), calling for radical rejection of the now-entrenched source criticism deriving from Wellhausen. A balanced summary of the literature is Childs, Chapter Five: "Introduction to the Pentateuch", esp. 132–5. A magisterial survey of the literature, concluding in rejection of the Wellhausen hypothesis, is R.K. Harrison, *op. cit.*, Chaps. I to IV (pp.3–82.)

10. Bright, 30–31.
11. M. Finley, *Ancient History: Evidence and Models,* Chap. 2: "The Ancient Historian and his Sources," and Chap. 3: "Documents", 7–46.
12. W. F. Albright, "The Biblical Period," in Louis Finkelstein (ed.), *The Jews: Their History, Culture and Religion*. Fourth Edition, (New York: Schocken Books, 1970), Vol. I,3.
13. George Ernest Wright, *God Who Acts: Biblical Theology as Recital* (London: S.C.M. Press, 1952). Emphasis in the original.
14. Karl Barth, *Church Dogmatics* [hereinafter cited, "C.D."] (Edinburgh: T. and T. Clark), Volume III, Part Two [1960], 248.
15. Abraham J. Heschel, *The Prophets* (New York: Harper and Row, 1962), Volume II, 45.
16. Heschel, *Prophets*, II, 43.
17. Herschel, *Prophets*, II, 44.
18. Theodore Gaster, *The Oldest Stories in the World*, (Boston: Beacon Press, 1958.)
19. Mircea Eliade, *Gods, Goddesses and Myths of Creation: a Thematic Source Book of the History of Religions* [being Part One of *From Primitives to Zen*] (New York: Harper and Row, 1974.)
20. W.F. Albright, "Judaism, the Ancient Near East...," in Cantor, I, 42.
21. Fritz A. Rothschild, (ed.), *Between God and Man; An Interpretation of Judaism, from the Writings of Abraham J. Heschel* (New York: Macmillan, Free Press, 1965), 217.
22. Rothschild (ed.), [Heschel], 272.
23. Rothschild (ed.), [Heschel], 217.

24. Rothschild (ed.), [Heschel], 216.
25. Rothschild (ed.), [Heschel], 216.
26. Albright, *From Stone Age*, 250–1. Consult further: Y. Aharoni and M. Avi–Jonah, *The Modern Bible Atlas* (London: Allen and Unwin, 1979), 21 (map #15); W.F. Albright, *The Archeology of Palestine*; W.F. Albright, *Recent Discoveries in Bible Lands* (New York: Funk and Wagnalls, 1955); D.J. Wiseman (ed.), *Peoples of the Old Testament* (London: Oxford U.P., 1973); and other works already cited, by Bright, Hayes and Miller, and Lapp.
27. Kant, "Idea...," in Friedrich (ed.), 116–131.
28. Solomon Grayzel, *A History of the Jews*. Revised edition (New York: New American Library, 1968), 25.
29. A brilliant proof of this is to be found in Robert Alter, *The Art of Biblical Narrative* (New York: Basic Books, 1981), *passim*.
30. I refer especially to the work inspired by the premises of the *Annalistes* school. The principal theoretical statement of the school is in Fernand Braudel, *Ecrits sur l'histoire* (Paris: Flammarion, 1969.) See esp. the essay, "Histoire et sciences sociales. La longue durée," 41–84.
31. Ulrich Simon, *Story and Faith in the Biblical Narrative* (London: S.P.C.K. Press, 1975), x.
32. Eliezer Berkovits, *God, Man, and History: a Jewish Interpretation* (Middle Village: Johnathan David, 1959), 12–15.
33. See esp. his *The Philosophy of History* , 1766 (New York: the Citadel Press, 1965), Chaps. 38–49.
34. The quotation is from the abridged version of the *Study of History*, and is cited by Emil Fackenheim, *Encounters Between Judaism and Modern Philosophy* (New York: Schocken Books, 1980), 255. Toynbee's summary of his views on this theme, and his response to critics is in *A Study of History*, Volume XII: *Reconsiderations* (London: Oxford U.P., 1961), Chaps. xiii and xv.
35. Ludwig Feuerbach, *The Essence of Christianity,* ("Torchbook", 1959), 118–9.

36. Barth, *C.D.* IV, 3 [1961], 62–3.

Chapter 5: The God of Israel and the History of World Empires

1. James B. Pritchard, *Ancient New Eastern Texts Related to the Old Testament*, Second edition. (Princeton: Princeton U.P., 1955), 315–316.
2. The extra-biblical evidence for this story is discussed in Bright, 360–373.
3. Josephus, *Antiquities*, Book XI, Chapter 1:3. I use the translation of William Whiston from *The Works of Flavius Josephus* (Grand Rapids: Associated Publishers and Authors, Inc., n.d.)
4. Bright, 365–6
5. F.F. Bruce, "Between the Testaments," in D. Guthrie *et. al.* (eds.), *The New Bible Commentary: Revised* (Grand Rapids: Eerdmans, 1970), 59.
6. Bright reviews this, 360–373.
7. Bright, 370–3.
8. Bright, 370–1; Harrision, Part Fifteen: "The Apocrypha," 1173f.
9. Bright, 373.
10. *Inter alia*, Bright, 220–4.
11. Heschel, *Prophets*, I, 185.
12. Heschel, *Prophets*, I, 184.

Chapter 6: Convergence of the Graeco-Roman and the Ancient Jewish Theories of History

1. Max Radin, *The Jews Among the Greeks and the Romans* (Jewish Publication Society, 1915. Reprinted, New York: Aron Press, 1973), Chapter vi: "The First Contact Between Greek and Jew", 76–89. The statement is attributed to Theophrastus of Lesbos, a pupil of Aristotle (Radin, 81–2.) Also, Martin Hengel, *Judaism and Hellenism: Studies*

in their Encounter in Palestine During the Early Hellenistic Period. Translated by J. Bowden (London: S.C.M. Press, 1973), 255–267.
2. Radin, 86; Hengel, 255–8.
3. Hengel, 65–82.
4. Emil Schürer, *The Literature of the Jewish People in the Time of Jesus* [original edition, ii vols., 1907–1911.] Edited, and with an introduction by Nahum N. Glatzer (New York: Schocken Books, 1972), 196.
5. Schürer, 197–222;Hengel, 83–106.
6. Hengel, 100.
7. On Josephus, see Grant, Chapter 15 (pp. 243–268), which stresses the links with the Graeco-Roman tradition, but has only a line or two (261, and a note on 449) on Josephus' links to Jewish historiography. On Philo, see Schürer, 321–381.
8. *Inter alia*: Stanley Brice Frost, "Apocalyptic and History", in J.P. Hyatt (ed.), *The Bible in Modern Scholarship* (Nashville and New York: Abingdon, 1965), 93–113.
9. If any part of what appears in the Christian "apocryphal" literature as *I Esdras* belongs to this period, as some scholars think, it is an exception to this generalization. See the "Introduction" to the Anchor Bible Edition: *I and II Esdras*: Introducton, Translation and Commentary by Jacob M. Myers (Garden City: Doubleday, 1974), esp. 8–15.
10. A collection of all of the major items in this literature is James H. Charlesworth (ed.), *The Old Testament Pseudepigrapha*. Two Vols. (New York: Doubleday), 1984 and 1985.
11. See *New York Times*, April 16, 1980, VII:27.
12 Eusebius [263–339], *The History of the Church*. Translated by G.A. Williamson (Harmondsworth: Penguin, 1963.) Consult: Henry Chadwick, *The Early Church* (Harmondsworth: Penguin, 1967), Chaps.1 through 3.
13. Consult W. F. Albright and C.S. Mann, "Anchor Bible" translation of *Matthew* (Garden City: Doubleday, 1971), Introduction, esp. xxxvii.

Endnotes 275

14. Livy, *History of Rome*, 1:16. Cited by Lidia Storoni Mazzolani, *Empire Without End: Three Historians of Rome*. Translated by J. McConnell and M. Pei (New York: Harcourt, Brace and Jovanovich, 1976), 7.
15. Mazzolani, 9. The author is citing Livy, 31:21.
16. Mazzolani, 15–17. I have altered the order of the passages which make up this citation. The quotation from Cicero is from *Academica Priora* 2.37.119, and that from Vergil is from *Eclogue* 4.4–6.
17. Mazzolani, 9–10.
18. Mazzolani, 13.
19. Eclogue 4:18–22. Reinhold Niebuhr, *Nature and Destiny of Man*, Vol. II, 17 cites this passage from Vergil, in connection with a profound discussion of theories of history which has greatly influenced my own views. See especially his chapter One, subchapter ii: "Where a Christ is Expected", 15–34. See also Mircea Eliade, *Gods, Goddesses...*, 27–31.
20. Tacitus, *The Histories* I:78. I have used the translation by Kenneth Williams (Harmondsworth: Penguin, 1975.) Suetonius, *Nero*, 57 . I have used the translation by Robert Graves: Suetonius, *The Twelve Caesars* (Harmondsworth: Penguin, 1957.) Some commentators see a trace of this theme of Nero *redivivus* in *Revelation* 13:3. *Inter alia* see R.H. Mounce, *The Book of Revelation [New International Commentary on the New Testament]* (Grand Rapids: Eerdmans, 1977), 252–3, 316.
21. Mazzolani, 135.
22. Mazzolani, 14 and notes on 212.
23. *The Sybylline Oracles*. Translated from the Greek into English blank verse by Milton S. Terry (New York: Eaton and Mains, 1899. Reprinted, New York: AMS Press, Inc., 1973.) See Mazzolani, 57–62 and 135–6, and Alfred Edersheim, *The Life and TImes of Jesus the Messiah*, Third Edition, 1886 (Grand Rapids: Eerdmans, 1971), I, 6f, 38f, 172–3, and II, 655–6.

24. Mazzolani, 135. For the figure of "the Widow" and related images associated with Cleopatra, see *Oracles* 3:75–96; 8:190–212, 11:290.
25. Suetonius, *Augustus*, 31.
26. Mazzolani, 58.
27. The stories and the citations from Cicero are in Mazzolani, 56f. and 215.
28. Mazzolani, 58. Mazzolani cites as sources: Vergil, *Georgics* 1:466–8; Ovid, *Metamorphoses* 15:782f; Suetonius, *Caesar*; 88; and *Sibylline Oracles* 3:334–6. See also, Michael Green, *Evangelism in the Early Church* (London: Hodder and Stoughton, 1970), 47–49.
29. Mazzolani, 135–6.
30. Mazzolani, 180–2.
31. Suetonius, *Julius Caesar*, cap. 6.
32. Suetonius, *Julius Caesar*, 32.
33. Suetonius, *Augustus*, 5–6 and 94.
34. Suetonius, *Augustus*, 97–100.
35. Suetonius, *Tiberius*, 14.
36. Suetonius, *Claudius*, 7.
37. Suetonius, *Gaius Caligula*, 22.
38. Suetonius, *Galba*, 1.
39. Suetonius, *Nero*, 40.
40. Suetonius, *Vespasian*, 5.
41. Tacitus, *The Histories*, I:86.
42. Suetonius, *Galba*, 2.
43. Suetonius, *Vitellius*, 1.
44. Suetonius, *Vitellius*, 1.
45. Suetonius, *Vespasian*, 5; Tacitus, II:78.
46. Suetonius, *Vespasian*, 4.
47. Suetonius, *Vespasian*, 4. There is a more elaborate version of this story about Vespasian at Carmel inTacitus, II:78.
48. Flavius Josephus, *The Jewish War*. I use the translation by G.A. Williamson, revised 1970 (Harmondsworth: Penguin, 1970) The quotation is from VI:v:4 (Williamson edition, p.350).

49. From the so-called "Slavonic additions," Williamson translation page 401. On Josephus see Michael Grant, Chapter 15. On the Jewish revolt and Vespasian's triumph, see Robert M. Grant, *Augustus to Constantine: The Thrust of the Christian Movement into the Roman World* (New York: Harper, 1973), Chapter Two.
50. Tacitus V:13.
51. Bury, 237–8.
52. Bury, 13–14.
53. Bury, 240.
54. Bury, 191–223.
55. Bury, 235f.

Chapter 7: The Gospels as Historical Testimony

1. I recommend as a succinct, scholarly presentation of the facts of this case, F.F. Bruce, *The New Testament Documents: Are They Reliable?* Fifth edition, 1960 (Grand Rapids: Eerdmans, 1978.)
2. Bruce, 7–8.
3. Bruce, 81–2.
4. Bruce, 81–92.
5. Moses Finley summarizes the extent and character of evidence for reconstruction of the history of the Roman Empire in this (and earlier and later) periods in *Ancient History: Evidence and Models*, *passim*, but esp. chaps. 2 and 3.
6. Frederic Kenyon, *The Bible and Archeology* (London: Harrap, 1940), 288–9.
7. Bruce, 19–20.
8. Bruce, 16–17.
9. Eric Auerbach, *Mimesis: the Representation of Reality in Western Literature*. Trans. by W.R. Trask, 1953 (Princeton U.P., 1953), esp. 40–49. See also, Hans W. Frei, *The Identity of Jesus Christ: the*

Hermeneutical Bases of Dogmatic Theology (Philadelphia: Fortress Press, 1975.)

10. Non-specialist summaries of the present archeological knowledge regarding places and events described in the New Testament are: Jack Finegan, *The Archeology of the New Testament* (Princeton: Princeton U.P., 1969); Christopher Hollis and Ronald Brownrigg, *Holy Places* (New York: Praeger, 1969); Clement Klopp, *The Holy Places of the Gospels* (New York: Herder and Herder, 1963); Eugene Hoade, *Guide to the Holy Land*. Tenth edition, 1979 (Jerusalem:Franciscan Printing Press, 1979); Gonzalo Báez-Camargo, *Archeological Commentary on the Bible* (New York: Doubleday, 1984); Jerome Murphy-O'Connor, *The Holy Land: An Archeological Guide from Earliest Times to 1700* (New York: Oxford U.P., 1980); G. Cornfeld and D.N. Freedman, *Archeology of the Bible: Book by Book* (New York: Harper and Row, 1976.)

The *Biblical Archeology Review*, published bi-monthly in Washington, D.C., provides learned evaluations for non-specialists of ongoing archeological research. An example bearing on our present interest (recent evidences tending to confirm the authenticity and specificity of New Testament allusions) is: Dan Bahat, "Does the Holy Sepulchre Church Mark the Burial of Jesus?" B.A.R., XII: no. 3 (May/June, 1986), 26–45.

11. Marc Bloch, *the Historian's Craft* (Manchester: Manchester U.P., 1954), 135.
12. See my article, "New Quests for Old; One Historian's View of a Bad Bargain," *Canadian Journal of Theology*, XVI: 3 and 4 (1970), 203–218. A part of what follows is drawn from that article. I admit to being less familiar with the academic literature appearing on this subject since 1970. I have read enough of it to feel confident that, while the names of many new scholars appear, and many new and formidable words have been coined, the issues have not changed at all. While I would stand by the critique in that article of Bultmannian and post-Bultmannian hermeneutics, I now see quite differently the question

Endnotes 279

of the relationship between "scientific" and "historical" knowledge, and herewith repudiate that portion of the argument of the article (see esp. pp. 212–218.)

13. Convenient summaries of their arguments are in James M. Robinson and John B. Cobb, jr. (eds.), *New Frontiers in Theology*, Vol. III: *Theology as History* (New York: Harper and Row, 1967); Carl E. Braaten, *New Directions in Theology Today*, Vol. II: *History and Hermeneutics* (Philadelphia: Westminster Press, 1966); and John MacQuarrie, *The Scope of Demythologizing* (London: S.C.M. Press, 1960.)

14. Frank Kermode, "Deciphering the Big Book;" a review of Raymond E. Brown, *The Birth of the Messiah* [and other books], *New York Review of Books*, June 29, 1978, 39–42.

In the 1970's Roman Catholic scholars appropriated these "discoveries" (by then long familiar in Protestant seminaries). An enthusiastic summary of Catholic literature on "the historical Jesus", is to be found in Hans Küng, *On Being A Christian*. Translated by Edward Quinn (London: Collins, 1977), section B:II: "The Real Christ," 145–165, and C:V: "The New Life," 343–410.

15. C.S. Lewis, "Modern Theology and Biblical Criticism," 1959. Reprinted in C.S. Lewis, *Christian Reflections*, edited by Walter Hooper (Grand Rapids: Eerdmans, 1967), 152–166.

16. Lewis, 154–5.

17. A summary of the unutterably tedious "debate" on this, the favourite theme of contemporary academic philosophy of history, is the article: "Historical Explanation", by Rudolph Weingartner, in P. Edwards (ed.), *Encyclopedia of Philosophy*, volume 4, pp. 7–12. To understand what is at stake, this article should be read in tandem with the article, "Explanation in Science", by Jaegwon Kim, *loc. cit.*, volume 3, pp. 159–163.

Some of the prestigious texts figuring in this debate are: W. Dray, *Laws and Explanation in History* (London: Oxford U.P., 1957); Carl G. Hempel and Paul Oppenheim, "Studies in the Logic of Explanation",

Philosophy of Science, volume 15 (1948), 135–175; Sidney Hook (ed.), *Philosophy and History: A Symposium* (New York: New York U.P., 1963); R.G. Collingwood, *The Idea of History* (Oxford: Oxford University Press, 1946); Maurice Mandelbaum, *The Problem of Historical Knowledge* (New York: Liveright,1938); Patrick Gardiner, *The Nature Of Historical Explanation* (Oxford: Oxford University Press, 1952); Morton White, "Historical Explanation", *Mind*, volume 52 (1943); W.H. Walsh, *An Introduction to Philosophy of History* (London, 1951. Revised edition, London: 1958); Patrick Gardiner (ed.), *Theories of History* (New York: Free Press of Blencoe, 1959).

18. Section X, "Of Miracles", in his *Enquiry Concerning Human Understanding*. (1748).
19. His *Das Leben Jesu*, 1835; translated into English as, *The Life Of Jesus Critically Examined*, 1848.
20. R.R. Niebuhr, *Resurrection and Historical Reason* (New York: Scribner's 1957), 26.
21 R.R. Niebuhr, 55.
22. Braaten, 69–70. Braaten is here summarizing the views of Käsemann and others.
23. Robinson, *A New Quest*, 47.
24. A valuable summary is W.F. Albright, "Judaism, The Ancient Near East, and the Origins of Christianity," in N.F. Cantor (ed.), *Perspectives on the European Past: Conversations with Historians* (New York: Collier-Macmillan, 1971), I, 38–62; or at greater length, Albright, *From the Stone Age to Christianity*.
25. William Nicholls, *The Pelican Guide to Theology*, Volume I (Harmondsworth: Penguin, 1969), Chapter Three: "Bultmann's Existentialist Theology, " esp. 155f; and Heinz Zahrnt, *The Question of God: Protestant Theology in the Twentieth Century* (New York: Harcourt, Brace, Jovanovitch, 1969), esp. 222f.
26. Voltaire, *The Philosophy of History* , 1766 (New York: Citadel Press, 1965), 151–2.

27. Gerhard Maier, *The End of the Historical-Critical Method*. Translated from the German by E.W. Leverenz and R.F. Norden (St. Louis: Concordia Press, 1977), 16. This book offers an excellent critique of the trends in Biblical hermeneutics which I have reviewed above, but does not (with the exception of a few observations like the one just quoted) get into general questions of theory of history.
28. R. G. Collingwood, *The Idea of History*, 210–231.
29. Collingwood, 213.
30. Rudolph Bultmann, *History and Eschatology* (Edinburgh: Edinburgh U.P., 1957), esp. 130–7.
31. Paul Tillich, *Systematic Theology*, Vol. II (Chicago: U. of Chicago Press, 1957), 105.
32. Harvey, 172. Harvey is offering here a summary of these theologians' case, rather than his own case. The quotations are from Robinson, *A New Quest*, 86.
33. For the actual technique of applying Collingwood's "inside/outside" formula to the problem of the Resurrection, see *inter alia:* Macquarrie, 81–86; and Braaten, 100–102.
34. Hugh Anderson, *Jesus and Christian Origins: a Commentary on Modern Viewpoints* (New York: Oxford U.P., 1964),9.
35. Anderson, 12.
36. Macquarrie, 81; *cf.* Robinson, 67, and Anderson, 181.
37. Collingwood, 304.
38. For what follows, see: Matthias Gelzer, *Caesar: Politician and Statesman* (Oxford: Basil Blackwell, 1968), 193–4; and M. Cary, *A History of Rome* (London: Macmillan, 1954), 396.
39. Plutarch, *Caesar*, 32:7.
40. Suetonius, *Julius Caesar*, 32.
41. See Frank Morison, *Who Moved the Stone?* (London: Faber and Faber, 1967.)
42. Here I accept the traditional attributions of authorship and witness behind the four Gospels, as these are found in Eusebius (*History of*

the Early Church, II:15, III:24 and 39.) Any challenge to these traditional attributions must be strong enough to override the unanimous tradition of the early Church, for which there is documentary support too strong to admit of serious doubt. Scholarly-academic objections to these attributions, originating in the early Nineteenth century, are various but contradictory, and none, taken singly, has won the undivided allegiance of the scholars. An outsider to the guild, without specialized investment in its dynastic-scribal rivalries, is obliged to apply Occam's razor to the question. And that test clearly favors the traditional attributions.

43. Alfred Edersheim, *The Life and Times of Jesus the Messiah*. Third edition, 1886 (Grand Rapids: Eerdmans, 1971), II, 369–70.
44. Oscar Cullmann, *Christ and Time: the Primitive Christian Conception of Time and History*. Revised edition, 1964. Translated by Floyd V. Filson (Philadelphia: Westminster Press, 1964), 42.

Chapter 8: Christ the Lord of Time

1. E.H. Carr, *What is History*? (Harmondsworth: Peguin, 1964.)
2. Carr, 119.
3. Carr, 112.
4. Carr, 110–111.
5. Carr, 120–121.
6. Carr, 109.
7. Carr, 121.
8. Carr, 125–7.
9. Carr, 121.
10. Carr, 123–4.
11. Carr, 130.
12. Carr, 132.
13. Carr, 108. Compare, Augustine, *Confessions*, Book XI.
14. Carr, 108.

Endnotes 283

15. Carr, 108.
16. Carr, 108.
17. Carr, 109.
18. Carr, Chapter Five: "History as Progess."
19. Carr, 87 and 109.
20. Carr, 110.
21. Carr, 110.
22. Carr, 110.
23. Karl Popper, *The Open Society and Its Enemies*. Second edition, 1950 (New York: Harper "Torchbook" edition, 1963), Vol. II, 269–272.
24. Peter Gay, *The Enlightenment: An Interpretation*, II Volumes (New York: Knopf, 1966 and 1969.)
25. Carr, 110–111.
26. Gay, I, Chapter Six, and II, Chapters One and Two.
27. Arthur S. Link, "The Historian's Vocation," in C.T. McIntire (ed.), *God, History, and Historians* (New York: Oxford U.P., 1977), 375–6.
28. Barth, *CD, III, Two*, 455.
29. Barth, *CD, II, One*, 627–9.
30. Barth, *CD, III, Three*, 167.
31. Barth, *CD, IV, Three*, 224.

Index

A

Albright, W. F., 20–21, 73, 81–2, 91
Alexander, 153, 156, 173
Amos, 124–26, 130
Anderson, Hugh, 225
Antiochus IV ("Epiphanes"), 157
Antony, Mark, 173
Apocalyptic literature, 160–64
Auerbach, Eric, 209, 212
Augustine, St., of Hippo, 162

B

Barth, Karl, 82, 114–15, 142, 258, 262–3
Berkovits, Eliezer, 108–9
Bible,
   formation of the OT canon, 69–71, 159; a historical source: antiquity of, 71–73; scepticism re Bible as historical source now corrected by archeology, 73–4, 95–6
Biblical References:

Genesis

1 to 2:4	94	10:22	99
1:1	82–3	11:1–9	97
1:16	87	11:22–32	103
1:27	88	12	98–105
2 to 5	94–5	12:1–3	99, 112, 201

2:2–3a ... 91	12:4a ... 103
5:1 ... 82–3	16:11–16 ... 111
5:1–2 ... 98	17:5 ... 99
6 to 9 ... 112	17:18–21 ... 110
6 to 10 ... 94–5	19:1–5 ... 98
8 and 9 ... 139	21:8–10 ... 111
8:21–22 ... 112	25:19–34 ... 111
9:1 ... 96–7	27 to 31 ... 111–12
9:7 ... 97	27 ... 111
10 ... 80–1, 95–6	35:11 ... 97
10:1 ... 83	

Exodus
6:5 to 7:4 ... 105–8
7:3 ... 106
14:4 ... 106
14:5–6 ... 107
15 to 22 ... 110
17:18–21 ... 110
32:11–14 ... 139

Deuteronomy
6:4 ... 90

Joshua
23 and 24 ... 120

I Kings
12:25 to 14:20 ... 120
13:1–4 ... 120

II Kings
22 and 23 ... 120
23:25 ... 120
23:26–7 ... 120–1

I Chronicles
28 ... 141

Index

II Chronicles
36:22–23 128
Ezra
1 to 6 132
1 and 6:3–5 128
6:13–18 134
Nehemiah
12:12 128

Isaiah
2:2a–4 143
10:7 142
10:5 143
10:12a 143
10:13–4 142
10:15 142
11:1–9 145
14:13a 142
19:23–5 144
40:11 138
41:2a, 4 135

41:8–9 136
42f 130
42:9 147
44:24 to 45:4 137–8
46:8–11 137
46:11b 117
48:6–7 147
48:14 138
49:6 136
51:15–16 90
65:17 147

Jeremiah
5 124
5:1f 124
7:4 122
7:5–7 127
7:21–25 123
7:31–31 123
14:13–14 123–4
51:7 141
Ezekiel
3:15 128
7:23 259

14:15f 125
20 and 21 125
21:8–9 126
21:10–12 126–7
30–33 125
31:35–37 146
33:25–26 125

Daniel 160–64, 176
Hosea
8:2–4 141
9:1 141
Amos
5:21f 124
5:27 125
8:1f 124
9:7–8 124
9:9–15 125
Jonah 112–4
1:1–2 112
1:3–16 113–4
4:2–11 113
Haggai 130, 133–4
Zechariah 130, 133
4:10 132
Matthew 166
1:1–7 237
1:18–25 217
4:1–11 237
14:12–13 237
14:33 237
22:19–20 180
Mark
1:15 204
14:33, 36 237
Luke 204–07
1:1–4 233
1:5 204
2:1f 204
3:1f 204
3:23–38 237

10:18 241
19:39–44 .... 237, 242–43
21:5–38 237
21:29–31 261
23:30–31 261

John

1:1–3, 14	256	7:19–20	239
4:22b	115	7:25–33	238–9
4:23	259	8:14, 21	239
4:35	261	18:52–58	235, 240
6:66–67	241	16:28–29	241
7	244	16:32–33	231
7 to 10	238–41		

Acts

11:28...........................204
17:26–7.......................28
18:2............................204
25:11..........................204

Romans

8:19............................260

I Corinthians

4:1..............................235

I John

1:1–2..........................199

Biblical theory and philosophy of history
  Biblical theory and Greek theory compared re universality of content, 28–9; *ditto* re its moral meaning, 47: *ditto* re historical research, 55–6; Biblical history not available to Herodotus, 70–1; prestige of history in Biblical view (74f), linked to issue of "authorship" of Biblical text, 74–82; use of multiple "sources", 77–9; Creation account gives clue to primacy of historical thinking, 82–90; the redemptive work of time, 90–4; assumptions about historical process in early chaps. of *Genesis*. 94–8; history "centred" on story of Abraham, 98–105; the radical freedom of the human will and the sovereignty of God, 105–9; the "offense" of God's electon of Israel, 110–14; how covenant with Israel is linked to God's purpose for all mankind, 114–48; the humiliation of Israel, 117–125; the gentile empires as instruments of God's purposes, 125–27; Israel's hope in the light of return from Babylon, 127f; the controversy over the "meaning" on Cyrus, 128–38; the controversy over the meaning of the restoration of the Temple, 132–35; Isaiah's message of universal

hope, 135–38; the "inner" and "outer" visions of Hebrew prophecy, 138–48; historical realism, 140–45; realism linked to hope, 145; the purposes of God shown in covenant with Abraham are overcoming the present order in nature, 145–48; historical reflections in Hellenistic period, 152f., Jewish intellectuals in Hellenistic period attracted to Hellenistic models of historiography, 153–56; Greek and Roman intellectuals are drawn to Jewish historiography, 156–198; apocalyptic literature, 160–64; convergence of Graeco-Roman and Jewish speculation on end of times, 164–66, 192–198; speculation on rise fall of empires, 176–79.

Bloch, Marc, 210

Bornkamm, G., 210

Bossuet, J. B., 47

Bright, John A., 71–2, 80, 134

Brown, Raymond, 209

Bruce, F.F., 203–5, 206–7

Bultmann, Rudolf, 209, 210, 216, 224

Bury, J. B., 21–2, 52–3; cited and discussed, 192–97

C

Caesar,
    Julius, 74, 179, 182–83, 206, 228–30
    Augustus, 174–75, 179–80, 183–85, 204
    Tiberius, 185, 204
    Gaius Caligula, 185–86
    Claudius, 185
    Nero, 173, 187–78, 204
    Galba, 187–88
    Otho, 187–78
    Vitelius, 187–88
    Vespasian, 189

Caesar-crossing-the-Rubicon as an instance of accredited historical fact, 221–234

Index   291

Cambyses, 50, 133
Carr, E.H., cited and discussed, 246–56
Cassuto, Umberto, 270–71, n.9
Cataline conspiracy, 179
Childs, B.S., 70
Christian theory and philosophy of history,
    based on dogmatic investments in events, 199–201; accepts paradoxes
    in Jewish theory, adds paradox that these meanings fulfilled in time
    in Christ, 201–03; stands on historical reliability of Gospels, 203–34;
    the "mystery" of Incarnation, 234–44; the premises of Christian
    theory of history derive from history itself, 245–46; its linear
    character and its positive attitude toward time, 251–56; it stands on
    dogma, not philosophy, 257–58
Cicero, 179, 205
Cleopatra, 179
Collingwood, R.G., 16, 222–28, 230
Cyrus II (the Great) of Persia, 68–9, 127–31, 135–38

D

Demythologizing of the Gospels, 224–27
Dilthey, W., 224–25
Dio, Cassius, 205
Diodorus of Agyrium, 63–66

E

Ebeling, G., 210
Edersheim, Alfred, 242–43
Eusebius, 80, 155, 282 (n. 42)
Explanation,
    an issue in recent philosophy of history, considered in the context of
    New Testament as historical text, 212–21
Ezekiel, 127

F

Feuerbach, Ludwig, 111, 113
Finley, Moses I., 53–55, 56, 254 (n. 5)

G

Gandhi, M. K., 3–4
Gaster, Theodore, 91
Gospels,
    as historical testimony, 199–234; the writers of the Gospels conscious of presenting an historical case, 204–08; manuscript evidence for present text, 206–07; recent academic literature denying standing of Gospel texts as historical sources, 208–16; definition of "historical testimony", 217–19; historical testimony is *kerygma*, 219–20; resurrection as historical event, 221–22, 230–34; "demythologizing" the Gospel accounts, 224–28; "incarnation", 230–34.
Grant, Michael, 19–20, 22, 51
Grayzel, Solomon, 104
Graeco-Roman historiography
    (See first "Greek theory and philosophy of History")
    convergence of Graeco-Roman and Ancient Jewish historiography, 149–98; early knowledge of Jews, 152–53; Jewish interest in Hellenistic historiography, 153–56; Gk and Rn intellectuals discover Jewish historiography, 156f., the impact of Jewish apocalypse, 160–64; convergence of Jewish and Roman "messianism", 164–98; Roman historians preoccupied with meaning of their empire, 164–66; Rn historicans co-opt eastern messianism, 166f.; Rn historians co-opt Gk interpretation of history of empire, 170–71; *ditto* Jewish interpretation of empire, 171–79; Augustine co-opts all eastern messianic expectations to his theory of empire 180–82; Rn historians interpret dynastic history in terms of messianic expectations, 182–91;

supernatural premises of Graeco-Rn historical philosophy, 191–98; ms. evidence of present texts of Rn historians, compared to that for NT, 206–07

Greek theory and philosophy of history

Herodotus, "father of history", 15–58 (and see "Herodotus"); the words *histor* and *historie*, 15–16; predecessors of Herodotus, among Ionian Gks, 20–22; Hecataeus and the problem of chronology, 23–24; the universal regime of the Gk gods, as key to universal history, 25–34; Herodotus' failure to impress his philosophy of history upon his successors, 51–66; Gk–Persian crisis no longer serves to "centre" history, 52; loss of seriousness about historical research, 52–56; Gk philosophical interest uncongenial to historical spirit, 57–66; cyclical concepts militate against historical spirit, 59–66; "uses of history", 63–66; Gk and Jewish visions of history compared, 145–48. (See further, "Graeco-Roman historiography").

H

Haggai, 130, 133–34
Hay, Denis, 74
Hecataeus, 22–26
Hegel, G.W.F., 46
Heidegger, Martin, 216
Hellanicus of Lesbos, 53
Hellenic historiography. See Graeco-Roman historiography.
Hengel, Martin, 155–56
Herodotus, 15–58:

he defines his task as *histor*, 15–16; origins and life-span, 17; occasion for his *Histories*, 17; his task to "fix responsibility", 17–18; undertakes whole story of mankind, 18; his credibility, 18–20; primacy of Asiatic Gks in intellectual inquiry, 20–22; "historical enquiry" before H., 21–22; Hecataeus and the problem of chronology,

23–26; universal jurisdiction of Gk deities as key to universal history, 27–34, 100–102; the Graeco-Persian conflict as *kairos*, 34f; H's views on "purpose" in history, 34–44; "fortune", "luck", "destiny", and the problem of theodicy, 44–47; H's theory and practice of history summarized, 47–48; H's claim to inclusiveness of his history, 49–50; H's vision of history lost, 51–52; H's motive for historical research lost, 52–58.

46. 67. 70, 74, 88–89, 91, 99–101, 117, 127, 131–32, 152, 219 passages from H's Histories cited or noted:

I:1	15, 17, 34	IV:24f	27
I:7–25	41	IV:255–56	49
I:32	41–42	VI:29	37
I:34	37	VI:107	37
I:90–92	43–44	VII:6	37
I:91	37, 91	VII:8	46
I:107	37	VII:10	46
I:209	37	VII:14–20	37
II:37, 104	152	VII:101–105	50
II:141	37	VII:133–8	38–40
II:145	25, 33	VII:152	19
III:80–88	50	VIII:77	37
III:100–118	49	VIII:144	51
III:124	37	IX:7	51
III:149	37	IX:65	40
III:210–12	50	IX:100	41
IV: 17–50	49	IX:101	34

Heschel, Abraham J., 87, 90–91, 91–92, 93, 93–94, 143–45
Hesiod, 25
Hosea, 130
Hume, David, 213, 257

Index 295

I

Incarnation, 235–64: as key to understanding claims of Jesus Christ in Gospels, 235–43; as dogma, it cannot be systematized, 243–44; the premise of our theory of history, 258–64
Isaiah, 127, 130, 135–38, 142–45
Israel, History of :.
  chronology, 67–69; reign of Cyrus links Herodotus' story to history of Israel, 69 (see also, "Cyrus II, the Great of Persia); origins linked to earliest civilizations, 71–3, 81–2; excessive scepticism of 18th and 19th centuries re Bible as historical source now corrected by archeology, 72–4; Abraham seen as father of Israel, 98–103, 110–14; world history seen as centered on history of Israel, 99–103, 114–16; as history of humiliation, 117f: against background of Mesopotamian and Egyptian empires, 117–19; the threat of annihilation by Assyrian and Babylonian empires, 118f; reign of K. Josiah, 119–21; the alliance with Egypt in defiance of Babylon, 121-27; Babylonian captivity, 127; return from captivity, 127–28; the period of restoration, 128–38; Jewish reflection on Israel's history in the period of restoration, 138–48; Israel in Hellenistic age, 149f; chronology for Hellenistic and Roman periods, 149–57; in time of Alexander, 156; under Ptolomies and Seleucids, 156–57; Hasmonean (Maccabean) period, 157–60; ambivalent Roman attitude twds Judaea, 174f; Rome co–opts Jewish messianism, 180–81, 187–91;. Jewish insurrection and destruction of Temple, 190–91

J

Jaki, Stanley, 267–68 (n.12)
Jeremiah, 122–27
Jeroboam I, King of Israel, 120
Jeroboam II, King of Israel, 124
Josephus, Flavius, 55–6, 128, 137, 155, 156, 160, 189–91, 205, 242–43
Josiah, King of Judah, 69, 119–121

K

Kant, Immanuel, 35-6, 97
Kasemann, E., 210
Kermode, Frank, 211
Kierkegaard, S., 263

L

Lewis, C. S., cited and discussed, 211-12
Lindsey, Hal, 162
Link, Arthur, 2, 257
Livy, 24, 74, 167, 207

Luke, author of *Gospel* and *Acts*, his concern for historical detail, 204-5

M

Maccabeans (Hasmoneans), 157-58
Macquarries, John, 225-26
Maier, Gerhard, 220, 281 (n. 27)
Manual, Frank, 62
Mazzolani, Lidia, 174-75, 179, 180, 181-82
Micah, 187
Moses,
  his "authorship" of Pentateuch? 79-81; the rabbinical tradition of Moses as source of Greek philosophy, 155

N

Nahum, 130
New Testament, manuscript evidence of present text, 206-07
Niebuhr, Reinhold, 97, 202, 275 (n.19)
Niebuhr, Richard R., 214

Index   297

P

Pannenberg, W., 210
Patrides, C. A., 62–3
Paul, St., 28, 204
Philo, 154–55
Plato, 60–61
Plutarch, 19, 229, 229–30
Pollio, Asinius, 229, 230
Polybius, 38–9, 74, 193

R

Ranke, Leopold v., 209, 216
Resurrection,
　as historical event, 221–22, 230–34
Revelation, Book of (Apocalypse of St. John). See "Apocalyptic literature"
Robinson, James M., 210, 214–25, 225
Roman historiography. See Graeco-Roman historiography

S

Sallust, 74
Schürer, Emil, 154
Simon, Ulrich, 108
Strauss, D. F., 213–14
Southern, R. W., 57–8
Suetonius, 74, 183, 183–85, 185–86, 187–89, 229
Sybilline oracles, 172, 174, 178–79

T

Tacitus, 74, 187, 191, 206–07

Thucydides, 74, 205, 207
Tillich, Paul, 225
Toynbee, Arnold, 110

V

Van Groningen, B. A., 30–2
Velleius, Paterculus, 229
Voltaire, F. M. A. de, 19, 110, 219

W

Woodcock, George, 3–4
Wright, G. E., 82

X

Xenophon, 74

Z

Zechariah, 130–34
Zephaniah, 130
Zerubbabel, 128, 133–34

TORONTO STUDIES IN THEOLOGY

1. Robert Ross, **The Non-Existence of God: Linguistic Paradox in Tillich's Thought**
2. Gustaf Wingren, **Creation and Gospel: The New Situation in European Theology**
3. John Meagher, **Clumsy Construction in Mark's Gospel: A Critique** of *Form-* and *Redaktionsgeschichte*
4. Patrick Primeaux, **Richard R. Niebuhr on Christ and Religion: The Four-Stage Development of His Theology**
5. Bernard Lonergan, **Understanding and Being: An Introduction and Companion to** *Insight,* **Edited by Elizabeth Morelli and Mark D. Morelli**
6. *Geffrey Kelly and John Godsey, editors,* **Ethical Responsibility: Bonhoeffer's Legacy to the Churches**
7. Darrell J. Fasching, **The Thought of Jacques Ellul: A Systematic Exposition**
8. Joseph T. Culliton, editor, **Non-Violence — Central to Christian Spirituality: Perspectives from Scripture to the Present**
9. Aaron Milavec, **To Empower as Jesus Did: Acquiring Spiritual Power Through Apprenticeship**
10. John Kirby and William Thompson, editors, **Voegelin and the Theologian: Ten Studies in Interpretation**
11. Thomas Day, **Dietrich Bonhoeffer on Christian Community and Common Sense**
12. James Deotis Roberts, **Black Theology Today: Liberation and Contextualization**
13. Walter G. Muelder, **The Ethical Edge of Christian Theology: Forty Years of Communitarian Personalism**
14. David Novak, **The Image of the Non-Jew in Judaism: An Historical and Constructive Study of the Noahide Laws**
15. Dan Liderbach, **The Theology of Grace and the American Mind: A Representation of Catholic Doctrine**
16. Hubert G. Locke, **The Church Confronts the Nazis: Barmen Then and Now**
17. M. Darrol Bryant, editor, **The Future of Anglican Theology**
18. Kenneth Cauthen, **Process Ethics: A Constructive System**
19. Barry L. Whitney, **Evil and the Process God**
20. Donald Grayston, **Thomas Merton: The Development of a Spiritual Theologian**
21. John J. McDonnell, **The World Council of Churches and the Catholic Church**

22. Manfred Hoffmann, editor, **Martin Luther and the Modern Mind: Freedom, Conscience, Toleration , Rights**
23. Erich Voegelin, **Political Religions,** Translated by T. J. DiNapoli and E. S. Easterly III
24. Rolf Ahlers, **The Barmen Theological Declaration of 1934: The Archeology of a Confessional Text**
25. Kenneth Cauthen, **Systematic Theology: A Modern Protestant Approach**
26. Hubert G. Locke, editor, **The Barmen Confession: Papers from the Seattle Assembly**
27. Barry Cooper, **The Political Theory of Eric Voegelin**
28. M. Darrol Bryant and Hans Huessy, editors, **Eugen Rosenstock-Huessy: Studies in His Life and Thought**
29. D. Thomas Hughson, editor, **Matthias Scheeben on Faith: The Doctoral Dissertation of John Courtney Murray**
30. William J. Peck, editor, **New Studies in Bonhoeffer's** *Ethics*
31. Robert B. Sheard, **Interreligious Dialogue in the Catholic Church Since Vatican II: An Historical and Theological Study**
32. Paul Merkley, **The Greek and Hebrew Origins of our Idea of History**